ACQ 5666
W9-CCW-612

By Different Paths to Common Outcomes

Marie M. Clay

Stenhouse Publishers
York, Maine

Stenhouse Publishers, 431 York Street, York, Maine 03909
www.stenhouse.com

Credits

Page 193: "The Sea" from *Laura's Poems* by Laura Ranger. Copyright © 1995 Laura Ranger. New Zealand: Godwit Publishing. Reprinted by permission.

Chapter 1: "Sailing On-Course: Language Development" by Marie M. Clay. Copyright © 1987 Marie M. Clay. *New Zealand Child Care Quarterly* 7, 3: 21–27. Reprinted by permission.
Chapter 2: "Conversation as One Model of Teaching Interactions." Copyright © 1998. In A. Watson and A. Badenhop, eds., *Accepting the Literacy Challenge.* Ashton Scholastic. Reprinted by permission.
Chapter 3: "Tomai, the Storyteller" by Marie M. Clay. Copyright © 1992 Marie M. Clay. Reprinted by permission of the publisher, Early Years, Inc. From the May 1992 issue of *Teaching K–8 Magazine,* Norwalk, CT 06854.
Chapter 5: "Developmental Learning Puzzles Me" by Marie M. Clay. Copyright © 1991 Marie M. Clay. *Australian Journal of Reading* 14, 4: 263–276. Reprinted by permission.

Credits continue on page 278.

Published simultaneously in New Zealand and Australia by Heinemann Education, a division of Reed Publishing Ltd., 39 Rawene Road, Birkenhead, Auckland. Associated companies, branches, and representatives throughout the world.
ISBN 0-86863-294-5

Published simultaneously in Canada by Pembroke Publishers, 538 Hood Road, Markham, Ontario L3R 3K9

Library of Congress Cataloging-in-Publication Data

Clay, Marie M.
By different paths to common outcomes / Marie M. Clay.
p. cm.
Includes bibliographical references.
1. Language arts (Early childhood education) 2. Children—Language.
3. Child development. 4. Literacy—Social aspects.
I. Title.
LB1139.5.L35C53 1998
302.2′244—dc21 98-15079
CIP

Cover and interior design by Cathy Hawkes, Cat and Mouse
Typeset by Technology 'N Typography

Manufactured in the United States of America on acid-free paper
03 02 01 00 9 8 7 6 5

to all my teachers—family, colleagues, teachers, and young learners—for they have all immensely increased my view of what is possible

CONTENTS

Foreword by Margaret Mooney vii

Acknowledgments ix

PART ONE *Children Come to School by Different Paths* 1

1 *Children's Language* 5

2 *Conversation as One Model of Teaching Interactions* 13

3 *Tomai, the Storyteller* 37

4 *Literacy Awareness: From Acts to Awareness* 41

5 *Developmental Learning Puzzles Me* 85

6 *A Fable* 98

PART TWO *Understanding What Children Know* 103

7 *Looking and Seeing in the Classroom* 105

8 *Using the Concepts About Print Task with School Entrants* 109

9 *Concepts About Print in English and Other Languages* 119

10 *The Power of Writing in Early Literacy* 130

11 *Fostering Independence in Writing* 162

12 *Introducing Storybooks to Young Readers* 171

13 *Constructive Processes: Reading, Writing, Talking, Art, and Crafts* 185

PART THREE *The Challenge of Helping All Children to Become Literate* 195

14 *The Challenge of Literacy Improvement* 197

15 *Ashok's Story from India* 220

16 *Accommodating Diversity in Early Literacy Learning* 223

17 *Child Development and Literacy Learning* 248

References 263

FOREWORD

I, LIKE MANY OF MY TEACHING colleagues, my career can be divided into pre and post "Marie Clay." Her message of asking "Why" struck me like a thunderbolt. It changed the way I perceived my role as a teacher and my understanding of the learning process.

Of course I knew why I was teaching x, y, or z at a particular time: they were the next books in the series, skills in the curriculum document, exercises in the handbook, or activities in the file. They were what everyone was teaching. But as I listened to Marie Clay and read more of her work and chatted with colleagues in various stages of questioning practices, I realized I had been operating on a very shallow understanding of the role of a teacher. I couldn't really answer the why questions beyond the superficial. My teaching was on automatic pilot and, worse still, the automatic pilot was under remote control. It seemed sufficient, given that my view of learning saw children as "vessels to be filled" rather than "fires to be lit."

And so began a transformation, one that has been, and still is, an exciting and challenging learning journey, changing the way I view the learning process and the way I plan, teach, and assess. The journey has brought an understanding that effective teaching is dependent on one's ability to make informed decisions about the most appropriate learning opportunities for a particular child at a particular time while still juggling the complexities of managing a class of exuberant individuals. For me, the initial and continuing challenge is having the confidence and competence to make *informed* decisions about children based on qualitative and quantitative data that drives and justifies my planning, selection, and presentation of resources and instruction which, of course, forms the basis for further assessment and evaluation. My attitude toward teaching has changed from seeing a need to compensate for skills children lack to one of enhancing the competencies and experiences they already have. I have come to realize and appreciate that teaching offers a responsibility and an unparalleled opportunity to help every child achieve his or her potential as a learner and a user of that learning.

I am sure readers of this collection of Marie Clay's thought-provoking writings will find themselves on a similar journey. The journey will not be along a speedy freeway, but will involve detours and crossroads, exploring new vistas and revisiting some so familiar that the signposts are in danger of being ignored. I am also confident that the resting spots will include reconsidering and re-evaluating beliefs and practices about learning and teaching and about the interdependence of learning and language, all the time emphasizing the importance of nurturing adults within and beyond educational parameters. Another detour will review the interweaving of planning, teaching, and evaluation and of research and practice.

It is likely that the journey will cross some rough terrain and the traveling will bring some discomfort. But readers can rest assured they will be guided back to the highway and the vision ahead. Marie Clay knows how to ask the niggling questions and to prompt and probe the uncomfortable issues. But readers of this collection will realize she is equally skilled in providing practical examples and well-researched, reasoned discussion for the road she chooses.

I have twice read the manuscript for this book and some parts several times. Each reading confirms some past journeys or leads me to new ones. And each reading reinforces my understanding that while we travel, visit, and revisit in different ways at different times, we will all find the journey but a beginning, and we will know we are not traveling alone. This book is not a one-read-is-sufficient publication. It is a companion for frequent dipping and delving, thinking and questioning, challenging and confirming. We'll all find different paths to common outcomes.

Margaret Mooney

ACKNOWLEDGMENTS

MY PERSONAL THANKS ARE DUE to the editors and publishers who made this collection of papers possible and to the dedicated readers who checked and advised on new material. Particular thanks to Dr. Barbara Watson who is always willing to be perceptively critical of texts that could affect the quality of teaching or the learning of children.

PART ONE

Children Come to School by Different Paths

If children are to achieve common outcomes after two or three years in school it will be necessary to recognize that they enter school having learned different things in different ways in different cultures and communities. I assume that what one already knows is important in determining what one will come to know and, if teachers believe that, they would search for what each new entrant to school, or any slow-to-get-started learner, already knows about how one can learn.

As educators focus on early literacy they tend to look backward from desirable literacy outcomes and ask, "What are the precursors of success in school literacy learning, and how can we ensure that they are part of children's preschool experiences?" Such a backward look must etch a narrow view of a limited set of activities. Most early-years educators look forward from the preschool years and seek to provide rich environments that feed into every aspect of each child's development. Literacy enthusiasts, through oversight and overemphasis, are in danger of narrowing the interpretation of what contributes to school progress, while early childhood educators are in danger of setting literacy aside until children get to school.

Remarkable learning has already occurred before children pass through the school doors. Even those who are most reluctant to speak have learned a great deal about the language of their community—how to name many things, how to construct a grammar for language with very little help from us, how to obey the social rules of speaking to certain people in certain places, and even something apparently as simple as putting their own thoughts into words. You can hear the construction of grammar going on in every conversation you have with little children. It shows up in the questions about the bedtime story, and the struggle of trying out different versions until they make themselves understood. They are already wise in the ways of communication. Chapter 1, "Children's Language," is a brief reminder of how talented children have proved themselves to be before they begin school learning. The very foundation of literacy learning lies in the language the child has already constructed, and it is so easy for us to listen to that we take talking for granted and attend to other things. After children enter school oral language learning will expand under the influence of school, home, and community, but all teachers need to create rich opportunities for this to occur. I have included the story of Tomai to show how one little boy with severe limitations on his language use at entry to school was able to be a great communicator, given the opportunity to be a storyteller. Conversational interactions are invaluable for learning to the enrichment of language use also.

A general concept of literacy awareness leads us to look and listen for the precursors of things to be learned in school; to become aware of the immature, tentative initiatives made by children that provide openings for learning. Preschool children are clearly taking hold of fragments of the complex literacy jigsaw, and we need to tune in to these—to their questions about the stories we read, to their play with oral language, to their primitive concepts about print, and to their ingenious attempts at writing. We need to learn how to observe how this learning is changing, especially among the children who seem the least well prepared for school or who are slow to adapt to the school's ways. Good conversations with children will be good teaching exchanges, for in conversation a teacher as speaker has to try to work out what his or her listener is understanding.

I think of children learning to be constructive, problem-solving doers and thinkers, each working towards more complex ways of responding. They initiate, construct, and actively consolidate their learning as they interact daily with their own special worlds. If we enlist their initiatives, and let them bring prior knowledge and ways of learning to new tasks, then we will have to teach less in school because they will take much of the learning load on themselves. If a child has even a half-formed concept of what the teacher is introducing, then all the teacher has to do is help the child complete the learning. Of course the teacher has to find out how the child is understanding the task to begin with.

It seems to me that what we thought could be a new, helpful view of children's learning—what people call developmental learning and developmentally appropriate learning—is sometimes reduced to a checklist of milestones derived from some average performance of a group of children. These can be checked off as a child passes a describable hurdle. And sometimes the small one is unchallenged by what interested the maker of the checklist but startlingly competent at something that has no place on the list. I have raised some questions about these concepts in Chapter 5, for I am interested in having schools be ready for the differences that their school entrants will display across the entire range of competencies. If we notice children taking different paths we can interact with their different journeys just as we would alter our talking to adapt to our listeners, and in a couple of years expect them to arrive at common outcomes.

Teachers who try to find out what children do not know (and much testing is directed to this) are looking for initial points of contact in the wrong places. What they need to do is find points of contact in children's prior learning, the things that children *can* do, and spend a little time helping children firm up their grasp of what they already know. Students who are active, independent learners go on adding to their competencies in all their different environments, not just in school. Learner-centered instruction is less about interest and motivation than it is about starting where the learner already is and helping that learner to move toward a new degree of control over novel tasks, teaching so that learners are successful and are able to say, “I am in control of this.” From there they go on to extend their own learning. Even at a low level of simple performance a sense of control and a sense of being effective will generate attention, interest, and motivation.

A close look at early literacy awareness shapes up an understanding of how diverse the literacy foundations are from child to child, how important interactions between teacher and child become if new kinds of awareness are to emerge and, when we understand where the child is, how easy the next step becomes.

This section ends with a fable, a fanciful genre for sending an unwelcome message. Across the world in many countries children experience little continuity between how they learn in the preschool years and how they are made to learn in schools. Why is it so difficult for us to provide continuity for the individual child learner as he or she makes those transitions through the preschool years, into school, and up through the first years of school?

1 Children's Language

Millions of children around the world begin to speak their mother tongues each year without any formal instruction. Natural language learning is infinitely more effective than any special programs we have been able to produce.

In the natural course of events we provide children with rich opportunities to learn language in their homes and communities. A little child's life seems especially well adapted in all cultures for language learning.

When we provide for preschool children to be cared for in play schools, kindergartens, nursery schools, or day care, studies show that we have changed the "natural" characteristics of the environment and that there are some gains in enrichment of experiences and some losses as far as language experiences go.

If a child has not been getting good opportunities for talking to people and learning more about language, going to preschool may be helpful. There will be people to play with and interesting activities that will create opportunities to talk. The horizons seem to be wider.

However, when observers ask "Who talks to whom?" and "What do they talk about?" and "How often does the child get to talk with an adult?" we find that although going to preschool may increase the average child's opportunities to play and socialize, it has been found again and again that children have fewer exchanges with adults than they do at home.

Barbara Tizard and Martin Hughes (1984) claimed that mother-child talk among a low socioeconomic group of families was adequate and valuable for children to learn what they needed to learn about language. Preschool teachers may think that findings about less opportunity to talk in preschool groups are wrong because they know that they spend their days in busy interaction with children, talking, talking, talking. It must be remembered that there are many children and few adults, and it is easier to exchange three turns in a conversation with a good talker than to struggle to get one response from a nontalker. Also, there are many interesting things to do in preschools, like bike riding, and block building, and water-play, which absorb the child in the doing and leave less attention for talking at the same time. One of my favorite stories is of a little boy, sitting alone, apparently not engaged in any activity. The teacher sat beside him, waited a moment, and then tried to engage him in some activity. He scowled, and growled at her, "Go away. I'm waiting for a bus." Wisely she left him to his imaginary play.

Studies show that teachers are busy making something like fourteen talking moves every minute. Most interactions are group affairs rather than one-to-one conversations. At home the child would engage a caring adult in conversation for much of his or her waking hours.

When staff are particularly good at conversing with children each child gets two to four conversations per morning session, but some children might only have one or not even one turn during the whole morning.

Children talk to each other. However, it seems from research that what is important for a good, natural learning situation is for the child to have a conversation with a person who uses simple language in correct forms and who is flexible enough to change his or her language to suit the language of the child being spoken to. Playmates do that, but adults do that better and for more of the time.

It is true that the longer children stay in preschools the older they get and the better their language. And when you are a good talker you can make your own opportunities for being heard. Older children on the whole talk more, so we might have to discipline ourselves to make room for the younger children to have their say.

Here is an extract of an interesting child-to-child exchange among five-year-olds in an American kindergarten class, told by Vivian Paley in a book called *Wally's Stories.* The class was about to act out Jack and the Beanstalk when Wally and Eddie disagreed about the size of the room's two rugs.

Wally: The big rug is the giant's castle. The small one is Jack's house.

Eddie: Both rugs are the same.

Wally: They can't be the same. Watch me. I'll walk around the rug. Now watch—walk, walk, walk, walk, walk, walk, walk, walk, walk—count all these walks. Okay. Now count the other rug. Walk, walk, walk, walk, walk. See? That one has more walks.

Eddie: No fair. You cheated. You walked faster.

Wally: I don't have to walk. I can just look.

Eddie: I can look too. But you have to measure it. You need a ruler. About 600 inches or feet.

> *Wally:* We have a ruler.
>
> *Eddie:* Not that one. Not the short kind. You have to get the long kind that gets curled up in a box.
>
> *Wally:* Use people. People's bodies. Lying in a row.
>
> *Eddie:* That's a great idea. I never even thought of that.

The problem and the conversation continue over several days, and the episode is very funny. I recommend Paley as enjoyable reading.

The mature speaker of the language is the language resource required by the little child. I have seen a multilingual preschool with children from several language backgrounds where between them the staff were able to respond to a child in Spanish, English, Navaho Indian, or French, whichever language a child chose to use. The mature speaker provides the child with the opportunity to speak and with the model of the language.

Tuning in to the Under Threes

Language begins with being talked to in the first days of life and throughout the first year, but I want to start this account at a time when the child is using language to talk to his or her family and is understanding something of what they say. Here are four examples from under threes.

> He is peekabooing from everywhere—under the coffee table, through the banisters, and around the corner. Each time we see him we are supposed to light up with surprise and joy and cry, "Here he is!"
>
> She gives a big smile and says "Hi!" whenever she sees you, all day long, a hundred times a day.
>
> He pushes the bottle into Teddy's mouth and says, "All gone."
> She climbs on her father's back and cries "Ride the horse!"

Joseph Church reported the diaries kept by three mothers of the development of their babies. His book *Three Babies* captures the progress made by Benjamin between 1 year 10 months and 2 years 10 months. Just before two years Benjamin was putting words together in little sentences.

> Benjy go upstairs sleep.
> All gone Frank bicycle.
> See you water [later].
> Go Benjy's house.

A year later Benjy talks a great deal to himself or to anyone else he knows. He is nearly three and he can explain ahead of time what is going to happen—first we go to school, then we come home for lunch, then we have a nap. It is now easier than it was earlier to capture this three-year-old's thinking as he tries to express his ideas, but he is finding the ideas hard to express. Not all the things in the real world are understood, and he is trying to find the words to express his thinking. One day around this time Benjy comes into the house howling because of a bee sting.

"Didja bump your toe on a fwy [fly]?" he said.

To understand him you would have to know that Benjy at this stage was likely to use a question instead of a statement (Didja?). "Bump your toe" conveys the notion of pain. Only those close to him would be able to understand his message. About this time his mother wrote in her diary that Benjy sneezed loudly and announced, "I sneezed my nose." When he caught sight of a covered wagon on a TV program with a twenty-mule team pulling it along he described this as "Horsies pulling a mixer truck." Between two and three years children are helped to put observations into words and to make the progress that Benjy made over that year because, and only because, someone bothers to know two things: how the child refers to things and how he or she puts ideas into language. That person who understands the talking replies, and in that conversation is the seed of the next steps the child will try to take with language. Family and familiar friends are more likely to be able to understand such colorful expressions; preschool teachers might puzzle over the references.

Children do not learn language by imitation. They learn to talk by talking to people who talk to them, understanding what they are trying to say. "Didja bump your toe on a fwy?" needed to be understood.

From Three to Five

Rapid development of language between three and five years is related to the amount of conversation that occurs between child and adult. Children who talk a lot with adults who know them well develop mature language at earlier ages. Play with other children is great for many reasons but does not produce the same accelerated language development.

How does talking with adults improve language? An example will help. The child here uses a way of asking questions common for three-year-olds.

Child: When Daddy comes home?

Mother: Daddy will come home soon when it gets dark.

The mother does not correct the child directly but responds to the question. The child not only gets an answer but also gets an opportunity to learn something more about the language he was trying to put together in his question. He did not imitate the mother, and she did not make him repeat a "good" sentence. Yet it would not be surprising to hear him use an acceptable question form the next day, as in "Daddy will come home soon?" or the more advanced form, "Will Daddy come home soon?" Although the mother did not think of it this way, the question form was implied by her reply.

If the child had asked a slightly older brother the same question he might have got the reply "At dinnertime," which would not have modeled a new sentence structure for him. And if he had asked a same-age playmate, the equally immature talker might well have given him a response matching the structure of his own question, so that "When Daddy come home?" might have been answered with "When Daddy bus come," which does not advance the control of English very far!

Children work hard at trying to find out the systems that operate in their first language. Regular words are mastered first; and irregular words are treated as if they were regular. We hear some strange verbs—doed, comed, buyed, tooken, breaked—and when they are put into sentences we might hear "Are these the best pictures you ever sawn?" or "Not a single one of them hadn't went." These novel sayings catch our ear. They are signals that a massive amount of learning is going on.

The constructive work that children do with language before they get to school is astonishing enough, but even more amazing is the ease with which they do it and how, unthinkingly, adults do just the right things to make it possible. They talk with children.

I am particularly fond of this example of a child struggling to straighten out an important message for an adult. The child had been playing outside with his brother Mark and came into the house to get a ball.

Adult: You're covered in mud. What happened?

Child: Falled me. Markie me. Markie me pushed. Markie pushed me . . . falled me.

The child struggled, but we get the message. The pauses and reconstructions are the result of a willingness to grapple with the problem of how to express the event that explains the muddiness. The mud is explained by the fall—"falled me"—but the fall also has to be explained by the push.

Children try out the meanings of words in different ways, and they know they are getting close to correct if you seem to understand. Our favorite examples uncover children's explorations, like

You should stay your dog in his kennel.

or the very specific meanings they have acquired, like this one:

Child: What are you doing, Mummy?

Mother: I'm watching you.

Child: Don't be silly. I'm not a television.

To understand the young preschooler's meaning it helps to know about their everyday lives. One mother noticed this.

> Sometimes when her Dad is answering her questions I see that because so much of what happens to her is out of his sight and so many of her references are riddles to him, he cannot, try as he will, see what point her question is trying to reach. (White 1984)

It is only when we know our children well and listen closely to their use of language that we can get inside the child's frame of reference and support the child's next forward moves. We must spend time talking *with* children, not *at* them. We must arrange our programs so that particular adults know particular children well, including the ways in which they use language.

The Adult's Response Is Very Important

The way in which we respond to children's talk determines whether they will continue their efforts or not. One way to encourage a child to go on talking is just to nod, smile, and say "Mm" or "Yes" in tones that say, "Go on talking—I'm listening with great interest." What we might call "I'm still listening" devices sustain conversation.

If we ask children questions that can be answered by "yes" and "no" or a single word, we stop a conversation in its tracks. It is a good idea to learn to recognize "yes" and "no" questions, and try to avoid them if we want to encourage language development.

Two big risks in preschools and schools is that a few busy adults will not have time to hold conversations with children about what they, the children, are finding interesting. The press of numbers often leads to activities that reduce talking time. The article "Who Talks to William?" (Meade 1982) tells what many research studies have found: that children in preschools do not get enough opportunities to talk with adults who have time to attend to their meanings. That is regrettable if a child attends a half-day preschool, but it is serious if he is in care all day long.

A great deal of talking can go on over routine activities, like getting clothes off or changed, eating, going to the bathroom, getting out toys and putting them away. These are times when adults can be chattering away to children.

One of the great things about talking with children is that many people in the community are good at doing this, and if they can be encouraged to come into a preschool center to spend time talking, this provides enrichment to the program. It requires no extra equipment. The extra resource is a person who can talk and share meanings with little children.

The wonderful thing that happens between one and five years is that children all over the world master the language of the community. We know from our later schooling in English that there are many tricky things about language, and grammar, and meanings, and idioms, but children learn it all without any hassle in conversations. If preschools do not create opportunities for conversation then more of the language learning is left to schools and they are not good at spending time on conversation with children.

The reality is that children do not all have similar opportunities; some enter school without nearly enough chance to put their experiences into words. If they are one or two years behind their classmates they may not get enough opportunity to converse in school, and be unable to catch up to their peers. In that case they will try to do what teachers ask them to do as they learn to read and write, and read math and science books, but they have to do this with a smaller grasp of the language's possibilities.

It is important that children develop a rich control of their home language as their first language, even when the language of the school is English; schools can build from there. Teachers and caregivers must talk to particular children one to one, more often. Talk to the ones who are least able to talk to you. Talk when the going is hard. Listen when the child wants to talk to you. Reply, and extend the conversation. How many times do the turns go back and forth? Just once, or more than that? Good talkers will talk among themselves, but adults in preschool and school settings should identify the children they need to spend time with.

The language of children has been the big discovery of the last two decades of research in child development, allowing educators to be so much more helpful as they interact with children. Language is a gateway to new concepts, a means of sorting out confusions, a way to interact with people, or to get help, a way to test out what one knows. It enters into every activity we can envisage. It is the source of much pleasure for the child and the adult. It is a pervasive, persuasive, perpetual fountain of learning—and there is no equipment that will give children the interactive experiences that will power their progress.

Every child becomes for a short time a linguistic genius and with great creativity learns to construct his or her first language (Lindfors 1987). To do this, children must talk, talk, and talk more, with an occasional "Mm-hmm" from whoever is talking with them.

References

Butler, D. 1980. *Babies Need Books.* London: Bodley Head.

———. 1986. *Five to Eight.* London: Bodley Head.

Butler, D., and M. M. Clay. 1979. *Reading Begins at Home.* Auckland, NZ: Heinemann.

Church, J. 1966. *Three Babies: Biographies of Cognitive Development.* New York: Random House.

Clay, M. M. 1987. *Writing Begins at Home: Preparing Children for Writing Before They Go to School.* Auckland, NZ: Heinemann.

Lindfors, J. W. 1987. *Children's Language and Learning.* 2nd ed. Englewood Cliffs, NJ: Prentice-Hall.

Meade, A. 1982. Who Talks to William? and Karla, and Susan, and Michael, and . . . ? Adult-Child Interaction, Particularly in Conversation, in Early Childhood Centres. SET No. 1. Wellington: New Zealand Council for Educational Research.

Paley, V. G. 1981. *Wally's Stories.* Cambridge, MA: Harvard University Press.

Tizard, B., and M. Hughes. 1984. *Young Children Learning.* London: Fontana.

Tough, J. 1975. *Focus on Meaning: Talking to Some Purpose with Young Children.* London: Unwin Education Books.

———. 1981. *A Place for Talk.* London: Ward Lock Educational.

Trelease, J. 1982. *The Read-Aloud Handbook.* Harmondsworth, UK: Penguin.

Wells, G. 1986. *The Meaning Makers: Children Learning Language and Using Language to Learn.* Portsmouth, NH: Heinemann.

White, D. N. 1984. *Books Before Five.* Portsmouth, NH: Heinemann.

2 Conversation as One Model of Teaching Interactions

ALMOST ANY ADULT CAN TALK with children in ways that teach. A famous student of children's language, Roger Brown, offered this guidance to parents:

> Believe that your child can understand more than he or she can say, and seek, above all, to communicate. To understand and be understood. To keep your minds fixed on the same target. In doing that, you will, without thinking about it, make 100 or maybe 1,000 alterations in your speech, and action. Do not try to practice them as such. There is no set of rules of how to talk to a child that can even approach what you unconsciously know. *If you concentrate on communicating, everything else will follow.* (Brown 1977)

The ease with which adults can talk to little children probably accounts for the fact that virtually every child without special training acquires the language of his community (Lindfors 1987). Anyone who can converse with a child can foster language development.

I want to develop the idea that one kind of teaching and learning proceeds like the everyday conversations you and I have. Just as a listener tunes in to a speaker, so *a teacher must observe, listen to, and tune in to a learner.* Being sensitive to the learner's thinking allows the teacher to draw the child's attention to things overlooked, to new aspects of the task, or to other possible interpretations. This type of teaching *must* be understood by those who work in preschools and in the first years of school, because this is a type of learning children have already participated in before they come to school. Because they already know how to engage in this kind of learning, it is a good place for them to begin their transitions into formal education.

My comments are the same for children who are monolingual in English, monolingual in another language, or bilingual.

Some Features of Conversation

How do two speakers communicate?

- In a conversation the two speakers cooperate.
- Speakers draw on their knowledge and their language, trying to make their ideas clear to their listeners.
- Speakers make listeners contribute. They leave so much unsaid that it takes a very active listener to leap from one sentence to another.
- Listeners have to bring considerable information to bear on the conversation, and they have to use it in rather subtle ways. Otherwise there would be no understanding.
- Speakers check to make sure they have been understood, and listeners have to check when they cannot understand the message.
- Speakers and listeners cooperate, for one does not tell the listener what he or she already knows. Each adapts a little so that both can understand the message.

Yet neither ever knows for certain what the other is thinking. Good teachers have to play both roles—sometimes speakers and sometimes listeners. Good learners have to play both roles—sometimes speakers and sometimes listeners.

There are several important conditions that apply to good communication, making speakers like teachers.

- The speaker has to get the attention of the listener.
- The speaker has to be sensitive to the listener. You have to adapt your message to take account of who the listener is, what the listener already knows, and what the listener needs to know. Then you have to monitor the listener's behavior to work out whether you are being understood and the message is getting across. You look for signs that your listener is understanding you.

- The message has to be adapted to the context or situation.
- The speaker has to listen when it is his or her turn to listen.

The same conditions hold true for many *teaching* interactions. Listeners are like learners.

- They can judge whether they are getting the message.
- They can recognize when the meaning has been lost.
- They can make this known to the speaker.
- They can ask for additional information.

Children have to know when they find someone else's message confusing and how to get a better message from the speaker. The children who find this easier to do than others get more opportunities to negotiate meanings. According to George Miller,

> Not only must conversationalists co-operate in turn-taking but speakers must wish to be understood; they must co-operate to make their contributions informative and germane to the hearer's interests by anticipating the hearer's problems . . . and by laying the groundwork for what they say. (1981, p. 134)

So there are important links between language, conversation, and thought. Miller put it simply. If a child asks what a zebra is, an adult in our part of the world may answer that it is a horse with stripes, assuming that the child knows what horses are, and expecting the listener to call up his or her knowledge about horses in order to understand the conversation about zebras. In parts of the world where there are zebras and no horses, the speaker would introduce horses as the new concept by making an analogy with zebras.

When we speak we do not assume that our listeners cannot think; we expect them to bring knowledge to bear on what we are talking about. Yet probably the most common error made by adults about the learning of young children is that we can bypass what the child is thinking and just push new knowledge into the child. We often assume that knowledge out here gets put inside their heads by means of the things we do. However, any learning situation is like a conversation, for it requires the learner to bring what he or she already knows to bear on the new problem being explored.

If we become observers of our own conversations—noting when they go well, when they get into difficulties, how we negotiate over our difficulties, and when and why communication fails—this may help us understand a little better how children learn.

Early Communications

JOINT ACTION FORMATS

Jerome Bruner, in *Child's Talk* (1983), called our attention to the joint action that occurs between mother and infant as they engage in certain activities. As the infant attends to mother's face, smiles and vocalizing are exchanged.

Bruner studied the ways in which communication develops in these situations. He looked at particular games, such as peekaboo, exchanging objects, and playing hide-and-seek. Games like these are made up of familiar routines. For example, the game format may be this:

1. First you focus on an object;
2. then it disappears;
3. then it reappears;
4. and then you touch it!

Over time the format changes because at first the child *observes* the routine, then comes to *anticipate* what will happen, then becomes able to *initiate* the game and then to *invent variations.*

Bruner's joint action formats can be seen as special communication situations. The infant learns to manage interactions and involve people in joint attention. It is communication without language.

One joint communication situation is created by pointing, indicating where to look for something. Babies learn to reach for things and then learn to indicate by pointing at what they want us to attend to. It is sometimes annoying that babies often cannot direct their gaze where you are pointing, but by one year of age children not only point but check to see whether their partner is looking in the right direction. That has the quality of a good communication.

If we study caregivers, we can find out how they teach children.

- They gain the child's attention.
- They support the child's entry into parts of the format.
- They encourage anticipation.
- They keep the format simple and conventional until after the child has control of it.
- They keep the challenge just right, so the baby is neither too sure of the outcome nor too upset by the complexity.

Good teachers in classrooms also do these things.

Have you tried to play ball with a little child? Talking with young children is very much like playing ball with them. It is a collaborative exercise, and if you do not allow your partner to be part of the collaborative exercise he or she will leave you, physically or attentionally. Reciprocity is the key to success.

I was reviewing a videotape recently showing the day-care procedures used in an Israeli kibbutz, and the dialogue was in Hebrew, which I do not understand. I was fascinated by the range of interactions that occurred between the adult and the five toddlers she cared for. She sang to them, talked at the meal table, played ball, shared books with them, talked all through the play in the sandpit, divided her attention and talked to several other children while bathing one. It was a day rich with interactions, sometimes language interactions and sometimes nonverbal interactions.

The naturally occurring routines of the child's day, related to dressing and feeding and moving around the family territory, can be seen in terms of these communication formats. Many of the early literacy activities like playing with nursery rhymes, sharing books, storytelling, and pretending to write, also fit into this idea of joint action formats.

NEGOTIATING MEANING

Preschool children, trying to understand their world, learn to negotiate meanings with people. For example, Mark, who was being studied by Gordon Wells (1986), was trying to understand why he should not touch the radiator. He offered the first comment: "Hot." His mother confirmed this and added: "Radiator." Mark then commented on why he should not touch the hot radiator: "Burn." His mother confirmed the completed proposition, saying, "The hot radiator will burn you." Many of our conversations with children involve such *negotiations of meaning.*

Another example, rather a favorite of mine, comes from Dorothy Neal White's *Books Before Five.* Dorothy was sharing a Little Golden Book with her daughter when they got to a picture of a father mending a chair with a close-up inset showing his hands on a saw. The child was puzzled.

> *Carol:* Whose are those hands *(pointing to the inset)*?
>
> *Dorothy:* Those are Daddy's hands.
>
> *Carol:* No! *Those* are Daddy's hands *(pointing to the main picture).*
>
> *Dorothy:* That's another picture of Daddy's hands, Carol.
>
> *Carol:* Daddy hasn't got four hands. Are those Mummy's hands?
>
> *Dorothy (weakly):* Yes. *(But the riposte came quickly.)*
>
> *Carol:* No-o. Mummy does not use a saw! (White 1984, pp. 47–48)

That book contains many fascinating negotiations of meaning between mother and child, observed and originally published in 1951, long before Bruner and Wells ever wrote about such things.

In the writings of Gordon Wells, such as *Learning Through Interaction* and *The Meaning Makers,* there are many examples of conversations in which adult and child negotiate meaning. Listen to Mark, when he was 28 months, trying to persuade his mother to break off from her household tasks to play with him. She, in turn, is trying to get him to put the lid on the clothes basket. A large part of the conversation is given over to each speaker, mother and child, as each tries to check that he or she has been understood. There are many turns in this short exchange.

(Mark is in the kitchen with his mother. He is waiting for her to finish washing the dishes so that she can play with him.)

Mark's Speech	*Mother's Speech*
1. Play, Mummy.	
2,3. Shish *(finished)* wash up, Mummy?	Pardon?
4,5. Shish wash up?	Yes.
6,7. Oh.	Let me just dry my hands.
8,9. Alright. In there *(wanting to put towel in laundry basket).*	Here.
10. 'ere-you-are *(said all as one word as he hands towel to Mother).*	
11.	Just a minute. Will you put the top back on the washing basket, please?
13. Uh? Uh?	
14.	Put the *top* back on the washing basket.
15. *(Pointing to laundry basket)* On there, Mummy? On there?	
16.	Yes.
17. *(Mark goes to put the towel in the basket.)*	No, not the towel in there. The top of the basket on it.
18. Alright. On there? Uh? Uh?	
19.	Put the *lid* on top of the *basket.*
20,21. Oh. On there?	Yes, please.
22. All right.	
23,24. *(Commands)* You dry hands.	I've dried my hands now.

25. Put towel in there. *(He wants her to put the towel in the basket.)*	
26.	No, it's not dirty.
26,27. It is.	No, it isn't.
28. 'Tis.	
29,30. Mummy play. Play Mummy.	Well, I will play if you put the top on the basket.
31. All right. *(He finally puts the lid on the basket.)* There. There. (Wells 1986, pp. 25–26)	

This was a successful negotiation even though one of the participants was linguistically immature. What are its features?

- Each takes turns to speak, listening while the other speaks.
- Each turn is understood, and the conversation flows.
- The exchange relates to the situation in which it occurs.
- Both understand the contract, and they work in collaboration.
- Each participant has a purpose, and they negotiate to achieve those purposes.

TODDLERS IN CONVERSATION

As the child becomes more of a talker, conversations provide many opportunities for the joint action format. Conversations are really negotiations between the adult and the child, with each member dependent on the prior response of the other, right through a whole series of exchanges.

A study of two-year-olds talking to other two-year-olds (Wellman and Lempers 1977) showed how skilled these young communicators were. The child initiating a conversation did several things to make sure they were effective in getting the attention of the listener. He or she

- talked when they were engaged together at play,
- or when the listener was not involved with someone else,
- or when they could see each other,
- or when they were physically close together,

and 79 percent of these initiatives met with an adequate response from the listener.

These young children also adjusted to the difficulty of communication situations, for when the situation was difficult (when an object was hard to locate, for example) they talked more, but when communication was easy they used shorter messages. When they received an adequate response they did not repeat things, but if the listener only looked or gave a negative verbal reaction the two-year-olds would try again.

This study shows a surprisingly sophisticated display of competence in communicating among children so young. As communicators young children are sensitive to the situations in which they find themselves; some situations help them to communicate, while novel situations and strange people make them clam up.

We signal the beginning and end of our communication in subtle ways. We do not interrupt the sender but wait until the message has been completed. Nothing is said, but we send and receive some kinds of signals that tell us that it is now permissible to reply. The following anecdote shows that young children learn about turn-taking early.

> A mother and her friend were deep in conversation. The mother's three-year-old daughter rattled something loudly.
>
> The mother asked, "What does that mean?"
>
> The child replied, "It means I want to say something."
>
> At the end of the statement the child rattled the thing again.
>
> The mother asked again, "What does that mean?"
>
> The child replied, "It means you can talk to each other."

In this case it was the mother who had to negotiate the meaning.

Sometimes the message you receive does not make sense, as when you have a bad telephone line, and you, the receiver of the message, frantically search for what would make sense, and make a judgment as to whether the message sent was the one you first received or the corrected message you think makes sense. Sometimes in a conversation, you do not understand, and so you tune out and think of something else.

As children gain more and more experience as communicators they can more accurately decide what is a good or poor message—whether it is their own message they are sending or the one they are listening to.

The following conversation between two four-year-old children was recorded in a playroom situation:

> *Girl (on toy telephone):* David!
>
> *Boy (not picking up the phone):* I'm not home.
>
> *Girl:* When you'll be back?
>
> *Boy:* I'm not here already.
>
> *Girl:* But *when you'll be back?*
>
> *Boy:* Don't you know if I'm gone already, I went before so I can't talk to you! (Miller 1981, p. 115)

You will find a whole book of five-year-old negotiations of this kind in Vivian Paley's book *Wally's Stories,* about a Chicago kindergarten. The teacher (Paley) leaves most of the negotiating of meaning to the children, who straighten each other out. (See, for example, Wally and Eddie's discussion of rug size related in Chapter 1.) Occasionally she joins in.

Conversation Formats for Learning

As children move into school, teachers introduce them to new formats within which learning will occur. Here are some examples I have collected in my research on early reading.

EXAMPLE 1: CREATING A ONE-TO-ONE FORMAT

An obvious format is the one-to-one format for learning in school.

Teacher: What have you done there, Karl? It's an interesting drawing. Show me the top.

Child: (Points.)

Teacher: Is this your elephant? Tell me about it.

Child: (Whispers.)

Teacher: I can't hear you very well.

Child: (Still whispers, but the teacher listens harder.)

Teacher: What a good story. *(She writes.)* Can you write *is?*

Child: (Shakes his head.)

Teacher (reads): The elephant is going for a bath. The zookeeper is scrubbing him. *(Child and teacher reread the story together, both pointing to the words as they do so.)* Lovely. That's a good story. Would you like to make the fullstop?

Child: (Nods, takes the pen, and writes a period.)

Teacher: We'll read it one more time because it's such a good story. *(They read it together.)* Lovely. Good. Now you write it underneath.

That is very like one of Bruner's learning formats. In the weeks to come the child will take an initiating role in the writing of his stories. But at this point the teacher is helping him learn the format, encouraging him to join in. When he is more competent the teacher will leave him more room to initiate his writing himself, but she will be there to support his attempts. Teachers negotiate meaning as they work with children. Like Mark's mother, the observant teacher gathers information of what has been understood, and perhaps where the explanation lost the listener. Let's look at why teachers need to negotiate over meanings and understanding.

EXAMPLE 2: CLARIFYING SOMETHING THAT IS UNCLEAR

Another example of a conversational format used in learning is that used for clarification.

Teacher: What is your story about?

Maria: A ball and pictures.

Teacher: Yes, that's at the end. What did the coach do?

Maria: He taught them how to scramble.

Teacher: How to—?

Maria: Scramble.

Teacher: What do you do when you scramble?

Maria: Get them on the ground.

Teacher (accepting this response, even though she is not entirely clear as to meaning): Scramble, yes.

EXAMPLE 3: TESTING READING COMPREHENSION

Conversation is also used to test what meaning the child is getting from a reading text.

Teacher: Where is Bill going [in the story]?

Rose: To bed.

Teacher: Good. How do you know he's going to bed, Rose?

Rose: Because he's got his pajamas on.

Teacher: You're clever. You're thinking hard. He's got his pajamas on.

Here, the teacher has discovered that the child is finding ways to make sense of what she is reading, and the teacher has reinforced the use of such a strategy by the child. Thinking about what you are reading is a clever thing to do. "How do you know he's going to bed, Rose?" is asking the child to reflect on the grounds of her own reasoning.

EXAMPLE 4: STAYING OPEN TO SURPRISES

It is also important in learning to be receptive to surprise, to unexpected turns.

Teacher: Sharon, come and tell me your story.

Sharon: I wanted to mow the lawn.

Teacher: Mmm. *(She writes Sharon's dictated story.)*

Sharon: Just for you.

Teacher: Mmm. *(She writes.)* Good girl. Read it to me.

Sharon: But I was too little.

Teacher: Oh! *(She writes the important qualification.)* Read it to me.

Sharon: I wanted to mow the lawn, just for you, but I was too little.

EXAMPLE 5: CHECKING ON WHAT EXPERIENCE THE CHILD BRINGS TO A TEXT

I watched an American teacher share a simple book with a beginning reader. The child was from a minority culture. The bear in the book was going on a holiday, and before he left he gave his mother a hug. The child looked puzzled. The negotiation went like this:

Teacher: You know what a hug is, don't you?

Child: *(Slowly shakes her head.)*

Teacher: When Mummy says "Good girl" and gives you a hug?

Child: *(No sign of recognition.)*

Teacher: Like this *(gives the girl a hug).*

Child: *(Still no response.)*

Teacher: Doesn't Mummy do that to you?

Child: *(Shakes her head.)*

This negotiation of meaning is successful in this sense: the teacher has found out that the child has no experience for understanding the word, but has provided her with the experience. Had she anticipated the child's difficulty she might have prepared differently or avoided the book as inappropriate. Under the circumstances she did an excellent negotiation and she, the teacher, now has more understanding of her listener.

Conversations involve the negotiation of meaning by either or both speakers, and so do teaching and learning interactions. Sometimes the expert sends the message and the child has to understand (receive) it. Sometimes the novice sends the message, and the expert has to try to understand it.

I have a story about a teaching conversation with an older child about mathematics. My daughter was about fourteen, almost at the outer reach of my ability to teach or converse with her about her mathematics homework. But her father was not available. So I shifted her problem into an area I felt I could talk about, and we began a good conversation. When I thought we were about halfway through and I was in full flight with what to me was only part of the needed explanation she said, abruptly, "OK, I've got it," and left the room. I sat with my mouth open, incredulous that my logic, my argument, my teaching plan for the negotiation was left in midair, unspoken . . . She was, of course, right; she had followed the negotiation to that point and completed it unaided. And she proceeded to complete her homework by herself.

That experience made me think: How often as a teacher had I played out an instructional phase to the bitter end? How often that must have been unnecessary!

The Social Rules for Language Use

Children learn how to converse and how to negotiate a learning task with us. In the following example, reported by a Play Center mother helper, the tables are turned. Listen to how the three-year-old mimics an adult way of talking.

> As I knelt quietly, watching a small girl of three, she finished painting and glanced at me.
>
> "Are you doing one today?" she asked.
>
> "Er—me?" I said.
>
> "Yes. Are you going to do a painting today?"
>
> "Oh . . . well . . . yes. I haven't done a painting for a long while," I said, managing to regain some poise.
>
> "Well, the paper's over there; get a sheet. Put it here. Here's the blue *(handing me the green paint pot).* Put it here *(pointing to an area on my paper).* Now here's the red *(handing me the yellow).* Put it over there."
>
> This continued until the paper was three quarters covered in blobs and stripes of various colors and sizes.
>
> "What is it?" she demanded.
>
> "It's . . . it's . . . it's my pattern," I replied, feeling my indignation rising.
>
> "Well, yes," she finished. "Are you going to take it home?"
>
> Can't say I enjoyed that painting session much, but I've heard it all before somewhere, haven't you? (Brogan 1981)

We set the patterns and children readily take them aboard.

My mind leaps to Ann Brown's and Ann-Marie Palincsar's reciprocal teaching with upper elementary children, which they used to develop comprehension in silent reading. The teacher models her own thinking about the text aloud, then helps the children use oral questions to guide their oral reading, which later become silent questions in silent reading (Bruer 1994, pp. 205–213). Reciprocal teaching takes the form of a dialogue.

> Dialogue is a game children understand, and it is a game that allows control of a learning session to alternate between teacher and student . . . When engaged in dialogue students are using their comprehension skills . . . [In the

> dialogue, while the talkers focus on understanding the teacher's talk inevitably models what students need to do.] Teachers and students take turns leading a dialogue about the portion of text they are jointly trying to understand. (Bruer 1994, p. 208)

An example of a kind of group conversation formalized in the reciprocal teaching format was provided by Palincsar and Brown (1986):

> *Student 1:* My question is, what does the aquanaut need when he goes under water?
>
> *Student 2:* A watch.
>
> *Student 3:* Flippers.
>
> *Student 4:* A belt.
>
> *Student 1:* Those are all good answers.
>
> *Teacher:* Nice job! I have a question, too. Why does the aquanaut wear a belt? What is so special about it?
>
> *Student 3:* It's a heavy belt and keeps him from floating up to the top again.
>
> *Teacher:* Good for you.
>
> *Student 1:* For my summary now. This paragraph was about what aquanauts need to take when they go under water.
>
> *Student 5:* And also about why they need those things.

Consider in what ways that example is like a conversation and where and why it differs from a conversational model.

Cultural Rules for Conversation

In most cultures there are specific rules about how conversations should be conducted—rules about who may speak to whom, when, with what kind of language, and who speaks first. Children in multicultural classrooms may have learned conventions for conducting conversations in their communities that are very different from the rules of the majority group or from a teacher's expectations. This can lead to misunderstanding. Jerome Bruner put this well.

> To speak . . . requires that one's utterances meet criteria of conventional appropriateness or felicity not only with respect to the context in which speech occurs but also to the acts of those with whom one is involved in dialogue. (1983)

Culture and context and the rules of conversation are very important, and little children have learned that before they come through the school doors. To some extent they are wary of using the wrong language in the wrong place or with the wrong person.

Children learn to communicate according to the rules of their home culture, which may be different from the rules of other groups in the same society. Their gestures and behaviors can be misunderstood. In their book *Talking Past Each Other* Joan Metge and Patricia Kinloch (1978) tried to help pakeha (white, majority) teachers understand some of the communication patterns of the Maori and Pacific Island children in their classrooms. I have only space to give you a few examples, which illustrate some of the reasons why conversations between teacher and pupil can and do break down.

The authors point out that pakehas, Maoris, and Samoans all talk with their bodies as well as their tongues, but that Maoris and Samoans emphasize body language more and verbalization less. Consequently pakehas may describe Maoris and Samoans as "hard to talk to" when in fact they are failing to pick up much of the communication directed their way because they are listening with their ears and not using their eyes.

Some of the cultural differences that could turn up in conversation between a teacher and a pupil, or a job applicant and an interviewer, mentioned by Metge and Kinloch are these:

- A shrug meaning "I don't know" is interpreted to mean "I don't care."
- A sniff meaning an admission of guilt and an apology is interpreted to mean disdain.
- Pakehas look at people when they converse, but such looks can be seen as confrontational, inviting opposition or conflict. Looking to one side or at the floor, the ceiling, or the distant horizon, or even closing the eyes may be more acceptable in Polynesian cultures than direct eye gaze.
- Samoans sit to show respect; pakehas stand to show respect.

Children learn these behaviors from those around them at early ages. The examples suggest ways in which communication can go awry because of the ways in which we conduct our communications.

A frequently quoted example illustrates how a teacher can fail to check what meaning a child's story has for the child and how, by ignoring the child's meaning, thinking, and understanding the teacher loses the child. The illustration is fiction, from a Maori author, but my point is not an ethnic one; it applies across cultural differences, class differences, and differences in rural and urban backgrounds.

Patricia Grace's story "Butterflies," which appears in her collection *Electric City and Other Stories,* provides an example of a teacher's response to a Maori girl's writing, and shows how easily miscommunication can occur. It tells of a little girl living with grandparents who have a garden where they grow their own vegetables. (A destructive moth that attacks cabbages and other vegetables is called a "white butterfly" in New Zealand.) The granddaughter goes off to school and returns.

> When the granddaughter came home from school her grandfather was hoeing around the cabbages. Her grandmother was picking beans. They stopped their work.
>
> "You bring your book home?" the grandmother asked.
>
> "Yes."
>
> "You write your story?"
>
> "Yes."
>
> "What's your story?"
>
> "About the butterflies."
>
> "Get your book then. Read your story."
>
> The grandmother took the book from the school-bag and opened it.
>
> "I killed all the butterflies," she read. "This is me and this is all the butterflies."
>
> "And your teacher liked your story, did she?"
>
> "I don't know."
>
> "What your teacher say?"
>
> "She said butterflies are beautiful creatures. They hatch out and fly in the sun. The butterflies visit all the pretty flowers," she said. "They lay their eggs and then they die. You do not kill butterflies, that's what she said."
>
> The grandmother and grandfather were quiet for a long time, and their granddaughter, holding the book, stood quite still in the warm garden.
>
> "Because you see," the grandfather said, "your teacher she buys *all* her cabbages from the supermarket and that's why."

This illustrates how easily miscommunication can occur in a busy classroom. As she made her teaching point the teacher ignored the child's meaning, thinking, and understanding. She lost the child.

As teachers work with children they can heed Roger Brown's sound advice quoted earlier to "concentrate on communicating to understand and be understood," but when teachers talk together about improving their conversations with learners they rightly point to how the numbers of children in their classrooms reduce the opportunities for dialogue.

Conversations in Classrooms

The literature on classroom discourse (see, for example, Cazden 1988a, 1988b) suggests that there are two ways to approach this challenge of improving classroom conversations; one is to plan for more opportunities to talk, and the other is to improve the quality of the teaching interactions that do occur.

OPPORTUNITIES TO TALK

Children of all ages, preschool through high school, need frequent opportunities to formulate their thoughts in spoken language. Too often school becomes a place where children write language down and teachers do the talking! Children need to ask *their* questions (like Mark did in the example given earlier), to explain things to other children, and to negotiate meanings between themselves and other children, and between themselves and adults. Children need to continue their oral language development during the school years, to expand their vocabularies and their control over the structures of the language, the patterns of sentences they can use. As Courtney Cazden writes,

> Teachers will never be able to spend as much time with each child as parents can do at home . . . but there is room for improvement for all children in some classrooms and for particular children in all classrooms. (1988b, p. 13)

Peers can be active partners in conversation: they can recognize when the message has been lost, make this known to the speaker, and ask for further information. In their conversations with children teachers should feel impelled to ask individual children to talk more. Vivian Paley's kindergarten children (see below) provide us with excellent examples from a classroom where talk has been allowed and encouraged.

IMPROVING THE QUALITY OF TEACHING INTERACTIONS

Schools are not able to provide all, or even most, of the teaching of children in one-to-one situations. If you are a teacher with thirty children in a class, all with different needs, at different levels of achievement, with different temperaments, from different homes and communities, then individual negotiations of meaning at the personal level with all of the children all of the time are not possible. Yet Vivian Paley (1981) was able to create some powerful learning formats for her class of five-year-olds from working-class homes in Chicago, allowing them to develop ways of negotiating meanings among themselves. Would you expect five-year-olds to be able to discuss why people speak different languages?

The personalized context of the topic of discussion in the next example was that Akemi, a classmate, was a fluent speaker of Japanese who was, at the time the exchange took place, preoccupied with learning English. The teacher merely begins and ends the exchange with her class of five-year-olds, contributing only one comment.

Teacher: Why are there so many different languages?

Lisa: Because some people don't know other languages.

Kim: They can't even talk the way we talk.

Eddie: Maybe when people are born they choose the language they want to know and then they go to special place to learn it. I mean their mother chooses.

Andy: Like a child could tell his mother and father to take him to a place where they can learn French if they are French.

Warren: God gives people all the sounds. Then you can tell you're in a different place because it sounds different.

Wally: When you're little you try to think what the name of something is and people tell you.

Eddie: Oh, yeah. Your mother tells you. You come out of her stomach and she talks English to you and she tells you a name for everything.

Deanna: If you live in a different country there's a different language there. Wherever you were born you talk that language.

Warren: Wherever your mother was born.

Teacher: Your mother was born in China, Warren, but you speak English. [Her only interjection challenges their thinking.]

Deana: But he never lived in China.

Warren: I'm going to Chinese school on Saturdays when I'm six.

Eddie: Someone has to teach you. My brother didn't know one word when he was born. Not even my name.

Earl: When I was little I said ca-see.

Rose: What does that mean?

Earl: "Take me in the car." Now I know every word.

Rose: Me too.

Teacher: Akemi was born in Japan and she speaks Japanese. How are you learning all these English words now, Akemi?

Akemi: I listen to everybody.

This very serious exchange of ideas illustrates opportunities to talk, the negotiation of meaning, the uncovering of confusions, and extended thinking. Paley's comment on the exchange was "As the children got closer to their own experiences they became more logical." She was interested in the quality of their thinking.

From many specific suggestions for overcoming the problem of numbers while increasing the opportunities for spoken language in classrooms, I have selected the following five:

1. *Wait time.* If the teacher allows some wait time to elapse in a conversational exchange it gives the children a chance to think and to search for other related information needed to get to the meaning of the conversation or, in the case of reading, to self-correct. Studies in the United States (Rowe 1986) have shown

that "when teachers ask questions of students, they typically wait one second or less for the students to start a reply; after the student stops speaking they begin their reaction . . . in less than one second." By contrast, when teachers wait for three seconds or more, especially after a student response, "there are pronounced changes in student use of language and logic as well as in student and teacher attitudes and expectations" (quoted in Cazden 1988b, p. 22).

2. *Joint focus.* Teachers should work toward joint focus with children on an action, in a real situation, on a shared task, and on a known topic. If we can assume that everything is known, it is easier to focus on and tidy up the language. I talk easily about the things I know and haltingly about the problems I am thinking my way through. This is true for most people. Teachers should anchor their interactions in something the learner knows or something he or she can act on.

3. *Teachers and students both negotiate meanings and uncover confusions.* Teachers need to find out what their students are understanding and can do this as students put their thoughts into words. Often the learning/teaching encounter creates confusion in learners' minds, which either party to the communication may need to test out. Where may the difficulties lie?

- Conversations may break down when teachers do not understand the home culture of the child because misunderstandings would cut off the flow of conversation.
- Topics from the child's experiences that are not shared or understood or valued by the teacher would not lead to educative thoughtful conversations unless the teacher has particular ways of coming to know about the child's out-of-school life. (Recall the "Butterflies" example.)
- Another problem arises where the teacher and child share knowledge of objects and events but give different meanings to them. This often occurs across cultures or social classes. As one white teacher reported to a researcher, "It always amazes me what children do know about the Maori way of life, which they never let out unless you really get into it deeply with them."

4. *Quality interactions personalize the conversation.* Cazden (1988b) emphasized that the key to quality conversations is not merely to individualize, but to personalize the learning. In some classrooms teachers move around the room helping children as they work at assigned reading and writing activities. Some manage extended conversations with children, but there is always the press of more help needed and too little time to give it. Then the interactions become abrupt and abbreviated, and do not extend the child's power to express thoughts in language. Cazden recommended that a teacher can personalize instruction and extend conversations with a single child in a small group lesson. She asked, "Is it possible that a teacher would be more apt to take the time to ask a thinking question such as 'How did you know . . . ?' when she is sitting down with three or four children

and knows she is going to stay there for a few minutes, rather than when she is stopping momentarily on her individualized rounds?"

The teacher may teach thirty children in his or her class, but the learning takes place in each individual differently. Instruction needs to meet an individual learner on a personalized level whenever the learning is challenging for that student. Cazden wrote, "It may be helpful to differentiate between individualization and personalization as a quality in the environment no matter how it is organized." Alan Watson, Robert Phillips, and Claire Wille (1995) discussed the need for teachers in composite classes to have, among other things, skills in the area of "the personalization of instruction." These authors emphasize the teacher's knowledge of the individual pupil's strengths and his or her history of learning, and the extent to which feedback on that child's work can be personalized. Cazden's discussion of personalizing the interaction in teaching related to classrooms where children came from very different cultural groups and were likely to bring very different experiences to their schoolwork. Her argument could have two thrusts: one argument, which refers to the effectiveness of learning in general, would be that understanding arises when the learner can bring personal and different cultural experiences to bear on a problem of understanding something novel; the other would relate to interactions involving cultural difference and learning. The first thrust requires the teacher to be aware of a learner's cognitive and learning history, and the second relates to the cultural or community backgrounds of both teacher and learner.

5. *Ground the talk in experience, but extend the learner.* In conversational exchange the teacher can support but can also extend the child's thinking and expression. To quote Cazden again, and at some length, because what she says is so important:

> [F]ollowing Vygotsky (1962) I would emphasize the value of children's talk about events and ideas for their understanding of the world, and for their growing ability to articulate that understanding orally and in writing. Creating links between words and the world, and . . . between words and other words, is the heart of the educational process. Children's expression of ideas in the classroom are thus not just the product in which they display the process by which much of that learning takes place. Teachers' "talk more" invitations can stimulate and encourage this important process . . .
>
> All children must take an active part in negotiating meanings, and we teachers are responsible for creating conditions that make such negotiation possible. Younger students, especially those just entering school, deserve encouragement and time to expand and explain. Older students should be empowered to assert "ownership" over their intended meanings and actively resist others' misinterpretations. (Cazden 1988b, pp. 13–14)

Teachers in classrooms have ways of fostering talk with children. In a study of children engaging with the school system (Clay 1985), I found there were many times when teachers sat alongside children and did some teaching. As an observer I could obtain five or six episodes of teacher-child interaction for each child on each of several mornings of observation. The teachers restated what children told them, they modeled new things children could do, they helped children try new things, they linked what the child was aware of to some other experiences known to the child, they shaped the child's product a little toward the desired goal, and they did some of the work for the child if that achieved the child's goal (for example, writing a new letter or a difficult word into the child's story). Often the teacher invited the child to elaborate on what he or she had already said—verbal elaboration that I called "talk more."

Sometimes the topic of the lesson is far outside the experience of the learner. Educators call for learning to be relevant to the learners. Cazden suggests that this really calls for seeing a relationship between the new topic and things the learner already knows. The teaching responsibility is to help the learner achieve the relationship. We know that. But if we use something like the conversation model in our teaching and think about how to link into the listener's knowledge every time we hold a conversation, we might be more helpful to children, and from our model they might learn how to make connections for themselves. Encouraging young children to talk more about their understandings is one way of helping them to make connections.

Cazden (1988b) wrote of three conversation topics teachers in New Zealand may find difficult when talking to Maori children—topics specific to the Maori culture, topics specific to the family life of the children, and topics familiar to both child and teacher that have different meanings in their different cultures.

It may be that we are able to find out what advantaged children know with fewer questions and less discussion with them, but unless we "talk more" with less advantaged children and encourage them to talk more we are very likely to make the wrong inferences about what they understand. In particular, any children with limited language skills need more opportunities for talk.

In Summary

As in conversation, both teacher and learner must adapt a little so that each can understand the message, remembering that neither quite knows what the other is thinking. Using models of conversation and communication as a guide perhaps we can improve our ways of reaching into the understandings that children already have. Research shows much room for change in the quality of our classroom discourse. But to make such improvements we must adopt a contract like the one Paley (1981) used with her five-year-olds:

> If you will keep trying to explain yourselves I will keep showing you how to think about the problems you need to solve.

Perhaps there are educational problems we can solve by applying the models of conversation, joint action, negotiation of meaning, and communication theory to teacher-student or teacher-students interactions at all levels of education, including adult learning and teacher education.

RESPONSIBILITY FOR CONVERSATION IN THE CLASSROOMS

The teacher bears primary responsibility for the quality of conversation in the classroom. Paley was able to achieve brilliant five-year-old conversations while saying very little herself. Cazden provided a synthesis of a great deal of research on talk in classrooms in her major work entitled *Classroom Discourse* (1988a), but the quote below is from a small booklet in which she reflected on New Zealand teaching and research on teaching:

> As we realize in all our conversational encounters—with colleagues, friends, spouse, etc.—it takes two to make a conversation. Talk is a *social* event . . . but in the special case of conversations in school, one partner—the teacher—bears primary responsibility. What she does—in setting the stage and then herself performing on it—will have considerable influence on how her student partners will play their role, and their actions will affect her perceptions of them as learners and her subsequent response. (Cazden 1988b, p. 19)

From many studies of classroom discourse Cazden summarized the negative characteristics of teacher-student interactions like this:

> In typical classrooms, the most important asymmetry in the rights and obligations of teacher and students is over control of the right to speak. To describe the difference in the bluntest terms, teachers have the right to speak at any time and to any person; they can fill any silence or interrupt any speaker; they can speak to a student anywhere in the room and in any volume or tone of voice. And no one has the right to object. But not all teachers assume such rights or live by such rules all the time. (Cazden 1988a, p. 54)

The teacher controls talk on a particular topic with the class or some subgroup of it. She talks two-thirds of the time, primarily asking questions to which she knows the answers, and the children know she knows. Ten minutes in a thirty-minute lesson is available for twenty-five to thirty pupils. Their talk is likely to get out of control, both because children have a hard time waiting for their turn and because lessons demand performance but give limited time for any one performer. Elaborate turn-taking routines are used to keep talk under control. If children try to participate too eagerly, more of everyone's time is spent on disciplinary talk and less time is available for academic tasks. But if children do not participate enough, teachers receive less information from which to make their judgments about the children's learning needs, and that in turn reduces the children's opportunities to learn.

A similar negative view of teachers came from research with New Zealand teachers and children. Hanlon summarized his data in much the same way as Cazden:

> The referee, the captain, and the star player in the classroom language game seems to be the teacher . . . she decides the topic, how the interaction will develop, and when the child would be allowed to play. [She had] the almost exclusive use of questions . . . controlling and directing the flow of interaction . . . the teacher was in communicative control. (Hanlon 1977, p. 247)

It is the teacher who needs to organize and control the classroom talk and to maintain order among the interactions, with the suppression of too much noise and unwanted activity. That produces an environment weighted against quality conversations.

The problem is exaggerated when the children come from different cultural backgrounds. At times of transition into another culture—from Polynesian home to majority pakeha school, from Asian homeland by immigration to an American school—there are new things about communication to be learned. How we use language, and how communication between speakers takes place, is an important area of language learning. It is not a matter of first learning the language and then learning how to make communication work. Rather, one has to get conversation under way in order to extend one's command of the language. It is the only way learning can take place.

THE NATURE OF COMMUNICATION

Communication theory is a larger canvas within which to set these discussions about, firstly, conversations and, secondly, teaching with the reciprocity of conversations in mind. In a way, examining the nature of communication brings some closure to this topic. Communication theory applies to a wide range of communications, not only to language exchanges. You can consider flag signaling, Morse code, smoke signals, drum messages, and flashing torches. You can think of sign language, telephone calls, television signals, tapping on the plumbing pipes by prisoners in cells—and so on. One film I saw even applied it to the canvas of an artist, because when you focus in on the painting with a magnifying lens you see dots of color, which can be thought of as collectively transmitting the message the artist wanted to get to you.

In communication theory there is

1. a source of messages used by the sender,
2. a sender of messages,
3. a channel along which messages flow,

4. someone who listens to or receives the messages,
5. and that listener's knowledge of the code.

The sender (2) selects a message (1) and transmits it using the channel (3) (often along the airwaves), and the receiver (4) gets the message and tries to understand it (5). Communication is a two-way process: a speaker is not effective unless the conversation flows and messages are exchanged. A competent speaker and a skilled listener are required (Miller 1981).

Notice how active the two parties to a communication are at all times. While the one partner is constructing the message and putting it into the language code, the other partner is actively working on receiving the message. When the roles are reversed, both partners are active again. In some ways the listener has to be more active than the speaker—and that is not the way one would normally think about it. Teachers can think of themselves as listeners and remind themselves how active they have to be to understand what is being said!

Using models of conversation and communication as a guide perhaps we can improve our ways of reaching into the understandings that children already have. Research shows that there is much room for improvement in the quality of our classroom discourse, and to achieve this improvement we must open avenues through which our children can reveal themselves to us. It is almost as simple as that; and whenever we do not bother to do that we will often fail to reach our targets.

> Conversation is thus the all-important context of language development. Although the child's earliest contributions are extremely rudimentary, they permit the adult participant to build around them; and thus to build a framework within which the child can learn by taking part in the interaction. (Wells 1981, p. 17)

Teachers have much to learn from serious consideration of conversation as one model of communication in teaching.

References

Brogan, M. 1981. *I'll Tell You About Your Painting.* Auckland, NZ: Play Centre Journal.

Brown, R. 1977. Introduction. In C. E. Snow and C. A. Ferguson, eds., *Talking to Children: Language Input and Acquisition.* New York: Cambridge University Press.

Bruer, J. T. 1994. *Schools for Thought: A Science of Learning in the Classroom.* Cambridge, MA: MIT Press.

Bruner, J. S. 1983. *Child's Talk: Learning to Use Language.* London: Norton.

Bruner, J. S., and H. Haste. 1987. *Making Sense: The Child's Construction of the World.* London: Methuen.

Cazden, C. B. 1988a. *Classroom Discourse: The Language of Teaching and Learning.* Portsmouth, NH: Heinemann.

———. 1988b. *Interactions Between Maori Children and Pakeha Teachers.* Auckland, NZ: Auckland Reading Association.

Clay, M. M. 1985. Engaging with the School System: A Study of New Entrant Classrooms. *New Zealand Journal of Educational Studies* 20, 1: 20–38.

———. 1987. Sailing On-Course: Language Development. *New Zealand Childcare Quarterly* 7, 3: 21–27.

Grace, P. 1987. *Electric City and Other Stories.* Auckland, NZ: Penguin.

Hanlon, N. 1977. Patterns of Verbal Interaction: The Effect of Situational Influences on the Language of Performance of Eight-Year-Old Children. Ph.D. diss., University of Waikato, Hamilton, New Zealand.

Jamieson, P. 1977. Adult-Child Talk. In G. MacDonald, ed., *Early Childhood Conference Papers.* Massey University, Wellington: New Zealand Council for Educational Research.

Kerin, A. 1987. One-to-One Interaction in Junior Classes. Master's thesis, University of Auckland.

Lindfors, J. W. 1987. *Children's Language and Learning.* 2nd ed. Englewood Cliffs, NJ: Prentice-Hall.

Metge, J., and P. Kinloch. 1978. *Talking Past Each Other: Problems of Cross-cultural Communication.* Wellington, NZ: Victoria University Press.

Miller, G. A. 1981. *Language and Speech.* San Francisco: Freeman.

Paley, V. G. 1981. *Wally's Stories.* Cambridge, MA: Harvard University Press.

Palincsar, A. S., and A. L. Brown. 1986. Interactive Teaching to Promote Independent Learning from Text. *The Reading Teacher* 39, 8: 771–777.

Rowe, M. B. 1986. Wait Time: Slowing Down May Be a Way of Speeding Up. *Journal of Teacher Education* 37: 43–50.

Tizard, B., and M. Hughes. 1984. *Young Children Learning.* London: Fontana.

Vygotsky, L. S. 1962. *Thought and Language.* Cambridge, MA: MIT Press.

Watson, A. J., R. D. Phillips, and C. Y. Wille. 1995. What Teachers Believe About Teaching Composite Classes. *South Pacific Journal of Teacher Education* 23, 2: 133–164.

Wellman, H. M., and J. D. Lempers. 1977. The Naturalistic Communicative Abilities of Two-Year-Olds. *Child Development* 48: 1052–1057.

Wells, G. 1981. *Learning Through Interaction: The Study of Language Interaction.* London: Cambridge University Press.

———. 1986. *The Meaning Makers: Children Learning Language and Using Language to Learn.* Portsmouth, NH: Heinemann.

White, D. N. 1984. *Books Before Five.* Portsmouth, NH: Heinemann.

3 Tomai, the Storyteller

IDEALLY STORYTELLING, LIKE CONVERSATION, IS also a two-way street. Tomai is one of my favorite storytellers. His parents came from one of the islands in the South Pacific and undoubtedly spoke their own island language at home. A radio interviewer was gathering material for a continuing education program aimed at helping parents to understand how children begin to learn to read and write when they come to school in New Zealand. She knew that part of becoming literate depended upon knowing that books have good things like stories in them, and also upon children wanting to hear stories. She asked a teacher of school entrants, who read to her children every day, if she had a child who might tell a story into the microphone.

The teacher chose Tomai, a good choice because he already knew much about the art of storytelling (and because he was not fazed by the recording technology). The teacher provided a picture-book version of "Goldilocks and the Three Bears," which she had read to the class the previous day. Just before Tomai left the classroom, a child had been reprimanded by the teacher for playing with an electric outlet. Suitable explanations and warnings had been given.

Tomai dodged the invitation to tell the Goldilocks story and asked the interviewer if he could tell another story instead. Wisely, she agreed.

Read this five-year-old's cautionary tale and his attempt to talk about something like artificial respiration and the application of oxygen. At the end of the story, he brings the victim back to life and sets him up like new.

A Cautionary Tale

> One day there was a little boy and there was a Muvva. And so Muvva was gone shopping. And brother, he saw a little—um, a light came on. And so he broked it and he put his hands in the thing and he died and he shaked and he died. And Mum came home from shopping and she looked for him and she said, "Oh! My God! He is died. I'd better ring up the police." So she rang up the police.
>
> And so the mans came. And so they got him—and they—and they put things in. And, and they put him in the, um, hospital and they do it. And, and he wasn't still up and they and they push his leg, squeeze him, squash him, and and he open his eyes like vis and he shaked again and died.
>
> An' you know what? He—his mother came. And the little boy waked up, and they made his hands new. And they—just cut his hands off. And they put new hands on—and they put—cut—his head off and they put a new head on and—cut his leg off and they put another leg on—a new leg on. And they cut in another leg and they put it on, and, and, and he was up and when they finished and, and, and they got a little things to put in his mouth—some drink of water and sugar in his tiny thing and he drinked it and the Muvva gave him some milk and he sucked it and he waked up.

Tomai's intonation and expression were very dramatic. It cannot be captured in print. He used different voices for different actors. He would pause to heighten the drama, and he used an immense range of pitch, from deep to high. All of this helped to make his story come alive.

Obviously, Tomai had a good "sense of story." I am certain that the teacher did not phrase her warnings in the terms Tomai used and that he was not copying her. Tomai imagined a "worst-case scenario." He enticed the listener into the story, killed the victim, introduced intense emotion with the mother's reaction ("Oh! My God! He is died") and then used what little medical knowledge he had to sustain the suspense of his plot. This five-year-old Polynesian boy was not retelling a story; he was creating one. He knew how stories go.

The urge to tell that story breaks through all of the barriers of his limited control over language. There is a wholeness to the encounter—a five-year-old on the way to becoming a more competent five-year-old. He describes shadowy concepts in very simple, cryptic language. Most of all, his strengths come together in this creative outpouring of what he understood the teacher to be warning the children about.

Where did Tomai get the art of the storyteller? Could he have heard it in his community and home culture? All children try to make sense of the things we tell them, but they bridge the bits they do not understand with fantasy, with what might be. Tomai does this all so well that I feel he must have learned from a family member who could tell stories wonderfully, or from people who held him entranced as they read storybooks to him.

Although little children think and talk differently from adults, they manage to talk to those adults quite well, and in those conversations they develop their home language and their understanding of the immediate world around them. Developmentally, the network of connections is from the child, through his family experiences and his mother tongue, spoken in the home, into the world of school and the world of literacy.

This may mean that the learner encounters a teacher who has a different way of talking, or perhaps the language of school is different from the language of the learner's home. And to be a reader and a writer, that learner must become familiar with these new languages and with the literary language used in storybooks.

Because of the many children in classrooms, learners get fewer opportunities to talk in these new "languages." If it had not been for the chance visit of the radio interviewer, Tomai would probably not have had an audience to listen to his story.

When I wrote to the producer of radio programs for the Broadcasting Corporation of New Zealand in 1982, asking about the little storyteller she had spoken to me about, she replied, "Being a bit of a squirrel when it comes to collecting goodies in the course of making programs, I'm delighted to say I still have Tomai telling his cautionary tale about the electric plugs. I'll dub it off onto a cassette for you and post it. When we made the recording Tomai was five years old and a new entrant to school of about five weeks . . . on the same tape I have Tomai's full version of 'Goldilocks and the Three Bears,' contrasting his retelling of that story as he turns the pages of the book (and not very well because he cannot remember how it went) with letting go with his own well-remembered tale" (Pam Carson, personal communication, 1982).

So all this happened a long time ago. The cautionary tale that Tomai created did not suit the radio producer's purpose. She wanted to demonstrate to parents what children got from stories when parents read to them. She wanted a retelling of a shared book. At her request, Tomai then tried to retell "Goldilocks and the Three Bears" in the words of the text, which he had heard read aloud more than once. He turned the pages and, guided by the pictures, tried to remember the words.

"Too hard," he said. "Can I tell you Goldilocks out of my head?" The interviewer agreed, and he told a good tale. It is the ending that I want to share with you because of its delightful cultural connections, as Tomai takes the opportunity to make some cultural adjustments. He allows Goldilocks' parents to take action to straighten out the social etiquette of the situation.

> . . . and Goldilocks ran home to mummy. And she said, "Mummy, I was naughty."
>
> "Oh, you shouldn't go there, little Goldilocks. I will give you a hard smack." Smack! Smack!
>
> And Father came home from work and he boot the little Goldilocks harder and harder . . . And then he said, "We're going to go there tomorrow." And they went there and Mother got some porridge and some apples and the little Goldilocks got some bananas. And so, knock, knock.
>
> "Who's that?"
>
> "It's only the big man."

"Come in right now."

And he hammered away.

And the little Goldilocks said to her Daddy, "Can I play with the little baby bear?"

"Of course you can." And they went out saying, "Bye-bye."

What an interesting way for a five-year-old to end a story in his second language and culture, giving it the kind of resolution that his first culture would require (taking food to the neighbors to restore good relations and mending the broken chair). Tomai could solve the problem of cultural differences. Educationally, it seems to me to be important that somebody gave him the opportunity to do so.

There are other good accounts of children of this age who were encouraged to be storytellers. If you want to "listen" to some other children creating stories, read *Wally's Stories* by Vivian Paley (1981). Paley writes about how children in a Chicago kindergarten learned to tell stories for their classmates to act. She's right when she says that the storyteller overcomes the limitations of world knowledge and language with creative twists to the plot and a good measure of magic.

Think how the effects snowball. The more children engage in telling stories, the more command they get over language. With more language, they can understand more detail in the stories they hear. That gives them a better idea of how stories hang together. So the better their own storytelling and retellings get, the more experience they'll bring to reading stories and to writing them.

When we add that story-making is one way in which children can bridge cultural differences in their various worlds, as Tomai did, we should turn again to the leadership that Paley provides and do more storytelling ourselves. But that is not enough, for there has to be a reciprocity in this. If we get to tell our stories, it's only fair that we become an audience to whom children can tell *their* stories.

Reference

Paley, V. G. 1981. *Wally's Stories.* Cambridge, MA: Harvard University Press.

4 Literacy Awareness: From Acts to Awareness

THE CONCEPT OF AWARENESS PROVIDES early childhood educators and first teachers with common ground for discussion. It serves parents, caregivers, preschool teachers and schoolteachers, researchers, and theorists well, because noticing awareness opens doors to further interactions if we know how to take up the opportunities. In this chapter I explore how young children demonstrate their awareness of literacy learning through behaviors that catch our attention, behaviors that relate to both reading and writing. Children's partly right and partly wrong actions or comments are unexpected, and cry out for explanation, making us ask, "Why did she or he do or say that?" Researchers, parents, preschool educators, and schoolteachers respond readily to signs of expanding awareness. My concern in this chapter is about how we can use these signs to promote further learning.

Accounts of preschool children's activities (Bissex 1980; Ferreiro and Teberosky 1982) and early school activities (Paley 1981; McKenzie 1981; Clay 1991) have clearly demonstrated that the beginnings of school literacy are falsely represented as merely learning letters, or sounds, or words, or letter-sound relationships. The first contacts that children have with written language are more complex than that, involving words, written messages, and storybooks, and children notice features of written language that adults would not think to teach them about.

The talk and printed texts in children's lives are most commonly made up of multiword utterances or multiword sentences rather than single sounds, letters, or words. If we did not think of the transition into literacy as primarily learning to decode letters and words to the sounds of speech, but rather thought of it as learning, from the beginning, to work with *any* features of written language (Vygotsky 1978), then we would need to take a broader view of experiences for young literacy learners.

Awareness

Awareness is defined here as being able to attend to something, act upon it, or work with it. I use the words *act* or *acts* to refer both to external, observable behavior and to internal psychological activity. Theories of activity and action provide a conceptual backing for my discussion. Most often a tacit awareness, rather than an explicit knowledge, is all that very young children have about any written language they are attending to. Human action is strongly influenced by the tacit understanding that people have about their worlds but are not able to discuss. In time children can discuss many things about literacy learning, but young children who speak very well are often unable to put into words what they know about language. On the one hand adults may often overlook what those children do know, and on the other hand adults may believe that teaching a child to name something or put it into words establishes the learning of some new concept, though frequently that is not the case.

The concept of awareness opens a door to interactions with children that promote literacy learning while avoiding an emphasis on one "chosen" way into literacy. Preschool educators do not agree on whether, and how, to foster literacy awareness; some are committed to having children learn their letters to give them a good preparation for entry to school, while others would leave children unaware of the existence of such things until faced with school instruction.

As we focus on early literacy should we look backward from school to preschool and ask, "What are the precursors of success in school literacy learning, and how can we ensure they are part of preschool experiences?" Such a backward look—including much valuable advocacy of reading stories to children—does not etch as rich a picture as most early childhood educators describe when they look forward from the preschool years and seek to provide rich environments that feed into every aspect of each child's development. Literacy enthusiasts are in danger of narrowing the interpretation of what contributes to school progress, while early childhood educators are in danger of setting literacy aside until children get to school.

Awareness helps us overcome the limitations of both the looking forward and looking backward views. It is a concept for parents in homes, caregivers in child care and preschools, teachers in the first two years of school, teachers giving extra help in literacy learning, researchers, and theorists. A forward thrust of learning can occur when

- adults provide opportunities for children to notice literacy events,
- children demonstrate awareness,

- adults grab the opportunity to interact with that awareness,
- and open up further opportunities for learning.

Children's awareness of literacy events provides common ground for people of different perspectives to discuss and share ideas. Both those who interact with children in homes, preschools, and schools, and theorists who search for explanations of how language and cognition develop can work with this idea of awareness. Children demonstrate awareness as they attend to new aspects of their world, and their comments from time to time on the printed language around them provide us with good examples of what they are attending to. Quite late in this noticing process children become especially curious about how different aspects of the oral code and the written code relate to each other, and the features of the two codes their young brains become aware of are many and varied.

When Downing and Leong (1982) provided a review of many theories of awareness (Mattingly 1972; Sinclair, Jarvella, and Levelt 1978; Read 1975; Chomsky 1969; Elkonin 1973) they concluded that

> Studies of awareness usually refer to situations where children will perform actions . . . and where they are encouraged to verbalize about how they perform these actions. Generally, awareness is shown to lag considerably behind success in action—the case of the child knowing more than he or she can tell. (p. 101)

Children do not find it easy to explain what it is they are learning about language in print, but Mark, aged five and in a (Canadian) kindergarten, managed to do this rather well, saying, "I know what it is in my brain but I don't know what it is in my mouth" (Brailsford 1985). A simple summary of extensive research on awareness is this:

> [R]esearch on "becoming aware" is to be interpreted as becoming aware of the how, and eventually the why, of specific actions, and of the how, and eventually the why, of certain interactions between objects. (Sinclair, Jarvella, and Levelt 1978, p. 193)

I would emphasize that it is common for most children to move from specific acts to awareness and thence to talking about awareness.

In a literate community most children become curious about some of the print they see, about people writing, and about how talking relates to printed language. Because codes for representing the world out there are complex, there are many different things the brain can attend to, but in young children curiosity usually arises from actions or activities related to getting things done. The first points of contact with literacy can be many and varied but whatever that point of contact may be, *one way of creating more literacy awareness is for adults to interact with children engaged in any kind of literacy activity.* The following sections illustrate how many different activities can be original points of contact with literacy for different children.

Awareness of How a Story Goes

A father was sharing a picture book with another boy named Mark and the interaction flowed like a conversation; but *notice how often Mark, aged 2 years 3 months, led the discussion.*

Mark: That? In the plane now.

Father: That's them all flying in the plane, now. Yes. Because the little baby is pretending he's flying in his plane.

Mark: Gone. Gone up.

Father: Yes, it's gone up. What will happen when it comes down?

Mark: Land.

Father: It'll have to land. Yes.

Mark (turning to the next picture): Landed now.

Father: Yes, it's landed now. Who is standing next to it?

Mark: Boy.

Father: Yes. That's the little boy, Louis. It's where he used to live.

Mark (pointing): Airplane. Mark been on that. Mark on that.

Father: Yes. Mark's been on one of those.

Mark (pointing to the moon in the picture and laughing): Mark been on the moon.

Father (laughing): You haven't been on the moon.

Mark (pointing): Gone up.

Father: Yes. You can see the people waving goodbye.

Mark: Going home.

Father: Yes, he's going home now. (McKenzie 1986, pp. 7–8)

As Mark's father reads, he stops to talk and respond to Mark's comments. This talk expands Mark's utterances into language structures that Mark is *not* yet using (Cazden 1972). Think how much time Mark still has ahead of him for learning about how stories work, before he crosses the school's threshold.

Margaret Meek (1988) wrote about how texts teach what readers learn, compiling "a list of ordinary things that readers do without seeming to have learned them as lessons," but she warned that if we look a little more closely these things may turn out to be less ordinary than we first believed. Things that children learn without instruction may be important constituent parts of a reading and writing process. McNaughton (1995) illustrated from several different cultures how children develop a knowledge base for how stories work, and how their knowledge and understanding of written narratives depend on the degree to which there has been extended discussion about the stories.

Children who are read to are "inducted into the contracts of literacy," according to Ninio and Snow (1988). Some of those contracts are

> that books are for reading,
> that the book is in control and the reader is led,
> that pictures represent things,
> that book events occur out of real time, often in a fictional world.

Social groups make somewhat different contracts with their children (Heath 1982). These contracts are as difficult for the three- and four-year-old as the ones my new computer forces me to buy into, and it takes a little time to learn them.

Around the world children enter school who have not had any experience of books being read to them, but most cultures have some tradition of telling stories. Listening to stories that are being told rather than read is a slightly different but excellent preparation for literacy learning. *Wally's Stories* (Paley 1981) is a convincing account of how young children can become storytellers who enact their stories, and discuss them, in a preschool setting. Vivian Paley's children enjoyed dictating stories to their teacher when they realized they would act those stories, and the activity created another kind of awareness: an awareness that their oral stories could be written down.

Awareness of How a Book Is Organized

In a research study one mother began a story reading with "This is where the story begins. *No more cakes.* That's the . . . that's the name of the story" (McNaughton 1995, p. 171). Everyday interactions like that make children aware of how what we say is written down. I made a detailed study of how children come to work with these concepts (Clay 1989, 1991, 1997). Some researchers ask young children questions like "What is reading?" and "What is a word?" expecting them to talk about things they may know only in a vague way (Reid 1966; Downing 1970). I wanted them to *show* me what they were aware of even when they could not talk about them, so I gave them a very simple storybook, and as I read it to them I asked them to *show me what they would do with the story.* I was interested in what children attended to rather than what they said about it. The distinction was important. To read, one has to know where to attend, in what sequence, and what sorts of things the pictures and marks on the page can tell you. I suspected that children could act within the conventions of written language before they could talk about what they knew, and five-year-olds in a research study demonstrated this. Children learn many of these things before they can do the particular kind of cognitive analysis that allows them to put their understanding into words.

How articulate do children have to be to "know something"? Must they put it into words? Do they have to act in response to particular words spoken by the teacher? Is it enough for the beginner to get the task done using some patterned response, or must he or she be able to deal with bits of the task in isolation? I needed a task that would let me answer questions like those, measuring learning that had a high relationship with reading progress before children could talk about it. I found a way of doing this with the Concepts About Print observation task (C.A.P.).

C.A.P. uses a short story told with a picture on one page and a text on the other. *The story is read to the child* (never by the child), and the child is asked to help the observer. In a book-sharing situation the child reveals what he or she knows about the front of the book, that print (rather than the picture) tells the story, what a letter is, what a word is, where the first letter in a word is to be found, pairs of upper- and lowercase letters, and when nonlegitimate changes have been made to the printed text. Five- and six-year-old children have some fun and little difficulty with this observation task, whether they are new to school, first-year graduates, or older nonreaders. One little boy who was aware what books were like was very puzzled by the changes made to the text in the C.A.P. test booklet, which broke the printer's rules, and he asked me, "Did you buy this book at a regular bookshop?"

C.A.P. shows teachers what children can bring to instruction, it points to children who may have particular instructional needs, and it can be used on more than one occasion to record progress. Confusions about the arbitrary conventions we use in print soon disappear with the help of early childhood teachers who know how to use the things that catch children's attention to best advantage.

C.A.P. was designed to capture various kinds of early literacy awareness. For example, how does one work within the directional constraints of the English language? It is relatively easy to get many children behaving as if they understood these rules, by modeling, sharing reading, and writing with them, and by talking a little (but not too much) about that behavior. Increasing awareness arises out of many successful performances or acts, as a result of which children become aware of what works. Acting in the world, they come to attend to more and more features and move toward better personal theories of the task by a series of slow changes. Some theorists argue that when children's early theories do not fit with some new experience, the conflicting evidence leads children to change their earlier primitive theories (Duckworth 1979; Tolchinsky Landsmann 1990; Grossi 1990); others challenge this and claim that learning progresses more often through successful performance and not necessarily because of conflict (Bryant 1982; Karmiloff-Smith 1992). As the complex patterns of literacy tasks are analyzed by children into finer detail the "cognitive haze," or confusion (which Downing and Leong 1982 described), diminishes. Late in this process of coming to know, talking about parts of the complex task might help learners discriminate further details. But articulation by the child is not the origin of the learning.

C.A.P. was intended to probe several sets of behaviors—book orientation skills, print and directionality, letter and word concepts, and advanced print concepts including letter position and letter sequence, all of which are challenges to the child grappling with understanding the written code. Like a standardized test, which needs a gradient of difficulty in the items, C.A.P. also contains tasks that challenge competent children towards the end of the first year of school. Concepts about print vary from language to language, particularly when the script is different; but rules for how to write down speech are necessary for every language. The redevelopment of the English C.A.P. test for Spanish (Escamilla et al. 1994) and Hebrew (Ministry of Education, Israel 1995) has illustrated in what sense concepts about print apply across languages, and how and why they vary. A young literacy learner in any language must become aware of concepts about print, and some biliterate children must learn two different sets of coding rules!

Print awareness is a general term used frequently today to include the visual features of print, often letter and word knowledge, as well as some concepts about how books work. Print awareness is used as if it were a synonym for what is assessed in C.A.P., but the understanding of the concepts of the printed code and what is measured as visual awareness of features in print are often very different when analyzed carefully.

Awareness and Writing: How I Write and How Adults Write

As more research has been reported on the transition into literacy it has become apparent that early writing provides some of the clearest evidence of how preschool children grapple with many of the rules and requirements of the written code. The accounts show us that children within any language group have varying exposure to print and come to attend to different aspects of this complex task.

To write a word, perhaps your own name, or a simple message, on several occasions is to bring the visual features of print into focus. A group of five girls, between four and five years of age, were sitting eating their morning snack at a (New Zealand) kindergarten. Monica held up her lunchbox, which had her name printed on it in black letters.

Monica: Can you read my name? Look, it's *M (points to the letter).*

Group (looking at Monica make the sound in unison): Mmmmm.

Monica (looking at each of her friends points to the next letter): A [sic].

Group (looking at Monica then one another): Aaaaa.

Monica: Now it's *n. (Puts her finger on that letter and traces it.)*

Group: Nnnnn. (One friend traces an n *with her finger, partly hidden in the fold of her skirt. Another puts her finger out towards Monica's lunchbox, tracing in the air the* n *shape.)*

> *Monica:* Here is *i (points to the letter and traces it).*
>
> *Group: Iiiii.*
>
> *Monica: C (looks at the letter* c).
>
> *Group: Ceeee.*
>
> *Monica: A* is the last.
>
> *Group: Aaaaa.*
>
> *Monica:* Monica, Monica *(running finger along the bottom of her name).*
>
> *Group: (They laugh, looking at one another. One friend touches the letters and murmurs "Monica." The others also murmur "Monica" to themselves. They all laugh again.)* (McNaughton 1995, p. 174)

We can think of this as an example of writing because the letter-by-letter approach, the tracing movements, and the movement of the hand gathering up the separate letters into one word are what must be done when writing. If we were to argue about whether this is a reading or writing example, that would serve to emphasize how close reading and writing are at this level of literacy learning. To read what one has already written or to write (reconstruct) something one can already read is to become aware of some common ground in these two experiences. An awareness of some vague kind emerges from such actions, which link marks on a page and words one can speak. Being able to draw on experience in both reading and writing adds another perspective to a learner's understanding of literacy. In addition to success and conflict situations, seeing the same thing in different places and acting on it in different ways adds further opportunities for comparison. The child will attend to the details and raise questions such as "Why does the teacher write my name like this [Ian] 'cause my name writes like this [IAN]?"

Even before the age of four, children often scribble in lines or produce strings of distinctive units, like circles and crosses in lines separated by spaces (Goodman 1990). Shifts occur from "letters" spread all over the page, to variations on the letters of the child's name, to several different ways of writing messages in one child's repertoire (Clay 1987). Children write "different words" with a different arrangement of the same letters (Jouuyi, Auudo, Joois). They become aware of representation, the fact that the notational system stands for the object. This is the central idea of a symbol code, but their initial theories of the basis of that representation are sometimes unusual. Lize, for example, believed that number of letters was related to age:

> My name has 4 letters because I am very young. My mommy's name must have 10 letters and my daddy's 15 because he is even older than Mommy. (Grossi 1990)

Children like Lize, who are presyllabic and presymbolic, have not yet connected written words to oral aspects of language. Another example is of the boy who was asked how many letters were needed to write the word *bread.* He said,

> It depends on the size of it. Bread standing for a loaf of bread is written with more letters than bread standing for rolls. (Grossi 1990)

Awareness of some features of the coding system is demonstrated in children's writing, showing us that much has been learned by children before they can relate their marks to talk (Ferreiro and Teberosky 1982; Goodman 1990, especially chapters by Tolchinsky Landsmann and Grossi). A growing awareness of the literacy code would include some of the following:

- a shift from producing drawing and writing together as if one is essential to the other to the substitution of written words for drawings, as when the written name of the child or of other people substitutes for a drawing;
- an awareness that writing is possible only with letters;
- a graphic sign or set of letters to represent a given word;
- real words constructed from a sequence of letters, without an understanding of how these letters relate to the syllabic structure of the oral form;
- a growing awareness of the uniqueness, stability, and variability of the written word (IAN versus Ian);
- a beginning sense of how to represent segments of the oral form of the word with letters.

That short list, selected from many other possibilities, represents an amazing set of coding features, which some preschool learners will already be aware of, and to which others will have paid no attention. That difference in awareness is the educator's challenge.

In schools where reading and writing are allowed to influence each other, early measures of writing will produce high correlations with reading progress in the first year of school (Robinson 1973). A teacher who sits with small groups of children to share their early writing tasks provides scaffolds for increasing awareness (Girling-Butcher, Phillips, and Clay 1991; Hobsbaum, Peters, and Sylva 1996). After a child has orally composed a sentence, the message gets built, letter by letter and word by word, as teacher and child together get a sentence or two written down. Teachers provide supportive scaffolds as learners work through a haze of possible relationships to early awareness. Their engagements with the task reveal bit by bit which features in the complex pattern the child is becoming aware of, with early effort directed more to the making and arranging of letters than to representing the sounds of oral language.

> Under reasonably good conditions children work themselves out of the initial state of cognitive confusion into cognitive clarity about the functions and technical characteristics of written language. (Downing 1979)

Some awareness of written language precedes schooled writing (Ferreiro and Teberosky 1982), and greater awareness follows from it. Most is forged during simple acts of reading and writing as learners become interested in texts. Part of a text may be temporarily raised to a level of conscious manipulation as some new feature or commonality is found. *A new discovery (today's "aha") will soon lapse into being merely the support system for new things to attend to.* A learner in action who works at attending to the text in some primitive way is a creator of awareness. That learner pays very close attention, tries possible responses, notices new features, puzzles over these, asks an adult a question or two, and makes a decision, selecting a word in reading or attempting to write. A correct response may have been achieved with what was only a primitive understanding which, within a day or so, can change as new encounters allow the learner to uncover previously unnoticed features. (A case study of Sally-Ann in Clay 1987 demonstrates how rapidly such shifts can occur.)

Awareness and Reading: What I Do When I Read and What Adults Do

It is difficult for a child to give a verbal explanation of what reading is. One little boy with high print awareness was thinking hard about this, but his attempt at explanation sounds like "cognitive confusion":

> You have to know the words, what the words say—and what the words spell. I mean, what the letters spell. You have to say the sounds they make and then make the whole word go together . . . like *B* says *book!* (King 1977)

Young children who are reading quite well often cannot define what they do. As long as they are sufficiently aware of the acts that will extract the messages from print, telling what they do is not essential to effective performance. Becoming able to explain what is done may be an outcome of many acts and a deepening awareness that arises from the experiences. Young readers even though they are expert have difficulty with explaining how they learn.

> Alex, [5 years 6 months], who could read at fourth grade level, was asked how he had become such a good reader. He responded that he "practiced a lot." When asked what he read, he replied, "Books." When asked a second time about how he learned to read, "Did you say your mother taught you to read?" Alex said, "No, I did." Persisting, the teacher asked, "Did you see anything around you that you learned to read from—signs or TV?" Alex said, "No, I just tried reading books." (King 1977)

Awareness of the Letter Forms in Both Reading and Writing

We talk about children knowing letters as if it were as easy as collecting stones. It is quite easy to learn to sing the alphabet, but visual recognition of many letters evolves quite slowly in young children. From alphabet books or magnetic letters or blocks, from simple things they ask us to write down, somehow one day they seem to know a number of letters. Careful recording will show that this is not a valid account of what happens. Most children separate out one or two easy-to-see or easy-to-write letters from their experiences, discover a few more in their scribbling, find them on things around the house, on important belongings, or in letters from important people.

> Stephen, aged four, came home from preschool with a large *S* which he had written himself on a painting. His three-year-old brother Timothy requested "his letter." Later Timothy was seen crouched on the floor in the kitchen, his face against the boards, peering at a tiny engraved plate at the base of the refrigerator. Suddenly, in a muffled but triumphant voice he said, "It's only got one Stephen but it's got two Timmies!" (Butler and Clay 1979)

Janice, even prior to (Canadian) kindergarten, was picking out letters and associating sounds with them. Her mother read the newspaper, and Janice would sit beside her and say, "Those letters say 'da' and those letters say 'o' and 'u'" (Brailsford 1985).

Cultural beliefs affect how much of this learning occurs before school and whether letter learning is seen to be important for later success. By the time children enter school their awareness of the symbols of the code can range from zero to all the lowercase and uppercase letters. *Efficient school programs allow children to expand their awareness of letters from whatever its level is when they walk in the school door.*

Should they learn the names or the sounds of letters? (Some languages, like Maori, do not have this problem, for the sound is the name, but this is not true in English.) In the beginning it makes sense to have children learn to identify letters by any means that works, because then the name or sound labels can quite easily be attached to them. The learner's initial task is to become aware that letters exist, that there is a set of these symbols, and that each can be distinguished one from the other, which means each has an identity. If the child is not aware that *m* is different from *n* there is little point in trying to learn a particular sound label (phoneme) for either form. The teacher's task is to know, through observation and interaction, what the child knows, and in what way the identity of the letter is known. In English we can count 54 letter forms, upper- and lowercase with two forms of *a* and of *g*. The child has to become aware that there is *a set of things* (the symbols); *after this initial insight the child can gradually learn about each and every one of the different members of that set.* The learner interacts with the literacy opportunities around him or her, distinguishing more and more letters one from another. Timothy began that journey by studying the maker's label on the refrigerator. When a teacher saw a child move from attempts like "C a" and "Ctsa" to a complete version of her name, "Christina," she observed that this showed a big leap forward in letter learning, among other things. To learn to distinguish all the letter symbols one from another is a massive task of visual discrimination learning, which takes place throughout the first year of school as the child reads and writes in primitive ways. Children will be reading text long before they can identify the entire set of symbols.

Once children begin the search for how their speech is recorded they will have many questions about letter-sound relationships, as in the following simple interaction of Paul and his mother.

> *Paul:* What makes the "uh" sound?
>
> *Mother:* In what word?
>
> *Paul:* Mumps.
>
> *Mother:* *U.* (Bissex 1980, p. 13)

A lecture on spelling was not necessary at that time. Paul was very aware of the sounds of letters and had done the phonemic analysis; he asked which letter he should use. Many things influence the expansion of the range of letters that a learner has become aware of.

Awareness of First Words

It is common for children to discover two or three favored words when they are preschoolers—their own name, that of another familiar person, a favorite food, an advertised product (Grossi 1990). Each word is known in some partial way before the full form is recognized or produced. I warm to children's versions of "look" and "see," which represent the semantics along with the code (as when children draw "two eyes" within the double letters).

> *Mark:* I can write names.
>
> *Paul:* Whose?
>
> *Mark (quietly):* Mine.
>
> *Paul:* *(Laughs.)*
>
> *Mark:* And I can write some first letters. I know the first letter of your name. It's a *P.*
>
> *Paul:* What's next?
>
> *Mark (quiet voice again):* I don't know.

Paul (confidently and loudly): It's *P-A-U-L.*

Mark: (Pauses.) Do you know how to spell my name?

Paul: (Points to Mark's name on the library chart and spells out the letters.) Yes, it's *M-A-R-K.*

Mark (surprised voice): That's right! (Brailsford 1985)

Many have noticed how children's own names can be of central importance.

Courtney: That's part of Vivi's name. [V]

Mark: That's the same as I am. [A]

Marcos: That's not my name (*even though there was an* A *and a* C *in it*). (McLane and McNamee 1990)

The learning may go in either of two ways, from reading to writing or from writing to reading. The child eager to reply to a birthday invitation may seek help by asking "How do you write 'come'?" so he leads with oral language and perhaps phonemic rendering and learns something about the visual equivalence (Clay 1991). Alternatively, the child may see the word *come* on the invitation and ask for help to work out the visual forms that make up the word he has used in oral language for several years.

Print in the environment provides many examples of attention-getting words—from STOP on the road signs, to the McDonald's logo, to a cereal packet or the name on the family car.

How Do Letters and Words Make Out Together?

The heading above is intentionally vague because, despite Paul's articulate example about the "uh" sound in *mumps,* the task he knew a great deal about is not clear to some learners after months of reading and writing. On the C.A.P. children are asked to show "just one letter" and "just one word" with the aid of masking cards. Children who would be considered successful readers and writers and who have been at school more than a year often cannot make these decisions. The hierarchical concept of using letters to construct words is still not clear to them, and is obviously difficult, even though they are actively constructing words.

Teachers sense an urgency to teach the child letter-sound relationships and they foster such learning in thousands of different ways, but those teachers must also at times hold back and become observers. Teachers are such fluent users of print codes that they devise letter-learning activities for the classroom from their own sophisticated level of understanding. They need to observe where the children are coming from. One little boy, John, whom I observed illustrated something of a child's awareness of how words work. He came into school at five years from a low literacy home, with a very low score on a standard readiness test; his level of preparedness was lower than 95 percent of school entrants. A year later he was a high-progress reader. As his reading and writing experience increased John became a commentator on the printed code. He showed interest in words and their possibilities, he made analyses that his school program would not have taught him to do, he actively verbalized what he was noticing about print and how he was categorizing words. In one weekly research observation session he spontaneously offered these comments.

> Look! If you cover up the *ing* in *painting* you get *paint.* (Inflections)
>
> If you cover up the *d* in *shed* you get *she.* (Phoneme deletion)
>
> If you cover *o* in *No* you don't get anything. (Word concept)
>
> *I've* is like *drive* but it's *have.* (Phonology, contraction, and meaning)
>
> That looks like *Will* but it's *William.* (Subword analysis) (Clay 1991, p. 194)

Perhaps there was a whisper of teacher talk in what he was saying, but at 5 years 9 months John was very advanced in his approach to taking words apart. He could use inflections, give alternative sound renderings, and was aware of contractions and proper name conventions. He was a successful analyzer of letter-word relationships, and was aware of many more features of the code than just letter-sound relationships. His flexibility and varied approaches to the code would be hard to build into a sequenced teaching program. John became aware, and then more aware, because he was a constructive learner who actively explored literacy activities for himself, driven by his own interest in letters and words. Acting so successfully, he came to know more about the way the cipher, or code, maps the printed words on spoken ones (Gough 1972), and created new opportunities for himself for noticing more things about how the code for English worked.

Teachers may facilitate or retard such learning. Many programs prescribe sequences of instruction that actually slow up letter-sound relationship learning, both because so much time is allocated to teacher-selected features of the coding system and because of what the teacher selects for emphasis. The more natural language of storybooks, as opposed to the contrived texts of many beginning reading books, may cover for the limitations of a sequenced curriculum because the natural-language texts allow children to go beyond the information given in the teaching sequence. They provide opportunities for children to learn those things that either the teacher or the learner has failed to attend to. If the program allows children to reread familiar natural-language texts, they will have opportunities to learn about the features of language not found in contrived texts. Given teacher support and opportunity, literacy learners can become more cognitively aware (as John did) and increasingly independent about pushing the boundaries of awareness. This is not to say that they can discover the code themselves; the environment and activities of the classroom must be supplemented by interactions with teachers, who scaffold opportunities for the expansion of awareness and assist the learner in pulling out more and more awareness from the experience.

Visual Perception: Awareness of Where to Look, What to Look at, and What to Look For

Important learning in the visual perception of letters occurs quickly for most children, but apparently rather slowly for a few. Features of the code discussed above challenge beginning readers and writers, but so does getting visual information from print. And visual perception of print calls for more than merely learning letters in isolation. The child must

- familiarize the eye and the hand with the graphic shapes in two-dimensional space in both reading and writing,
- look at single shapes and clusters of these shapes,
- scan from left to right, with a return sweep to the left, moving from top to bottom of a page,
- cope with the size of the print (larger print can help poor readers),
- adjust to the spacing of print between words and lines (more space helps young readers),
- find and use higher-order units (chunks), not just single letters.

The role of the space in printed language is important and is best illustrated by examples from Paul (Bissex 1980), who wrote his first message to his mother at five years: RUDF (Are you deaf?). A few months later Paul wrote the following long message, still without spaces between words.

EFUKANOPNKAZIWILGEVUAKANOPENR
(If you can open cans I will give you a can opener.)

What precisely was Paul aware of?

Being able to distinguish the shapes of letters will determine the quality of the information that the active reader has to work with. We might have many questions but few answers as to what learners perceive as they look at the letter symbols. "Scanning" the letter has been an attractive metaphor to use, as if the eyes trace an outline; but most exposures are too brief for tracing movements to occur (Frith and Volers 1980). Gibson's (1969) experiments began an exploration of the relationship between observable scanning movements and the internal scanning that goes on in the brain. Does attention make use of real scanning movements that are internalized? (This was a popular theory among Russian developmental psychologists, which Gibson challenged; see Pick 1992.) If stimuli are not absorbed in a unitary fashion, at a glance, and scanning does not take some path of successive analyses of parts, then what? Can large-scale movements be internalized and then applied to small shapes as well? There are no satisfactory answers to those theoretical questions, only suspicions and personal beliefs. A working hypothesis for reading adopted by some theorists (Juel 1991, p. 768) is that children select some cue within the word that enables them to read it correctly. *However, writing does involve actual scanning and production of detail and may provide important links to visual learning in reading.* Writing also reveals some of what the child is noticing when he or she does not put all the letters into the finished product.

In some way the brain must become aware of what it must do with these new kinds of stimuli. In reading and writing highly experienced, literate adults can apply what they know about printed symbols to learning a new script (and even they find this hard), but children have in addition to find out about *what to look at* and *what to look for* in print for the first time. Researchers have found an early phase after about three to six months in school when young learners seem to be "glued to print": they give it intense attention and slow down to read in a very deliberate way (Clay 1967; Biemiller 1970; Chall 1979). This may be an important phase in learning about what to look at and what to look for. There is no reading that does not pass through a visual perception system (with the obvious exception of Braille), and young learners must become aware of things to look at (seeking visual input) and things to look for (searching for input guided by expectancies of what could be found).

I repeated an experiment of children's visual perception of print each year for three years on the same children (Clay 1970) and found that how one responds to features of print changes over the first three years of school on different time schedules for different children, and that these responses are related to successful reading experiences (which makes sense). Children take time to learn how to apply their excellent preschool visual perception skills to the new task of attending to the variations in printed alphabets and word forms while working within the constraints of the spatial and directional rules of printed English. It is complex!

Phonemic Awareness, or How to Listen and What to Listen For

Does the currently popular term "phonemic awareness" have any conceptual and developmental similarities with "awareness" as it has been discussed above? The term is used with several different meanings in recent literature on reading, so that a "yes" answer to that question needs some qualification. Yopp (1995) defined phonemic awareness as simply "awareness of phonemes, or sounds, in the speech stream." Williams (1995), with equal clarity, defined phonemic awareness as the awareness of the sounds (phonemes) that make up spoken words. She added this important distinction:

> [T]raining in phonemic awareness is not simply phonics instruction but rather training that enhances concurrent or subsequent phonics instruction or other reading instruction. (p. 185)

Phonemic awareness has only to do with sounds one hears; it has nothing to do with letters one sees. However, the literature is littered with its use as a synonym for letter-sound relationships, a collapsing of two different things. And phonemic awareness is only one part of a larger range of phonological awareness of the features in a language that allows speakers to signal differences by varying the sounds and sound patterns of oral language.

Yopp argued that most youngsters entering kindergarten are not conscious that sentences are made up of individual words, let alone that words can be segmented into phonemes. By the end of their first year at school (that is, by the end of first grade in the United States) many (but not all) children have gained this awareness and can break spoken words into their constituent sounds. They can remove a sound from a spoken word, saying "rake" when asked to take the *b* off the beginning of the word *break;* and they can isolate the sound that they hear at the beginning, middle, or end of a word. Yopp thought that few would argue with the claim that this ability is essential for reading progress, and that authorities would expect teachers of young children to include experiences in their curriculum that facilitate the development of true phonemic awareness (the hearing aspect), and to pay particular attention to those children lacking this competence.

Research has demonstrated that phonemic awareness is necessary for success in learning to read and write. Juel and Leavell (1988) found that children who entered first grade lacking phonemic awareness were unable to induce spelling-sound correspondences from their exposures to print or to benefit from phonics instruction, and Adams (1990) concluded that children who fail to acquire phonemic awareness "are severely handicapped in their ability to master print" (p. 412).

The development of phonemic awareness was, historically, subsumed under a more general approach to auditory perception training, plus various ways of teaching letter-sound associations. The new concept identifies more specifically that young readers must become aware of sounds within spoken words, and raises questions about how essential awareness can be developed. Teachers provide children with opportunities to play with and focus on sounds in such preschool activities as:

- rhymes, jingles, poems, songs, and choruses,
- stories read aloud, some selected for their play with sounds,
- rereading aloud that emphasizes rhyme, alliteration, phoneme substitution, or segmentation,

- games like "What I'm thinking of begins with . . . ?"
- manipulative activities with buckets of letters, magnetic letters and boards, and masking cards; and demonstrations and shared activities that call attention to sounds as one kind of naming of letters (Chomsky 1975),
- any message writing the children do in which a teacher asks "What can you hear? What else can you hear? At the beginning? at the end? in the middle?"

Poetry and songs, jingles and rhymes, and inventing words in play are activities that break utterances and words into parts, and make words from parts. Together with slow articulation of some words in writing and reading, these activities can result in significant gains not only on tests of phonemic awareness but also in reading and spelling achievement.

Particular interest centers upon how phonemic awareness can best be fostered in those children who seem to have neglected to give attention to it.

AWARENESS OF SOUND SEQUENCES

Perhaps because of the kinds of experimental tests used by researchers, the literature stresses being able to hear and identify single phonemes; but Elkonin (1973), a Russian psychologist who gave early recognition to phonemic awareness, stressed a feature overlooked in many established practices used by teachers. Activities are needed that help learners think about *the order of sounds in spoken words* and that help them analyze a new word in their writing into *its sequence of sounds.*

Most beginning reading programs bring most children to the awareness of sound sequences in words rather effortlessly. Some children, however, find it extraordinarily difficult to hear the sounds that make up words. *A few children consistently focus on the final sounds of words, which causes them to miss the initial sounds.* This is something Reading Recovery teachers have to accept as a place to begin to develop phonemic awareness with low-achieving children, though this fact has not been reported in any phonemic awareness study I have read recently (with the exception of Elkonin's work) and is overlooked in theoretical discussions of phonemic awareness. The science of the experiment has masked the on-the-ground difficulty, but I found a clear example from a high-print-aware child in a research thesis (Brailsford 1985):

> Trevor engaged in word-building tasks independently. Initially he built words starting at the final letters, moving to the middle and then filling in the gaps (as in Piglet) but within two weeks Trevor had self-corrected his print directionality strategies.
>
> P I G L E T (but two weeks later) B R O N T O S A U R U S
> 6 5 2 3 4 1 1 2 3 4 5 6 7 8 9 10 11 12

It is pragmatic to teach sound awareness in writing because segmentation in order to write letter by letter is essential; that is the nature of the task. In writing, when the teacher acts as an analyzer of words, articulating the word slowly but naturally, this gradually develops the same skill in the students. Helping children to hear the sound sequence in the absence of printed letters or words has been helpful for children who find the task difficult. The child should hear the word, speak it, and try to break it into sounds *by slowly articulating it.*

Reading Recovery teachers who work with the lowest achievers in the first years of school find that one place where phonemic awareness is imperative and can be developed is in one-to-one writing sessions as the teacher and child together write a sentence the child has composed. The teacher helps the child attend to the sounds within a word by providing a slow articulation of the sound sequence. As the days and weeks go by, the teacher's help is reduced and the child writes more and more alone. After several weeks an important shift is made. Children who at first had difficulty hearing the sound sequence in a word make a shift in what they are attending to. It occurs about halfway through their lesson series. Teachers follow the children's attention as it shifts from sounds to letters. The teacher who used to say, "What can you hear?" begins to ask, "What letters would you expect to see?" So, within a short series of lessons, teachers of low-achieving children work first with *phonemic awareness leading to a sound-by-sound analysis, but quite quickly follow this with an orthographic or letter-by-letter analysis.* The transition to awareness of orthography occurs early (Seymour 1986), but both analyses remain in the reader-writer's repertoire of appropriate activities. Teachers can readily help the child become aware of how knowledge first learned in writing is also used in reading.

The phonemes that are easy to hear differ from language to language. In English, consonants are easier to hear than vowels, but in Spanish it is the reverse. When teachers share the task, writing for the child whatever is too difficult at that time for that child, children gradually take over the whole analysis. When sound awareness is developed in association with messages the child has chosen to write, the child isolates the phonemes from his or her existing resource of oral language, as distinct from an adult-devised curriculum of what should be learned before what.

Phonemic awareness, like each of the other kinds of awareness discussed earlier, passes from a phase of no attention (with zero scores on experimental tests) through perceptual and conceptual hazes as vaguely aware children become more certain of how they are acting and what they are attending to in a pattern. Slowly they become more verbal, though not very precise, about what they think they know. At this stage it is great to have a child say that a fullstop "tells you when you've said enough" (responding to the sound signal of juncture); or that *eat* belongs with *cat, fat,* and *hat,* "but it doesn't!", showing both phonological and orthographic awareness.

OTHER FORMS OF LINGUISTIC OR PHONOLOGICAL AWARENESS

I once saw a child trying to write the name of the game "I Spy" into her story: she wrote "Eye Spy." Her teacher would need to understand the child's analysis in order to interact effectively with that child's level of awareness. Try to explain to someone else what this child has done!

There are aspects of the phonology of language other than phonemes that budding readers and writers become aware of, like finding the breaks (which linguists call juncture) in a stretch of language like "apastate" or "brannew bike" or the syllable break in words like "away" and "along," which sound to some children like two words. Children who speak a regularly syllabified language like Spanish or Maori quickly become readers and writers of syllables. For a detailed example we can look at the "regular" forming of the past-tense verb in English by adding "ed." The following example shows a child's confusion arising from his awareness of the phonology of the language and the grammar of the language. George was reading a book called *Rosie at the Zoo.*

> *George (reading):* "Dad took us to the zoo.
>
> "'Let's go and see the monkeys.'
>
> "'Me, too,' said Rosie.
>
> "We lifd her up."
>
> *Teacher:* It's got some letters at the end.
>
> *George:* Lifd-d.
>
> *Teacher:* Lif-ted *(hoping this will be helpful).*
>
> *George:* We lifd her up. *(He rejects the help and matches the final phoneme to the orthography, the final letter. He then reads on, using the ending correctly in* looked, walked, roared, *and* cried.)

The teacher demonstrated that *lifted* was like *wanted.* How confusing for George, who correctly negotiates *looked, walked, roared,* and *cried* in the same reading lesson! Later in his lesson George was writing about a story he had read. He wanted to write "The kids lied to their mother" because the children pretended they were not afraid. George wrote "The kids li" and asked the teacher, "Is it -ed?" The teacher said, "You write it," and he did. Then he said something the teacher did not hear and did not respond to. He said, as if to himself, "That means yesterday." So George, at one time an at-risk reader, demonstrated several kinds of awareness of how the phonology of past-tense verbs is complicated, and he verbalized the meaning of the -ed grammatical marker! His problem was more tricky than his teacher realized: how to choose between giving his attention to a phonemic issue—*lift, lifd* (which seemed to him to do the job), *lifd-d* (which was awkward) or *lif-ted* (which the teacher modeled)—or to think about when the event took place and how to signal that! He did not see the analogy with *wanted* as a solution, and he went back to sounding the *t* like *d*—"lifd"! George demonstrated a complex knowledge of the phonemic nature of past-tense verb endings and how they are represented in print, but he had a little more to learn.

An unusually crisp example of a four-year-old's awareness of grammar was reported by Karmiloff-Smith (1992).

Yara: What's that?

Mother: A typewriter.

Yara: No, you are the typewriter, that's a typewrite.

It was as if she caught the English language out on an inconsistency, demonstrating in the process a very early awareness of how the language works.

Phonemic awareness may be critical for a learner linking the oral to the written coding of language, but it is one of several types of awareness that can be observed as children learn literacy, all of which are necessary for literacy performance. Teachers work to bring children to awareness of many aspects of literacy activities, and the ways in which phonemic awareness is learned and changes over time is not unlike what occurs in other areas of awareness.

Awareness and Some Issues It Raises

The diversity in young children's understanding of literacy is challenging. Caregivers and teachers are conscious of how much there is to learn about literacy and do not want to undervalue what children already know about stories, texts, books, reading, and writing. How can they judge what would be helpful ways to encourage children's engagement with literacy events?

Most talk and printed text around the preschool child is made up of multiword utterances. In these early years the forward thrust of learning occurs when adults provide opportunities for children to be part of literacy activities, and interact with the awareness they show, opening up further opportunities, as in this example.

> I was speaking with a mother in my home while her four-year-old son browsed through the pictures of the *NZ Listener,* which contained radio and television programs. Our conversation was becoming difficult to maintain, as her son wriggled and bounced, sang loudly, and interrupted us from time to time. She leaned over, turned to the television programming page and, pointing very specifically, said, "That is where it tells you when [his favorite program] is on." There was silence for a few minutes, as he searched the page, turned to another page, hurriedly turned back and with difficulty roughly located the spot she had indicated. "Is it now?" he asked. "No," she replied, "but it says we should turn it on at four o'clock." It was as if an awareness that written messages can tell you important things had been created. The program entry held his attention for a while before he went on to something else, but one felt that there were more interactions to come from that beginning.

CAN TEACHERS OBSERVE CHILDREN'S AWARENESS?

As preschool children engage with literacy events they seem to move from acts to awareness. The changes are influenced by their interactions with people in both informal and somewhat formal ways. Children already know a great deal when schoolteachers give them their first reading books or writing tasks, but what they know is tentative and in a formative stage so that they would be unlikely to score well on some formal test of knowledge. What they know will differ from one child to another depending on what they have become aware of in their preschool environments. My visitor in the example above refrained from explaining advertising, and programming, and time schedules to her son, none of which this four-year-old wanted to know about, but she opened the door to more exchanges later about his new awareness. How can we respond to the features of literacy that children are becoming aware of, the strengths in a limited repertoire, when what they know differs from child to child?

My descriptive research of new entrants, designed in the tradition of child development studies, allowed me to observe reading and writing behaviors closely each week, away from the classroom, and record and analyze gradual changes in literacy awareness across the first year at school. Those nonexperimental studies did not allow me to observe visual perception changes; for that I needed a separate experiment. My nonquestioning approach did not allow me to probe the children's responses below the surface behaviors that could be observed, and for error behavior analysis a linguistic theory was imperative. Different research designs produce different kinds of information.

A research design used at only one point of time, or even a two-point predictive or retrospective study, cannot map the processes of change in individual children, or the different ways in which different children change from different initial states of awareness. Yet this is the reality of the situation. The processes of change must be studied in themselves, tested by hypotheses about change, and they cannot be modeled by statistical analyses from data that are not change data. Numerical test scores or pass-fail data derived from group scores cannot guide teachers whose children show literacy awareness, but of different kinds. I believe that teachers need descriptions of the changes that occur during a time of very rapid learning once children begin formal instruction if these teachers are to interact effectively with learners. In particular, such descriptions cannot be limited to correct outcome performances because the imperative for teachers is to interact with the putative, half-right and half-wrong formulations of the learners—the primitive awareness—in order to support further learning.

It is the immature beginnings of awareness and partially correct responses that catch our attention. We might want research to describe a neat progression from preschool learning through a year or so of formal instruction in literacy (see Chapter 5), but researchers typically find large individual differences. When I shared an easy, small book with children I captured whatever range of literacy awareness they could demonstrate, including such common behavior as starting from the back of the book or having the book upside down. The task was not intended to predict future success in literacy learning (although it does that quite well for a year or so). The Concepts About Print task was one among six observation tasks used to capture changes in early reading behaviors over the first or second year at school. *All tasks in my observation survey are like screens on which are projected the immaturity or degree of control demonstrated by the young child's tentative responses to print and to books.* Allowance was made for immature beginnings in the scoring of each observation technique. For example, in the letter identification test the child is credited with any response that gives a letter an identity as distinct from other letters; in the writing vocabulary the child is given an open invitation to write all that he or she knows; in the dictated sentence the child receives credit for recording correctly in letters any phonemes he or she can hear in the words, even when he or she cannot spell the whole word; and most particularly in the running records of reading all the child says and does as he or she tries to give reading responses to simple books is recorded. If such tentative responses are absent the teacher has much less to build on, and that makes a vast difference to how and what the teacher teaches. A wide-ranging survey of print awareness is necessary to bring out the many things a beginning reader might know, and its array of results will help teachers to *avoid the error of looking at only one aspect of early reading progress and expecting to find in that one aspect an explanation of the beginnings of complex literacy behavior.*

To provide a specific example, let me narrow the discussion to a few items in C.A.P. that measured directional behavior in a short-term longitudinal study of change over time of *identical quadruplets* in their first year at school (Clay 1974, 1982). The children were given tests of abilities (general and specific); observations of home and kindergarten environments, and later school programs showed that life was much the same for all four healthy children, and that they had similar developmental histories. Yet they acquired control over the directional rules of printed English on very different time schedules during their first year at school, taking 12, 26, 38, and 46 weeks respectively. This acquisition of directional control over the sequences in print related closely to how the quadruplets performed as readers at the end of the first and second year of reading instruction. The link between directional control and being able to profit from literacy instruction is *being aware that order matters* when you are picking up information in print (although it often does not matter when one is looking at pictures or at a television screen).

Conventions for recording languages differ: scripts are different (for example, Chinese, Hebrew, Roman), some use similar signals differently (like the inverted question mark in Spanish), and directional conventions differ (moving right to left on a page or from the back of the book to the front, to take the view of a reader of English). These recording conventions determine the order in which we direct our attention to print once we accept that order is important: scanning a word carefully from left to right would indicate a great level of brain awareness for an English reader, but it would be disastrous for a Hebrew reader. And deciding that *k* and *y* are the same letter is not where the learner needs to be. The young learner is unlikely to be able to verbalize these things, but observant adults can interact with what they observe in ways that enrich something of importance to the child. That leaves the way open for new opportunities to increase awareness on another day. Sometimes children resist changing their awareness for a considerable time. This is when we realize that the task is more complex for the learner than it seems to us.

HOW DOES ATTENDING RELATE TO AWARENESS?

Take an example from the first year in school. If the school entrant's attention is on the wrong page, or the wrong part of the page, on a word instead of a letter, or on the back end of a word rather than the front end, it may be difficult for that child to profit from the talk of the teacher who is working with a group of children. It is important for the teacher to ask, "What is the child attending to?" and "In what order?" Substitute terms for *attending* might be *noticing, orienting,* or *scanning,* referring to turning toward and beginning to explore some new object or situation; but *attending* also describes what the brain does when it first begins to "pay attention" to some new kind of stimulus. The problem is that when teachers orally explain things about literacy tasks, they cannot assume that what they say will teach a child's eyes and brain to locate, recognize, or use this information, when what they are telling relates to some feature of the code which the child is not yet aware of!

The important question is, to what is the brain tuned? Children with little prior experience find it difficult to orient to features of the written language code for many reasons. Learning to move across print from left to right, for example, is at first complicated. It involves

- a movement, or motor component;
- a visual perception, or looking component; and
- a mental, or cognitive component.

Children who are at first only vaguely aware of a few features of print shift from vague awareness to clear understanding and even try to put what they are doing into words as their control over print increases. Not only do children get the items right, but they come to know why they are right and can check their decisions in more than one way. When asked how he or she can be confident of being right, a competent child after a year or more of learning may be able to say things like this:

- "Because you make it this way" (motor component).
- "Because you have a little rest" (time, linguistic juncture).
- "Because big *M* has points, not tunnels" (visual component).
- "Because you need more letters to make a word" (conceptual component).
- "That's *no* but if you start with *o* it's another word I don't know" (information about order in *no* and *on*).

Children *demonstrate* that they have verbal, visual, motor, and order information about reading and writing when questioned about a task. It is this information, tentative and primitive, that we build on when we interact with children's awareness.

Tasks like Concepts About Print work well as observation instruments for teachers to find out

- what children are attending to (by this I mean *looking at, looking for, listening to,* and *listening for*),
- whether progress is occurring,
- and what action teachers might take to try to change the child's responses
- or to change their way of interacting with the learner.

Although visual attention is hard to observe, special tasks (like C.A.P.) give teachers information about some aspects of learning to read at the time when it is important for formal school instruction to create links between oral language and reading. It is not the score on a test that the teacher needs to know, but rather how to interact with the child who has an immature level of awareness.

However, outward signs of attending are not enough. There needs to be some other evidence that the learner has responded to some part of the experience.

GETTING THE BRAIN'S ATTENTION

When I developed the C.A.P. task I put a book into children's hands and read it to them. I asked them to act, to make some nonverbal response showing me what they understood but not necessarily telling me in words. *In learning to read it is essential to know where to attend, in what sequence, and how to pick up different kinds of information. While this involves cognitive activity of a kind, it does not mean that children have to deal with the problem by talking about it, or that they should direct themselves by talking themselves through the task.*

Simple tasks capture children's tentative attempts to read or write and allow the child to project a range of behaviors, from immaturity to control, onto a "screen" for the teacher to observe. This information makes a vast difference to teachers, because what they must do in the absence of these tentative responses is very different from what they must do if the child demonstrates the behaviors.

As the child attends with hands, ears, and eyes, behavior may be temporarily brought to a level of conscious manipulation by the child or the teacher, and this may begin a new shift in the child's awareness. *The child is a creator of awareness* as he or she works at analyzing print and, in that analysis, pays close attention, tries new responses, notices new features, puzzles over them, and reaches understanding. The child may change the analysis within a day or so, as new encounters uncover previously unseen features.

Thus the route to awareness lies within the actions taken by the learner. The teacher's words, or the terminology of instruction, or the sequence of instruction dictated by experts may be grossly out of synch with the learner's actions, and when this happens the learner may seem to the teacher to be confused. Teaching helps some children because they are already "aware," but those who are "unaware" are readily confused by it. Because children act, they come to know how they are acting and what works well. Teaching needs to provide opportunity for activity, to create situations in which children become involved along a gradient of challenge, and then to provide scaffolds of support for increasing awareness, involvement, ways of knowing, and independent learning.

Children are highly successful in widely different instructional programs and they start at different times—between four to seven years in cultures that have different expectations. The set of behaviors children need in order to profit from instruction depend on the expectations in the culture, the age of entry to school, and the emphases built into the program. Only some of children's learning is done in school; much occurs in homes and communities. It is inevitable that children will develop literacy awareness through very different encounters in their preschool cultures.

It is, however, important for educators to get a sense of some starting points in what could seem to be an elusive process. Children's early attempts to write direct our attention to features the children are attending to. How they work out the rules of word order and letter sequence are possible starting points. C.A.P. points up other possible starting points in the learner's shift from vague awareness to conscious manipulation of ideas about books. Some systematic attention to children's awareness can be made by teachers if they do the following:

- Find out on the child's entry to school what book behaviors he or she brings to formal instruction.
- Monitor changing responses on book behaviors over the first year of instruction.
- Establish what is known and what might be taught (that is, inform the instructional task).
- Find out which children need special help with literacy awareness after the first year of instruction.
- Find out in what ways children are relating what they *see* to the single sounds and the patterns of sound in what they *say*.

Literacy learners will continue to discover novel things about both the oral language code and the written language code, and how to relate one to the other, for many years.

THE ISSUE OF INDIVIDUAL DIFFERENCES

Individual differences in literacy awareness, historically attributed mainly to differences in intelligence or maturity, have been shown to be highly related to social and cultural factors that limit or extend opportunities to learn. What children can do at entry to school is heavily weighted on the side of prior opportunities to learn. Playing safe, many kindergarten and first-grade programs are still organized as if most children come to school without any knowledge of literacy, and as if all children must be taught all components. Basal readers, workbooks, reading readiness activities, and prescriptive programming ignore the experiences children have with reading and writing before school and treat all children as empty slates (Goodman 1990). Those who are already competent are sometimes considered an embarrassment for "set piece" classroom programs. Staff teams should ask each other questions about what they have seen each child do and how best to build on each child's current strengths. The concept of awareness encourages us to think about the many ways individuals may start their literacy learning journey. How can teachers deal with children who have a high awareness of print and at the same time provide for those who have avoided literacy learning opportunities and have low awareness of print? These types of students will respond differently to the opportunities provided by schools.

Brailsford (1985) studied Canadian children as they entered school. Print-aware children managed to engage with the teacher's program even when it did not relate closely to what they already knew. Low print-aware children soon gave up trying to make sense of the teacher's requests and became passive in the teacher's presence, as if to say, "If I am to learn it is your responsibility and you have to put the learning into me." Obliging but passive learners did not show signs of literacy awareness and did not know how to act in this new situation. Perhaps intimidated by the degree of newness they believed that the teacher would somehow deliver the learning to them! A teacher using a concept of developmental learning might not actively assist such children to engage with the real learning in the classroom. If all that is offered the child is a time of waiting for maturity to arrive that would worsen the plight of those most in need of help.

Four- to seven-year-olds become aware of many sources of information in print relating to the written code. *Both depth of awareness in any area and breadth of awareness in several areas can profitably be used by learners as starting points for literacy learning in school. A foothold of some kind is a great advantage.* There is a gradual accumulation of expertise, moving from

1. orientation to literacy activities to
2. involvement in literacy activities to
3. developing awareness of some different kinds of information that lie within written language.

We could assume that each learner will move from acts to awareness of many aspects of written language, and later from awareness to being able to verbalize that awareness.

Increased awareness of the written code can appear in a short period of time after entry to school, when a large group of children eagerly demonstrate what they know. Another group of children have some well-developed awareness of selected aspects of written language before they come to school but find it difficult to bring that prior knowledge to bear upon the particular activities created by the teacher. The school program may not help them expand the awareness for literacy learning that they already have (see the example of Sally in Clay 1987; and that of Nicholas in O'Leary 1997). A third group of children have yet to even begin to discover that there is anything worthy of their attention in black marks on white paper. (Within each of these groups is a range of individual differences.) Educational packages of set curricula are usually ill adapted to the needs of the second and third groups described above. For these children, teacher interactions are crucial for learning to occur.

THE ISSUE OF TEACHING BY TELLING

Given my arguments above about children's moving through many immature attempts and partially correct acts as they shape up effective responding, it is not enough to have children adopt our verbal statements about what they are doing. We want them to think about their thinking and not merely parrot teacher talk. Some current educational instruction promotes explicit discussion, modeling, and practice of verbalization by the learner, a common approach to instructing children in the USSR in the early 1970s (Zaporozhets and Elkonin 1971). A Vygotskyan notion of "cognitive apprenticeship" is used in programs that espouse a gradual transfer of responsibility of regulating performance with spoken instructions from the adult later used by the child to guide his or her actions (Baker 1994, p. 229). This verbal guidance of learning might be worth exploring with older children, but it is not of great assistance to a teacher working with learners who are tentative, aware of very little, and finding footholds in different aspects of a complex task.

A helpful theory for teachers of young children would sensitize them to what a particular child is already aware of, lead them to interact with the child's activity in ways that call forth a new kind of response, and lead them into interactive teaching that

- consolidates awareness and reinforces what is known;
- opens up that awareness in new ways;
- awakens new awareness, interest, and action; and
- expands awareness and checks it out in another place and on another day.

The mother and four-year-old's encounter with the television programming guide foreshadowed a potential journey in those directions.

Cazden (1992) has written about three ways of teaching—by teacher telling, by teacher revealing, or by the learners working it out for themselves. For example, an expert can "tell" me how to solve my computer problem and talk me through it; or my colleague can "reveal" what needs to be done to get me into a new procedure, which I only come to understand as I try it under scaffolded support and use it effectively; or I can try to "discover" the solution on my own. Which is the "right" procedure? That depends on my expertise: the more I know, the more I can solve myself or work out from the expert's instructions; but the less I know, the more I need a helping hand from someone who sees where I am and *what my learning problem is.* A criticism of the "telling" that many teachers consider to be their professional contribution is that it proffers cognitive guidance that is liable to confuse some learners. A counterclaim, that children will learn best if they can and do discover what is necessary for themselves, has been criticized because some children would require a lifetime of immersion to learn this way (Delpit 1992, p. 296). A third position close to Cazden's concept of "revealing" is for literacy teachers *to actively support the early formative stages of perceptual processing so that children make successful responses, and through doing so come to know how to make them without external support.*

I think of a child's primitive processes, which form hidden processing relationships, passing through many extending and integrating changes as more difficult information is processed—and all this before a teacher has noticed that the child is beginning to learn something new. My view is developmental in the Karmiloff-Smith (1992) sense that a series of changes is occurring in the types of mediation used by novice readers as they become aware of the information sources in written language. Direct attempts to foster cognitive reasoning about literacy may threaten effective fast processing of information from print, which will allow learners to give attention to the content of the messages in the print. In due course young constructive children will become able to verbally comment on their actions, but teachers may be unduly eager to tell children how to find and use (i.e., process) information in print.

Adults who observe their own reading give explanations of what they do that are not necessarily a good account of what the brain is working on, because the brain is working very fast in intricate ways. In addition, adults are so expert at reading that what they do is little guide to what young readers need to learn in order to become experts. At this beginning stage teachers have to work with children's vague awareness and try to work out what "cognitive confusions" impede their progress. The goal is to build up the children's effective performance with a minimum of conscious intervention. Message-getting in reading is the goal, but if readers give conscious attention to how they control their cognitive processes, this may slow them down.

We need to have children successfully monitoring and controlling their literacy acts, but with minimal conscious attention. As processing becomes more successful, children may volunteer verbal comments on how they are thinking about what they are doing (see John, p. 54), and teacher-child dialogue about the processes can occur with minimal confusion. The distinction is easy to argue for on paper, but is often hard to maintain during a teaching interaction. Young learners often know how to act before they are able to talk with teachers about how they work on print.

I think of "processing the information on the printed page" as going in search of and finding information of many different kinds in print—that is, becoming aware of what is there to be used. In fluent reading the perceptual processing and message processing need to be fast; the slow, labored, and verbalized cognitive work is used on the hard parts (usually the new, the vaguely familiar, or the confused parts). The system expands in efficiency through extensive, fast, perceptual processing, which releases attention for more deliberate analysis of newer stuff. The foundational learning of perceptual processing that the young child is building is hidden from sight, involving as it does visual perception responses in milliseconds, vague linking associations, silent self-corrections, and other control processes, none of these adequately modeled by psychologists. The theory of co-construction, discussed later, overcomes the inadequacies of telling for the young child.

A spate of teacher's telling could confuse a child and delay the very learning it was designed to foster. It must be remembered that *teachers are often trying to develop awareness the nature of which they do not fully understand themselves.* In addition, our own analysis of what we do is often faulty, or not the whole story. How often, for example, have my friends left out an important part of directions of how to get from A to B. Finally, there are many reports of psychological testing and laboratory experiments where children are not able to "understand the instructions" well enough to do what is required. Telling can misdirect actions and learning.

Quality Interactions with Beginning Readers and Writers: A Light Touch

Teachers notice things the reader is attending to, they catch the child in action. They notice which foothold in print is being used and support it. They interact with the child using it, stretching out the opportunity so that the child can give it more attention. Sometimes they interact to enhance what can be attended to, expanding the teachable moment and the child's opportunity to notice something novel. Their interaction involves capturing the attention or awareness they noticed in the reader, sharing the experience. They may mark the feature with emphasis, or prolonged attention, or brief acknowledgment; they may perhaps model it by repeating it, or demonstrate it in another place, or help the reader make a clear link with something he or she already knows. Some of the teachers' interactions celebrate that things have been brought together and are going well; they do this with brief gestures or comments that let the child know that what he or she just did worked well, but without interfering with the ongoing reading or writing. All such teacher interactions serve to increase awareness. Too much explanation can make it difficult for learners to know what they did right, or where they should direct their attention. The youngest learners with the least preparation who are reaching for the lowest rungs of the ladder are not up to learning from a barrage of telling from teachers or invitations to talk about how they think.

AGE IS NOT THE INDICATOR

In discussing awareness I have been dealing with a set of behaviors children learn before or soon after entering school. The impact of schooling on C.A.P. scores was clear in one research study, which compared children from the United States and Denmark (Schmidt 1982). The children were aged five, six, seven, and eight; the American children began instruction at age six and the Danish children at seven. There were no significant differences among the five-year-olds in the two countries; the American children scored higher at six and seven; there were no differences at eight. Age of entry to school explained the differences; the Danish researchers concluded that as the C.A.P. behaviors could be learned in the first year of school paying attention to print awareness before school was not critical for success in learning to read. The research consolidated the interpretation that most children become aware, and gain access to, some information in print before they enter school, but they complete their learning (for example, of the total set of letters) under the pressure of learning to read and write in school. The more awareness children have of print before entering school the easier it will be for them to learn what is taught in their first year of school.

Nevertheless, schools must inform themselves of the risk areas created by the cultural settings of the populations of children they serve, and must identify for extra attention the children with low print awareness. Awareness is a key concept for educators who work with children who are making the passage from language heard to language seen (Bissex 1980, p. 119).[1]

WHAT DO QUALITY TEACHING INTERACTIONS LOOK LIKE?

How can adults be encouraged to interact with the various behaviors children are likely to display? It is easy to confuse learners with our enthusiasm when they are just beginning to form a new concept, the very time that parents and educators want to be most helpful. How can the natural response to tell, and have the child echo the instruction, be more profitably turned to *revealing with a gain in understanding?* It is easy to tell but hard to reveal. How can adults be encouraged to interact most effectively with children who demonstrate many different kinds of literacy awareness?

In preschool or at school entry, children may be able to "tell the story" from the pictures of a book. They may be able to point to some eye-catching words in print; if they point to each word and find they have spoken words to spare, they may be able to revise their "storytelling" response and try again to match the words in the lines with the breaks in their speech. It is unlikely that these learners would be able to talk about how they were doing what they were doing.

Six months later, in school, they may act with more assurance. They might "read" the word *telephone* correctly, using only the *t* and the picture as selected cues, and notice some other feature of the word, such as how long it is. They may make errors as they read a simple text, double back, and correct the errors without any prompting from teachers, but still they may not be able to say what they did or why they did it, and teachers know that they are not using all the information in print. Important learning is occurring without being put into words. Self-corrections are common, as if children even at this early stage are aware of, or have a sense of, mismatch or error (Clay 1969, 1991) and try to make repairs. Within a year of entering school the learner may be able to chat with a stranger in quite knowledgeable ways about some aspects of his or her writing or reading.

Yopp and Singer (1994) present a brief, but astute, summary of the role of teacher interactions with awareness in the first years of school:

> Although the teacher can and tends to assume the linguistic and cognitive requirements in the initial period of learning to read, a teacher phase-out from this responsibility and phase-in of students as they become ready to develop and mobilize their own resources and interact with more demanding stimulus tasks on their own is necessary in order to pace students' reading development at an appropriate rate. In short, an inverse relationship exists between the contribution of the teachers' resources and the demands that can be placed on students as their resources develop. The role of the teacher is to control this shift. (p. 388)

IS IT POSSIBLE TO CONTAIN THE MATTHEW EFFECT?

Some good readers become aware of features of the code in their preschool years; others are drawn into literacy actions when they enter school by their new teachers. Before long a kind of reciprocal learning takes over. As children learn to use more skills and strategies they become able to talk about them; as they come to talk about them they are more likely to use them and move on to more complex skills and strategies. This is a relatively late achievement.

In 1986 Stanovich used the term "Matthew effect" (derived from the Gospel according to Matthew xxv:29) to explain to educators that early achievement spawns faster rates of later achievement so that the rich-get-richer and the poor-get-poorer as learners advance in reading achievement. Stanovich outlined unchallengeable evidence. Then he developed two hypotheses to explain why these results occur. The first cause he suggested was a reciprocal relationship in which good reading ability strengthens cognitive processing and vice versa. In other words, individuals who have advantaged early educational experiences are able to use new educational experiences more efficiently. The second cause Stanovich suggested was that learners across time are exposed to environments that differ in the quality and quantity of literacy learning opportunities, and even when they learn in settings of comparable quality they "select, shape, and evoke their own environments" (1986, p. 381) by the choices they make in what to attend to. Stanovich identified as a major problem for future research whether instructional differences are a factor in generating the Matthew effect. A decade after his seminal article a clear issue for early childhood educators and teachers in the first years of school is still whether at the time of children's transition into school and for the first two years of school it is possible for teachers to turn the tables on either of those two purported causes of the Matthew effect. Yopp and Singer end their report quoted above with one answer to this challenge.

> If the pace of the shift is commensurate with the development of these [student] resources and toward higher levels of learning as required by "real reading" then students are likely to progress with a feeling of cumulative success toward independence in the acquisition phase of reading development. (1994, p. 388)

A New Challenge Emerges

Educators agree that children must develop awareness of many complex aspects of language in print. Phonemic awareness of the language they speak must be developed beyond what they already know. At the same time, print awareness, including visual discrimination learning and conceptual learning about the written code, must also expand; children must link hearing and seeing to an awareness of letter-sound relationships in all their variety, governed at all times by the road rules for attending to print. One teaching approach calls for these elements to be pulled out from rich natural language texts (somewhat like the child's own language used in dictated stories) and systematically monitored; another urges a systematic program of specific instruction, ensuring total coverage, "knowing in isolation," and explicit attention to letter-sound relationships.

The impact of teachers' attempts to teach through telling things children are not aware of, and to which they cannot easily turn their attention, must be studied closely. The worst scenario will occur when the not very well-prepared child is trying to hear phonemes, and at the same time distinguish between letters that look the same to him or her. That child can be misled by the teacher, who is further down the track, talking about letter-sound relationships, and words, and texts. The child is confused by the "I for ice cream" curriculum, perplexed by the emphatic and exaggerated "p-ing" or "puh-ing," the "t-ing" and "tuh-ing," at the very time when he or she is trying to hear indistinct phonemes and see visual differences within the print. Teachers' curricula and publishers' schemes often decontextualize letters and phonemes to make the task easy, and recontextualize them in gimmicky contexts, thereby removing children's attention from the important tasks of finding phonemes in actual speech and seeing letters in continuous text. When the teacher talk stems from years of knowing what must be done without observing where the child's awareness is directed, learning is at its most vulnerable. Mismatch between what children are struggling to attend to in the complexities of language in print and the instructional intent of the teacher talk will mess up the foundational learning of letter and phoneme awareness.

The early and basic challenge arising from my analysis is how to expand awareness of any child at any level in any direction. When teacher interactions are driven by observation, and the progressions on three fronts—phonemic awareness, letter identification, and letter-sound relationships—are paced by the child's awareness, cognitive confusion could be drastically reduced and gradual, cumulative gains made more quickly. One can assume—and teach—for reciprocal effects between reading activities and writing activities. It takes a year or more, and differentiation and refinement continue long after that.

Endnotes

[1]*Theories That Discuss Awareness*

What kinds of theory can guide adults who want to increase children's awareness of written language during early childhood?

SOME OLDER EXPLANATIONS

Cognitive Clarity. Downing and Leong (1982) described learning to read as the development of linguistic awareness of the functions and coding rules of the writing system and other features of communication and language. Because the set of learning is complex, and children have many new and arbitrary things yet to learn, Downing and Leong thought of young literacy learners as being in a normal state of cognitive confusion on entry to school; under reasonable conditions of instruction, they believed, children would work their way out of confusion into cognitive clarity. (They further proposed that cognitive confusion continues to arise throughout later stages of education as new subskills are added to the student's repertoire.) Their theoretical analysis resulted from careful scientific study of beginning readers. In my opinion, because the term "cognitive confusion" presents a negative view of what exists prior to some desired state of clarity, it tells teachers to be prepared for confusion and patient with learners, but it offers them little help about what to foster or facilitate. This general description must be picked apart and analyzed further (Hall 1987) if beginning readers are to shift from cognitive confusion to cognitive clarity as they become successful. Furthermore, the two terms "cognitive confusion" and "cognitive clarity" do no more than describe the degree of haze being experienced by the learner.

Instructional Language. Several researchers in the 1960s, including Reid (1966) and Downing (1970), drew attention to how the language of instruction used by teachers confused children. Teacher talk about literacy activities introduces many new terms and concepts to children ("letter," "word," "first letter," "space," "beginning of the line," "top of the page," even "next page"). When classroom discourse is filled with unfamiliar terms, many children do not know how to relate them to the features of the text or book they are trying to attend to, especially in group learning situations in schools. Research in the 1960s placed considerable emphasis on children's being able to comment on the code and use the language of instruction to discuss it, but some reports showed children talking effortlessly about print only *after* they had learned to work effectively with it, rather than by first learning many new terms.

Readiness Theories. The idea of readiness, like cognitive confusion, was also a theory that acknowledged children's lack of awareness of the significance of written code. It supposed a point at which the learner was transformed from being not-ready to being ready for instruction. Evidence became available that children come to school with extreme variability in their prior learning about literacy, that they are on the way to becoming literate but at different points in a multidimensional set of learning. Teachers and caregivers can notice an almost infinite range of things that different children can become aware of, things that adults can pick up on and take forward. This enriches a particular individual's repertoire of awareness at any level, enabling the teacher to take the learner to somewhere else within the complexity that encompasses literacy learning, rather than passively waiting for "readiness" to arrive. Such evidence has largely discredited readiness theories, and replaced them with the term "print awareness." New awareness can arise before entry to school, during a transition period following entry to school, and throughout schooling.

Visual Perceptual Learning. Theories of perceptual learning provide further support for the utility of a general concept of awareness. Some reading theorists understood that one must learn to operate effective visual perception strategies to make the necessary discriminations between letters and words (Vernon 1971; Gough 1972; Gibson and Levin 1975; Smith 1978)—that is, the visual perception of print has to be learned. Eleanor Gibson's (1969) synthesis, derived from a large body of empirical research, suggested that there are two components in visual perception learning: the improvement of the processes of perceiving as a function of experience and learning; and the acquisition of knowledge as a function of changes in perception (Pick 1992). In her view, the important process underlying perceptual development is differentiation, (as opposed to association). She saw perceptual development as an aspect of cognitive development and attributed the increasingly complex conceptual sophistication of learners in part *to their ability to detect more and more meaningful aspects of the rich stimulation impinging upon them.*

TOWARD MORE INFORMATIVE THEORIES

We have arrived at an important intermediate summary point. As the child's transition into early literacy learning has to do with linking oral language knowledge with spatial and visual forms of the written code, a double emphasis emerges on child action or activity and on adult modeling and demonstrating in order for the child to develop spatial and visual awareness of the code. As acts recur and the child's awareness sharpens, adults can shift to using verbal instructions to guide performance.

In either oral or written language, the process of differentiation is an apt way to describe the shifts learners make from awareness of one or two exemplars of letters, sounds, rhymes, words, stories, or concepts about print to completion of learning either closed sets (such as all the letters in a language) or foundational vocabularies of open-ended things like "words written" and "words read." In the area of oral language the differentiation must occur in the auditory perception of phonology and grammatical structures like inflections; in the area of written language there has to be differentiation of visual symbols, clusters, and spatial signals in the texts. Awareness that oral and written information must be linked leads on to awareness of regularities that exist between the oral and the spatial/visual components of language, and awareness of when irregularity occurs.

A Vygotskyan Approach. My earlier description of teachers interacting with awareness calls up the notion of scaffolds that support children's functioning and that can be removed as children become aware of how they act and of how their acts can be used and controlled. Support is lessened as awareness increases, or as attention is appropriately directed. Readers do what they know how to do independently. However, in actual fact the scaffolding of teacher support continues, for the sensitive teacher tries to work at the cutting edge of the child's competencies as the learner moves deeper into the consistencies of the coding system.

Vygotsky's concept of how the forms of mediation used by the learner in activities might change as competence increases can also be related to the general issue called by different theorists orientation/awareness/attention. As children move into literacy learning and gain more understanding of the written code, they presumably use new forms of cognitive mediation as they achieve "the integration of the semiotic codes of oral language and English orthography, plus world knowledge, into complex operations of reading and writing" (Berman and Slobin 1994). An example of this would be a shift from pointing to each word in sequence, to later internalization as visual and brain attention take over, at which time the teacher would discourage the use of the hand and invite the learner to "Try to work it out, but just with your eyes."

Such shifts might occur either on texts created by the child or on those given to the child in teacher-selected activities.

The orientation-awareness-attention issue is a special case of Vygotsky's conscious realization. As children become familiar with how to work with the teacher's lessons, and how to work on their own text-solving problems, teachers impose new demands for conscious realization by the questions they ask: "How did you know . . . ?" They may do this because they want to establish and maintain communication with the learner, or they may wish to know what information the child is trying to use; but the child, by being prompted to talk briefly and even ineptly about text processing, learns that we can know about how we know and thereby control our mental processes more effectively. The learner who is making important advances in reading and showing less need of earlier scaffolding must still not be confused by too much teacher talk, and has to be aware of how to utilize the interactions to best advantage.

I question whether conscious realization should be the goal in beginning reading. Although conscious attention to the signs that mediate higher mental functions should become available to a successful reader or writer for use when needed (for example, in problem-solving a difficult piece of text being read or written), *it should not displace the fast, perceptual processing required most of the time.* (It is not appropriate to drive in low gear when we do not need to.) Certain behaviors, developed and checked initially at an explicit level (such as directional behaviors and most of the early visual perception learning associated with writing), must run off as fast routines with some attention, but not conscious attention, during successful reading. Most cognitive psychology models of reading allow for the capacity for conscious manipulation at some time and in some form, but the perceptual, directional, sequential sign-reading operations used by the skilled reader should usually not receive conscious attention, but be available for deliberate problem-solving (for example, on harder texts, or with poor lighting, or on contrived texts, all of which should occur infrequently).

The Theory of Co-Construction. While the child's activity in reading and writing is a fundamental route to greater expertise, an alternative view has emerged as a contemporary elaboration of Vygotsky's work. This takes into account the interactions that occur with others as part of an activity. Interactions help to structure ways of doing and ways of thinking, and learning is mediated by interested others. The expertise of the child is *co-constructed* with others through social and cultural processes. As McNaughton (1995) put it, for example, "the participation patterns and the focus of the interactions when books are read to children in families carry meaning about social and cultural identity. Together these forces activate learning, and define and channel development." These arguments are rich with ideas as to why and how adults can interact with children's literacy awareness to enhance learning. I have emphasized children as creators of their own awareness for two reasons: for fear adults will set their interaction agenda from assumptions already in their heads and neglect to observe what the child is capable of doing; and for fear adults will talk too much about their own concerns.

Wertsch (1978) reminded his readers that *regulation by another is not the only precursor to self-regulation, for children make their own contribution to their learning processes.* Examples exist of repeated independent problem-solving (Kontos and Nicholas 1986; Watson 1994). Eventually children may be able to give some verbal account of how they are acting, but in important respects that is unnecessary and can even interfere with the balance needed for appropriate learning. The teacher's telling them and having them appear to guide their behavior by what the teacher said does not convince me that children have internalized the new learning.

The common but false assumption is that teachers can pull literacy behaviors apart, talk about them at length, have children verbalize about them, even have children direct themselves verbally, and then expect children to slide into a variety of "automatic" ways of responding. At-risk readers find it hard to give away procedures that they have devoted such effort to learning. For a variety of reasons it may be best to have children develop many early reading behaviors to a level of awareness *without* verbal analysis, in many cases leaving any dismembering until the behaviors are so well established that children begin to regulate their own activity by becoming aware of what has already been going on for some time under the direction of others. In Vygotsky's terms adults often take on the regulatory responsibilities for children, but research on cognition has still not adequately addressed the question of how children get to the point where they can function independently (Baker 1994, p. 209).

Instruction Directs and Channels Awareness. Katz and Singer (1982, 1984) wanted to know whether variation in instructional methods in the initial stages of formal reading development would differentially develop subsystems for attaining comprehension; and, in particular, if instruction emphasized one of these subsystems, whether that subsystem would become better developed than other subsystems and be a strength in the pattern of subsystems used for reading (as suggested by Barr 1984; Biemiller 1970; Chall 1967; Singer 1994). They designed a study in which children received their regular classroom program plus one of three supplementary treatments: (1) a graphophonemic treatment, including feature, letter, and letter cluster knowledge; (2) lexical level knowledge assessed by a morphophonemic subtest; (3) special attention to syntax and semantics. Predictably, they found that for beginning readers a treatment with a heavy emphasis on a particular subsystem created a strength in the beginning reader's development of that subsystem. The data confirmed the hypotheses: methods of instruction were functionally related to the pattern of subsystems that the beginning reader developed and could mobilize while reading. Differential methods did develop quantitatively different subsystems for attaining reading comprehension.

Katz and Singer described how the various subsystems underlying reading comprehension in the first year of reading could come about. They hypothesized that readers mobilize their knowledge, abilities, and cognitive processes into working subsystems for solving problems in reading, changing the roles of those subsystems according to their purposes for reading and the difficulty demands of the printed material being read. Further research by Yopp and Singer (1994) explored teacher interactions with the initial period of learning to read.

If the different programs that schools adopt create in children awareness of different components of literacy learning in the first year or two of instruction, then every adoption has risks and should be accompanied by an analysis of what these might be and what counterbalancing efforts can be made to minimize those risks.

Divergent Views and Few Answers About Linguistic Awareness, Metalinguistic Awareness, and Metacognitive Awareness. Mattingly (1972) described *linguistic awareness* as the process by which children develop knowledge about the nature of their own oral language and bring the grammatical and phonological knowledge that already guides their talking to bear on literacy learning. Linguistic awareness exists when oral language is far from mastered and continues to diversify through the interplay of written language knowledge and oral language. The awareness does not need to be conscious and verbalized but merely available, and its development continues throughout life. Awareness of phonemes and other linguistic features discussed in this chapter fit within Mattingly's description and broad theoretical framework (which could be paraphrased to apply to awareness of other features on the printed page).

Metalinguistic awareness and metacognitive awareness are issues of debate beyond the scope of this book. They were the subject of a study by Fletcher-Flinn and Snelson (1997), which explored two competing hypotheses about the emergence and change of metalinguistic abilities—namely, that changes over the years four to eight result either from some underlying change in cognitive capabilities or through the mediating influence of some third factor, like learning to read (and write, perhaps?). The researchers concluded that learning phonemic segmentation and gaining print awareness accompany learning to read and develop further as a result of reading, rather than being "strong" precursors for reading in children who have not been exposed to print. Teachers can bear witness to such effects being reciprocal and interactive, with one influencing the other in both directions.

Metacognition refers to a person's knowledge of his or her own cognitive processes (Brown 1980; Brown and Smiley 1978) and to conscious attempts to control one's own thinking, or to think about thinking. It is defined as "awareness and knowledge of one's mental processes such that one can monitor, regulate, and direct them to a desired end" (Harris and Hodges 1995). Metacognitive awareness may arise when some aspect of cognitive processing in literacy learning catches attention often enough that the child becomes able to talk about it, with teacher and student then talking together about the task. This gives the teacher new evidence of the child's growing awareness. But it arises in situated activity in very specific examples.

Baker (1994) identified two components within metacognition that theorists do not always clarify, and that are potential areas of confusion: knowledge about cognition; and regulatory processes that operate on cognition. Is it the knowledge or the control of the cognition that is accessible to consciousness? As literacy theories give more attention to literacy processing (what readers do in order to read rapidly and efficiently or to write quickly and correctly), more questions are raised about how much of this work needs to be accessed consciously (Paris and Winograd 1990; Campione 1987; Gitomer and Glaser 1987) and whether the speed and power of literacy acts are reduced by conscious cognitive processing.

The metacognitive questions are difficult ones, and they are only marginally relevant to the discussion of awareness in this chapter. They relate to how teachers might teach and what teachers might assume. Some think they can "train" learners in metacognitive awareness by having them talk about the concepts or relationships they need to understand: these teachers expect to tell children how to understand something (perhaps again and again), and that this will make them cognitively aware of what the task consists of. Verbal explanation comes readily to adults as a way of expanding awareness (and teachers are used to telling). Baker (1994), in an excellent review, criticized the uncritical acceptance of metacognition among educators who claim to teach it in their interventions.

References

Adams, M. J. 1990. *Beginning to Read: Thinking and Learning About Print.* Cambridge, MA: MIT Press.

Baker, L. 1994. Fostering Meta-Cognitive Development. In H. W. Reese, ed., *Advances in Child Development and Behavior,* Vol. 25, pp. 201–239. San Diego: Academic Press.

Barr, R. 1984. Beginning Reading Instruction: From Debate to Reformation. In P. D. Pearson, R. Barr, M. L. Kamil, and P. Rosenthal, eds., *Handbook of Reading Research,* Vol. 1, pp. 545–581. New York: Longman.

Berman, R. A., and D. I. Slobin. 1994. *Relating Events in Narrative: A Cross-Linguistic Developmental Study.* Hillsdale, NJ: Lawrence Erlbaum.

Biemiller, A. 1970. The Development of the Use of Graphic and Contextual Information as Children Learn to Read. *Reading Research Quarterly* 6: 75–96.

Bissex, G. L. 1980. *Gnys at Wrk: A Child Learns to Write and Read.* Cambridge, MA: Harvard University Press.

Brailsford, A. 1985. Kindergarten Children's Literacy Experiences. Ph.D. diss., University of Alberta.

Brown, A. L. 1980. Metacognitive Development and Reading. In R. J. Spiro, C. Bruce, and

W. F. Brewer, eds., *Theoretical Issues in Reading Comprehension,* pp. 453–481. Hillsdale, NJ: Lawrence Erlbaum.

Brown, A. L., and S. S. Smiley. 1978. The Development of Strategies for Studying Texts. *Child Development* 49: 1076–1088.

Bryant, P. E. 1982. The Role of Conflict and Agreement Between Intellectual Strategies in Children's Ideas About Measurement. *British Journal of Psychology* 73: 243–252.

———. 1984. Piaget, Teachers, and Psychologists. *Oxford Review of Education* 10, 3: 251–259.

Butler, D., and M. M. Clay. 1979. *Reading Begins at Home.* Auckland, NZ: Heinemann.

Campione, J. C. 1987. Metacognitive Components of Instructional Research with Problem Learners. In F. E. Weinert and R. H. Kluwe, eds., *Metacognition, Motivation, and Understanding,* pp. 117–140. Hillsdale, NJ: Lawrence Erbaum.

Cazden, C. B. 1972. *Child Language and Education.* New York: Holt, Rinehart and Winston.

———. 1992. Revealing and Telling: The Socialization of Attention in Learning to Read and Write. *Educational Psychology* 12, 3–4: 305–313.

———. 1995. Bernstein's Visible and Invisible Pedagogies: Reading Recovery as a Mixed System. Paper presented at AERA, San Francisco.

Chall, J. 1967. *Learning to Read: The Great Debate.* New York: McGraw-Hill.

———. 1979. *Stages of Reading Development.* New York: McGraw-Hill.

Chomsky, C. 1969. *The Acquisition of Syntax in Children Five to Ten.* Cambridge, MA: MIT Press.

———. 1975. How Sister Got into the Grog. *Early Years* (November): pp. 36–39.

Clark, M. M. 1976. *Young Fluent Readers.* London: Heinemann.

Clay, M. M. 1966. Emergent Reading Behaviour. Ph.D. diss., University of Auckland.

———. 1967. The Reading Behaviour of Five-Year-Old Children: A Research Report. *New Zealand Journal of Educational Studies* 2, 1: 11–31.

———. 1969. Reading Errors and Self-Correction Behaviour. *British Journals of Educational Psychology* 39: 47–56.

———. 1970. An Increasing Effect of Disorientation on the Discrimination of Print: A Developmental Study. *Journal of Experimental Psychology* 9: 297–306.

———. 1974. Orientation to the Spatial Characteristics of the Open Book. *Visible Language* 8, 3: 275–282.

———. 1975. *What Did I Write?* Auckland, NZ: Heinemann.

———. 1982. *Observing Young Readers: Selected Papers.* Portsmouth, NH: Heinemann.

———. 1987. *Writing Begins at Home: Preparing Children for Writing Before They Go to School.* Auckland, NZ: Heinemann.

———. 1989. Concepts About Print: In English and Other Languages. *The Reading Teacher* 42, 4: 268–277.

———. 1991. *Becoming Literate: The Construction of Inner Control.* Auckland, NZ: Heinemann.

———. 1993a. *An Observation Survey of Early Literacy Achievement.* Auckland, NZ: Heinemann.

———. 1993b. *Reading Recovery: A Guidebook for Teachers in Training.* Auckland, NZ: Heinemann.

———. 1997. *Using Concepts About Print with School Entrants.* In SET Special, Wellington, NZ: New Zealand Council for Educational Research.

Clay, M. M., and C. B. Cazden. 1990. A Vygotskyan Interpretation of Reading Recovery. In L. Moll, ed., *Vygotsky and Education: Instructional Implications and Applications of Socio-Historical Psychology,* pp. 206–222. Cambridge, UK: Cambridge University Press.

Delpit, L. D. 1992. Acquisition of Literate Discourse. *Theory into Practice* 3: 296–302.

Downing, J. 1970. Children's Concepts of Language in Learning to Read. *Educational Research* 12: 106–112.

———. 1979. *Reading and Reasoning.* New York: Springer.

Downing, J., and C. K. Leong. 1982. *Psychology of Reading.* New York: Macmillan/Collier.

Duckworth, E. 1979. Either We're Too Early and They Can't Learn It or We're Too Late and They Know It Already: The Dilemma of "Applying Piaget." *Harvard Educational Review* 49, 3: 297–312.

Elkonin, D. B. 1971. The Development of Speech. In A. V. Zaporozhets and D. B. Elkonin, eds., *The Psychology of Preschool Children,* pp. 111–185. Cambridge, MA: MIT Press.

———. 1973. Reading in the USSR. In J. Downing, ed., *Comparative Reading,* pp. 551–580. New York: Macmillan.

Escamilla, K., A. M. Andrade, A. G. M. Basurto, and O. A. Ruiz. 1994. *Instrumento de Observación de los logros de la lecto-escuritura inicial: Spanish Reconstruction of* An Observation Survey: *A Bilingual Text.* Portsmouth, NH: Heinemann.

Ferreiro, E., and A. Teberosky. 1982. *Literacy Before Schooling.* Portsmouth, NH: Heinemann.

Fletcher-Flinn, C., and H. Snelson. 1997. The Relation Between Metalinguistic Ability, Social Metacognition, and Reading: A Developmental Study. *New Zealand Journal of Psychology* 26, 1: 20–28.

Frith, U., and J. M. Volers. 1980. *Some Perceptual Prerequisites for Reading: The World of Two-Dimensional Space.* Newark, DE: International Reading Association.

Gibson, E. J. 1969. *Principles of Perceptual Learning and Development.* New York: Appleton-Century-Crofts.

Gibson, E. J., and H. Levin. 1975. *The Psychology of Reading.* Cambridge, MA: MIT Press.

Girling-Butcher, W., G. W. Phillips, and M. M. Clay. 1991. Fostering Independent Learning. *The Reading Teacher* 44, 9: 694–697.

Gitomer, D. H., and R. Glaser. 1987. If You Don't Know It Work on It: Knowledge, Self-Regulation and Instruction. In R. E. Snow and M. J. Farr, eds., *Aptitude, Learning, and Instructions: Vol. 3, Conative and Affective Process Analyses,* pp. 301–325. Hillsdale, NJ: Lawrence Erlbaum.

Goodman, Y., ed. 1990. *How Children Construct Literacy: Piagetian Perspectives.* Newark, DE: International Reading Association.

Gough, P. B. 1972. One Second of Reading. *Visible Language* 6, 4: 291–320. Republished in R. B. Ruddell, M. R. Ruddell, and H. Singer, eds. 1985. *Theoretical Motels and Processes of Reading,* 3rd ed., pp. 661–686. Newark, DE: International Reading Association.

Grossi, E. P. 1990. Applying Psychogenesis Principles to the Literacy Instruction of Lower-Class Children in Brazil. In Y. Goodman, ed., *How Children Construct Literacy: Piagetian Perspectives,* pp. 99–114. Newark, DE: International Reading Association.

Hall, N. 1987. *The Emergence of Literacy.* Portsmouth, NH: Heinemann.

Harris, T., and R. E. Hodges, eds. 1995. *The Literacy Dictionary: The Vocabulary of Reading and Writing.* Newark, DE: International Reading Association.

Heath, S. B. 1982. What No Bedtime Story Means: Narrative Skills at Home and at School. *Language in Society* 11: 49–76.

Hobsbaum, A., S. Peters, and K. Sylva. 1996. Scaffolding in Reading Recovery. *Oxford Review of Education* 22, 1: 17–35.

Johns, J. L. 1980. First Graders' Concepts About Print. *Reading Research Quarterly* 15, 4: 529–549.

Juel, C. 1988. Learning to Read and Write: A Longitudinal Study of 54 Children from First Through Fourth Grades. *Journal of Educational Psychology* 80: 437–447.

———. 1991. Beginning Reading. In R. Barr, M. L. Kamil, P. Mosenthal, and P. D. Pearson, eds., *Handbook of Reading Research,* Vol. 2, pp. 759–788. White Plains, NY: Longman.

Juel, C., and J. A. Leavell. 1988. Retention and Nonretention of At-Risk Readers in First Grade and Their Subsequent Reading Achievement. *Journal of Reading Disabilities* 21: 571–580.

Karmiloff-Smith, A. 1992. *Beyond Modularity: A Developmental Perspective on Cognitive Science.* Cambridge, MA: MIT Press.

Katz, I., and H. Singer. 1982. The Substrata-Factor Theory of Reading: Differential Development of Subsystems Underlying Reading Comprehension in the First Year. In J. A. Niles and L. A. Harris, eds., *New Inquiry in Reading Research and Instruction.* (Thirty-First Yearbook of the National Reading Conference.) Rochester, NY: National Reading Conference.

———. 1984. The Subfactor Theory of Reading: Subsystem Patterns Underlying Achievement in Beginning Reading. In J. A. Niles, ed., *Thirty-Third Yearbook of the National Reading Conference.* Rochester, NY: National Reading Conference.

King, M. L. 1977. Evaluating Reading. *Theory into Practice* 16, 5: 407–418.

———. 1980. Learning How to Mean in Written Language. *Theory into Practice* 19, 3: 163–169.

Kontos, S., and J. G. Nicholas. 1986. Independent Problem-Solving in the Development of Metacognition. *Journal of Genetic Psychology* 147: 481–495.

Mattingly, I. G. 1972. Reading, the Linguistic Process, and Linguistic Awareness. In J. F. Kavanagh and I. G. Mattingly, eds., *Language by Ear and Eye,* pp. 133–147. Cambridge, MA: MIT Press.

McKenzie, M. 1981. *Extending Literacy.* London: Inner London Educational Authority Centre for Primary Education.

———. 1986. *Journeys into Literacy.* Huddersfield, UK: Schofield and Sims.

McLane, J. B., and G. D. McNamee. 1990. *Early Literacy.* Cambridge, MA: Harvard University Press.

McNaughton, S. 1995. *Patterns of Emergent Literacy: Development and Transition.* Auckland, NZ: Oxford University Press.

Meek, M. 1988. *How Texts Teach What Readers Learn.* Stroud, UK: The Thimble Press.

Ministry of Education, Israel. 1995. *Concepts About Print: A Tool for Assessing the Buds of Knowledge.* Jerusalem: Ministry of Education.

Ninio, A., and C. E. Snow. 1988. Language Acquisition Through Language Use: The Functional Sources of Children's Early Utterances. In Y. Levy, I. M. Schlesinger, and M. D. S. Braine, eds., *Categories and Processes in Language Acquisition,* pp. 11–30. Hillsdale, NJ: Lawrence Erlbaum.

O'Leary, S. 1997. *Five Kids: Stories of Children Learning to Read.* Bothell, WA: Wright Group.

Paley, V. G. 1981. *Wally's Stories.* Cambridge, MA: Harvard University Press.

Paris, S. G., and P. Winograd. 1990. How Metacogntion Can Promote Academic Learning and Instruction. In B. F. Jones and L. Idol, eds., *Dimensions of Thinking and Cogntive Instruction,* pp. 15–51. Hillsdale, NJ: Lawrence Erlbaum.

Pick, H. L. 1992. Eleanor J. Gibson: Learning to Perceive and Perceiving to Learn. *Developmental Psychology* 28, 5: 787–794.

Read, C. 1975. *Children's Categorization of Speech Sounds in English.* Urbana, IL: National Council of Teachers of English.

Reid, J. 1966. Learning to Think About Reading. *Educational Research* 9,1: 56–62.

Robinson, S. E. 1973. Predicting Early Reading Progress. Master's thesis, University of Auckland.

Rumelhart, D. E. 1994. Toward an Interactive Model of Reading. In R. B. Ruddell, M. R. Ruddell, and H. Singer, eds., *Theoretical Models and Processes in Reading,* 4th ed., pp. 864–894. Newark, DE: International Reading Association.

Schmidt, E. 1982. A Comparison of United States and Danish Children's Emerging Learnings of Written Language. Reading by All Means: Selected Proceedings, 12th New Zealand Conference of IRA (Hvad ved skolebegyndere om bøgernes sprog? Serien Laese Rapport, 6. *Laesning.* Copenhagen: Danish Reading Association.)

Seymour, P. H. K. 1986. *Cognitive Analysis of Dyslexia.* London: Routledge and Kegan Paul.

Sinclair, A., R. J. Jarvella, and W. J. M. Levelt, eds. 1978. *The Child's Conception of Language.* New York: Springer.

Singer, H. 1994. The Substrata-Factor Theory of Reading. In R. B. Ruddell, M. R. Ruddell, and H. Singer, eds., *Theoretical Models and Processes of Reading.* 4th ed., pp. 895–925. Newark, DE: International Reading Association.

Smith, F. 1978. *Understanding Reading: A Psycholinguistic Analysis of Reading and Learning to Read.* 2d ed. New York: Holt, Rinehart & Winston.

Stanovich, K. E. 1986. Matthew Effects in Reading: Some Consequences of Individual Differences in the Acquisition of Literacy. *Reading Research Quarterly* 21, 4: 360–407.

Tolchinsky Landsmann, L. 1990. Literacy Development and Pedagogical Implications: Evidence from the Hebrew Writing System. In Y. Goodman, ed., *How Children Construct Literacy,* pp. 26–44. Newark, DE: International Reading Association.

Vernon, M. 1971. *Reading and Its Difficulties.* London: Cambridge University Press.

Vygotsky, L. S. 1978. *Mind in Society.* Cambridge, MA: Harvard University Press.

Watson, B. 1994. Facilitating Independent Learning Early in the First Year of School. Ph.D. diss., University of Auckland.

Weinberger, J., P. Hannon, and C. Nutbrown. 1990. *Ways of Working with Parents to Promote Early Literacy Development.* Sheffield, UK: University of Sheffield Education Research Unit.

Wertsch, J. V. 1978. Adult-Child Interaction and the Roots of Metacognition. *Quarterly Newsletter of the Institute of Comparative Human Development* 2: 15–18.

Williams, J. 1995. Phonemic Awareness. In T. Harris and R. E. Hodges, eds., *The Literacy Dictionary: The Vocabulary of Reading and Writing,* pp. 185–186. Newark, DE: International Reading Association.

Yopp, H. K. 1995. A Test for Assessing Phonemic Awareness in Young Children. *The Reading Teacher* 49, 1: 20–29.

Yopp, H. K., and H. Singer. 1994. Toward an Interactive Reading Instructional Model: Explanation of Activation of Linguistic Awareness and Meta-Linguistic Ability in Learning to Read. In R. B. Ruddell, M. R. Ruddell, and H. Singer, eds., *Theoretical Models and Processes in Reading,* pp. 381–390. Newark, DE: International Reading Association.

Zaporozhets, A. V., and D. B. Elkonin, eds. 1971. *The Psychology of Preschool Children.* Cambridge, MA: MIT Press.

5 Developmental Learning Puzzles Me

WHAT GUIDES OUR UNDERSTANDING OF developmental learning? I am a developmental psychologist, but I have to admit, the term "developmental learning" puzzles me! What is the distinctive meaning of this relatively new term? Does this "new" concept tell me that when I wish to interact with children I should take account of what they can already do or understand? Well, that was Dewey's claim early in this century.

Some explanations of this term seem to imply that my grandchildren are all moving through developmental learning sequences that have been described in research. When I observe these children I find that this is not so; what they learn depends on the times in which they live, the country in which they live, and what each child chooses to attend to. If they had been growing up somewhere else, at another time, with different learning opportunities, their developmental learning would have been different. This is cultural relativity, a concept we cannot ignore.

There are two major problems mixed up in this puzzle I am trying to solve. The first problem might be called "The Path," a proposed sequence through which all, most, or many children are thought to pass. Individuals rarely follow precisely the path described by researchers, and researchers have almost never produced complete sequences—only some aspects of learning have been documented.

The second problem might be called "Ways of Interacting." There is much disagreement as to how expert persons (like parents, peers, siblings, and teachers)

The author was introducing a symposium topic with this piece.

should interact with developing novices. Should we ignore the child? Or withhold help? Provide opportunities but no direction? Let the child lead? Share tasks and work with the child? Help, show, model, or point directions in helpful ways? Or give up on all these adjustments and instruct in overbearing ways? Where readers stand on that issue will depend on whether they see children as learning by their own actions or passively responding to teaching initiated by others.

If we had a passive child and passive expert, one wonders whether anything would happen. The passive child and active expert situation occurs when educators ignore differences between learners and, after deciding what shall be taught, set about putting the learning "into the children." That solution is too simple, but it eliminates both the path and the interaction problems. Children are passive, and experts do things to them, like teach and instruct from an expert-driven curriculum. I suspect that the reader will be asking questions about The Path and the Ways of Interacting while reading articles on developmental learning.

Most educators wish their learners to be active, bringing prior knowledge to new problems and actively searching out solutions, learning as much as possible by their own endeavors. Why? Because they hope this characteristic will bring about effective current learning and ensure continued success in learning. Now it might be argued that unless the expert adopts a passive role, an unhelpful, holding-off role, an expert can too easily induce passivity in the child. As the learner becomes passive, having failed to understand what is wanted, the expert becomes more directive. If the expert takes a passive role in order to show children that they are expected to be active, learning for themselves, this danger is reduced. However, so is the chance to be helpful.

The active child working with an active expert is the most recent model to be written about (Vygotsky 1978). This configuration encourages an independent and active child learner, but it also assumes an active, interacting expert. Cazden (1991) has recommended that the best mix for development and learning supported by teachers is to have active learners (actively hypothesizing and teaching themselves) who, at the same time, have teachers who actively support, model, encourage, provide answers, and even correct children occasionally. *Active learners and active teachers!* Cazden suggested that we now know much about the active child, but we still have much to learn about the active teacher. She believes that "the descriptive research which we have seems to paralyze teachers, and make them give up even reasonable and helpful aids to helping children."

What Would a Support System for "Developmental Learning" Look Like?

If we accept a model of learners actively constructing what they understand, then we need to be observers of what children already understand. Vivian Paley understood this: as mentioned earlier, she made an agreement with her kindergarten class:

> Our contract read . . . like this: if you will keep trying to explain yourselves I will keep showing you how to think about the problems you need to solve. (Paley 1981)

Eleanor Duckworth (1984) advised us to engage learners in activity and keep trying to find out what sense they are making of what they are doing. For her, curriculum can be taken to be the things we do to engage students with matters we think are important. Minds get engaged, children see their own confusions, they learn to be tentative, and they learn the excitement of owning ideas. Understanding is complex, not simple, and it is not to be smoothed over and left hanging, unconnected. The teacher's task, Duckworth says, is to learn to understand someone else's understanding.

So Dewey's advice deepens in meaning. We observe what children are already doing, assume they are actively constructing some understanding of complex tasks, and try to understand how they are thinking about the activity. Then, responding tentatively, knowing that our assumptions could be wrong, we open up opportunities for children to take that thinking further. While this approach takes care of the interactions with an individual child, it is difficult to apply to the agendas of schools for groups or classes of children.

In general terms the goal is to help children move from where they are to somewhere else by empowering them to do what they can do and helping them engage in activities through which they can learn more. Helping may involve doing the hard parts of a task while children do the easy bits, and I cannot understand why some educators find that unacceptable. It is how experts interact with preschool children. Teachers and children both need opportunities to negotiate meanings, to uncover confusion, to extend each other's thinking in the interaction, and both need wait time to actively solve problems. In Paley's words, we need to "open avenues through which our children can reveal themselves to us."

Vygotsky's theories of the support system provided by others for learners at the growing edge of their competence come almost as a confirmation of recent developments in literacy learning. Teachers scaffold budding reading skills through prompts and examples and then foster individual control of reading by gradually removing social supports (Pintrich et al. 1986). There is more than a scaffold involved, however, because learning in the language and cognitive areas leaves the learner not only with the production of performance but with inner structures and functions capable of generating that performance (Karmiloff-Smith 1979). We have very vague notions about such inner structures of literacy learning at this point in time.

Learning Opportunities

Young children learn to do amazing things with oral language; all they need are opportunities to produce language in situations that are meaningful to them, to be understood, to be part of conversations, and to have a model of the language to learn from. Conversation provides for: (1) a chance to learn language; (2) a chance to learn how to learn language; and (3) the available "expert" talker who undoubtedly, if unknowingly, provides the means to achieving the first two things (Lindfors 1987).

Close recording of what children say reveals that they have traveled differently along the path of language acquisition, and they are not all at the same place in their learning: some have gone further than others. Their individual differences probably arose from different kinds of learning opportunities in their real-world contexts, and the only place to start further language development is to work with what they already control.

Does literacy learning in early childhood develop in some analogous way? When we found ways to probe what children understood about literacy tasks, research uncovered a wealth of data. Emerging literacy concepts underpinning the learning of the school's curriculum have been described in reading, writing, and spelling; concepts about books and print; directional learning; and word forming, message making, and rhyming. Are these emerging literacy behaviors really literacy learning? They are now accepted as legitimate and necessary responses, like the young child's approximations of the grammar of oral language. "Nobody don't likes me" is an attempt at a complex piece of grammatical construction. It isn't wrong so much as only partway along in its rule construction.

Do the differences in school entrants' achievements arise through different exposure to learning opportunities? We can be certain that children whose opportunities for literacy learning have been limited before they come to school will have to do that learning in school. Will they have to follow the same path as the preschoolers? And take as much time?

Cazden cautions against unwarranted celebration of what we have learned about language acquisition:

> For us as teachers, this descriptive research on first language acquisition can be paralyzing or energizing. There is no question that young children's remarkable success contrasts dramatically with the considerably less universal success of much language-learning—reading as well as writing—in school. As one response to this disheartening contrast, we can let exaltation of the power inherent in children's minds divert our attention from problems in the schools. (Cazden 1991)

Developmental Descriptions

Could we teach to descriptions of "the developmental path" described in research reports? This apparently simple solution is highly problematic.

Educators are able to draw on many studies and describe markers along the way as if there is a route to be traveled and achievements that can be checked off. However, I have many problems with developmental curricula:

- Research reports the average achievements of groups, but that average performance does not reflect the actual performance of any one individual;
- or it reports what the median child of the group was able to do, which also is not a model for all children;
- or it describes a longitudinal path taken by a particular child, but it is unlikely that any other child will travel precisely that path.

Enough markers of progress seem to plot a developmental route, a guide to teaching, but no one child has passed from marker to marker. I can give a specific example. Brown (1973) described the fourteen grammatical morphemes acquired during Stage 2 of his language acquisition description, but when these were used in an intensive program with a profoundly deaf child learning Australasian sign language the description provided no guidance as to which forms should be introduced in which order. From time to time the researcher was fairly certain she had to leave a form and reintroduce it later in the program.

No authority on oral language acquisition can tell you what usage to expect for a child of a particular age nor what precisely that child should learn next. It is possible to take a sample of current language usage and analyze it for achievements, and to make a statement about what the child already controls, and even to state a range of possible next changes that might occur in the near future, but the precise sequence is unpredictable (Bloom and Lahey 1978). This is so because oral language learning is very complex: like choosing among roads that crisscross on a route map, one can take any number of possible next steps. One can record samples that hint at what a child controls at this point in time, but no research description will predict where he or she will go next without being misleading more often than it is useful.

A child will attend to some aspects of a complex task before others, and developmentalists suspect that this has something to do with the cognitive complexity of what is being learned, but it also has to do with what the child is choosing to attend to, or what people in the environment are stressing. For example, I think we see a vast amount of something called "invented spelling" these days because teachers are making it clear that they expect it and want it. Why? Because what we have read suggests that this is a developmental step in learning to write. Did not Charles Read show this? I do not believe so. What Read (1975) showed so clearly was that children use what they know to solve new problems and that, young though they are, they form hypotheses about what might work in print. I have a sense that many teachers are directing children to write nonsense and children are obliging them, as they typically do.

Only performance is observable, and it must serve as a basis for inferring the nature of the underlying learning process. When teachers observe and listen, and try to understand what it is that the child understands, they are trying to work with the child's perspective in mind. This is very different from having a curriculum (preschool or school) where there is a sequenced plan of instruction and what the child is allowed to learn next is controlled by adult assumptions driven by the curriculum. But the blatant mismatch between an imposed curriculum and what individual children can do is not overcome by gathering together from research reports some averaged description of sequence of acquisition. Such research-based sequences can drive the expectations of teachers while individual children are working their way along various different paths.

Different Developmental Descriptions

The "developmental curriculum" may have been culled from average achievements of individuals learning in another culture. For example, children in the United States tend to know far more about the alphabet on entry to school than New Zealand children. I presume this is because New Zealand society does not see any particular advantage in this knowledge: it has long been a cultural assumption in New Zealand that such learning can take place easily within the reading and writing tasks in school. On the other hand, longitudinal research in New Zealand in the 1970s showed a strong correlation between writing in the first year of school and early reading progress (Robinson 1973), whereas in the United States Juel (1988) published longitudinal research showing little relationship between these two activities. I interpret that to mean that the two longitudinal studies showed different paths to achievement related to different educational practices in timing, emphasis, and expectations. What is described in these comparisons are different paths to similar goals, and a large role for learning opportunities to shape the apparent sequence of development.

There is a problem, however, in establishing this point. Science relies on replication of results, so countries with a large research community will provide many confirmations of their paths to acquisition, and countries with a small volume of research will be hard pressed to demonstrate that the world could be otherwise.

CONTEXTS

In the 1970s and 1980s in education we became very aware of the power of contexts, physical and social, and their influence on our behavior and what we are able to learn. The people around us, the setting we are in, the strangeness of a culture that does not match that of our own community can create a breakdown in what we can learn. Context and culture also influence sharply how the teacher understands, and interacts with, the learner. Cazden and Mehan (1989) provide advice to teachers on using community resources to overcome such problems. Just being in a class of children may change Johnny's power to learn from what it was before he came to school. The work of a particular classroom may change the power to learn for some children more than others because of where the program is started and whether the child can get to that starting point or not. Even the teacher's style of helping may prevent Johnny from bringing to the task what he has already learned.

If you were to compare writing samples of preschool children from the United States with New Zealand samples and with Argentinean samples you would see differences. Spanish-speaking children tend to write in vowels and omit consonants, while English-speaking children find vowels harder to identify and consonants easier. What children can hear in their own language differs by language spoken. I think the print forms in children's writing samples differ from New Zealand and the United States, and I do not yet know how or why. Context has an effect. One of my favorite examples is from a little Thai girl who spent her preschool years in the United States. Writing as a five-year-old in English she placed curls on every English letter as one would if writing in Thai script (Clay 1987). These culture, language, and context effects suggest that we can collapse developmental descriptions across settings and across time only with extreme caution. Can one write a general description of writing development and ignore such important differences?

INDIVIDUAL DIFFERENCES

Beyond the problem of cultural diversities there is a deeper and more pervasive conflict between described progressions and individual differences. A basic developmental "law" laid down in the early days of developmental research concerned the genotypic and phenotypic relationships. In simple terms it means children may develop from different genetic origins towards the same behavioral outcomes, and when they appear to go from the same origins they may reach different outcomes (see the discussion of identical quadruplets in Chapter 4). A similar logic applied to the effects of experience might be this: Children can go through different language experiences and yet end up with the same control over the grammar of their mother tongue; or children work through the same spelling program and end up with very different understandings of what it is to spell.

Descriptions of developmental progressions will be only a very rough fit as descriptions of individual progress. We need to think about what a teacher can do to accommodate the rich diversity of children's ways of exploring and using written language (Dyson 1990).

TIME DIFFERENCES

Knowledge about children gained from research should be reviewed and checked at quite short intervals since today's research populations may be responding differently from the original research populations, or conversely we may have more background knowledge to interpret those findings and would do so differently in the light of further information. Although we would not want outdated information to limit the learning opportunities we provide for today's children, in fact it always does!

I suspect that what was described in my book *What Did I Write?* (1975) as things children were able to discover about print in my country in the 1960s and

1970s is not what new entrants are producing today. There are marked differences in the writing samples consistent with a popular version of process writing and a misinterpretation of Charles Read's research. The developmental progressions are clearly influenced by what teachers expect to see and therefore what they, the teachers, pay attention to.

Educators should be wary of old theories constructed on the basis of old research, such as the early writing of Gesell, Piaget, and Vygotsky. In the past twenty years, research has shown how all learning is affected by specific contexts and cultures, and we must critically evaluate the current relevance of older theories for children in today's society. Gesell and his colleagues paid very little attention to children's writing (Ilg and Ames 1950): and both John Bowlby and Piaget have been criticized for paying too little attention to oral language development while making important contributions respectively to emotional and cognitive development.

Making What You Already Know Work in School

When children enter school, what they can do is determined by their different experiences in particular contexts, with particular learning opportunities provided and others unavailable.

I was disturbed by a report of Argentinean children in the first year of school in which the authors looked at the least prepared children.

> Group 1 children persistently refuse to write words they have not been taught. [One said] "I don't know. I have rocks in my head. I'm a dummy!" (Tengo la cabeza como un burro. Soy un burro!) Hearing this from the mouth of a six year old after one year of school is distressing. It reveals two of the most serious problems of the instructional system: a) if children do not learn it is their own fault and responsibility, and b) the instructional method has a restraining effect on children's creative possibilities [experimenting with and testing ideas with all the risks and errors this implies] and establishes a total dependency on the teacher. A significant observation is that resistance to writing increases toward the end of the school year. (Ferreiro and Teberosky 1982, p. 242)

In Canada, Brailsford (1985) presented a similar picture. Print-aware five-year-olds managed to engage with their teacher's program even though it did not relate closely to what they already knew. Low print-aware five-year-olds soon gave up and became passive in the teacher's presence. They do not help the learning process because they do not know how to act in this new situation. How does what they already know fit into this thing called schooling? They are cowed by the degree of newness into believing that the teacher will deliver the learning unto and into them. Is the passive role they adopt learned? It is frequently assumed to be "developmental," and something that time will do something about. As a result of holding this view, some teachers might not actively assist such children to engage with learning in the classroom.

How Do We Know About Child Development?

Are the theories and methods of research in child development suited to producing descriptions of "developmental" progressions to be used by educators?

The Child Study movement in the early 1900s emerged as a branch of psychology in the 1930s (Senn 1975). By the 1980s it had become the study of change over time, across the human life span; people of any age could be studied. It sought: (1) to describe what occurs; (2) to explain how and why change takes place; and (3) to optimize opportunities for enhanced development (Baltes 1983).

Systemic and sensitive observation techniques were worked out for studying change over time in learning and development. Some studies took place in homes, preschools, and play settings; others used a standardized situation, as in Piaget's questioning experiments and Donaldson's (1979) revisions of these experiments. The studies gave rise to detailed accounts of oral language and children's primitive, emerging ideas about reading and writing.

Historically, developmentalists searched for laws that governed the unfolding of competencies in children across times and cultures. When you had grown enough (developed) you could run fast. It was easy to form a "grow first, learn later" hypothesis about development. The best indicators of having "grown enough" were taken to be what average children of given ages could typically do, or normative descriptions. Normative statements underestimate what high-achieving children can learn and overestimate what low-achieving children are likely to be able to learn.

Theories about change over time were generated, and since education can be thought of as a myriad of interventions in children's lives during years of rapid change, educators tried to apply developmental theories to their enterprise. Developmental theorists and educators, however, share some goals but not others. While developmental psychology must take time to pose its questions and systematically test its explanations in a scientific way, education must act on today's best available knowledge for current programs and tomorrow's plan for changes. The teacher's job is to work with all aspects of the child's functioning as they impinge on a single task. Teachers know that it is the individual child who interacts in some holistic way with the specific task at a particular time. In contrast, developmental psychologists search for explanations in specialized areas, tease out the specific, eschew the complex, explicate processes, avoid global theory, and oppose unwarranted generalization, thus tending to exclude holistic theories (see Chapter 17).

An example of the educator's challenge lies in the concept of orchestrating many types of responses in a single production task (Dyson 1987; Clay 1991). Children do not control all aspects of writing or reading at once; but, mastering some of the task, they slowly win control over the whole task. As Dyson (1987) put it:

> [T]here are individual differences . . . in how students get a handle on the process, that is, in which aspects of the process they do or do not attend to at any given writing moment. Moreover, to this orchestration, students bring varied resources—different understandings of the encoding system, the text structure, and the literary purposes—and they bring diverse ways of interacting with other people and with other symbolic media.

This calls for an integration in pedagogy—not the time-honored analyzing of tasks into small pieces, but finding ways of letting children bring what they know together in a single problem-solving action or process. Dyson uses a metaphor of the child learning to weave the complexities of writing together and the teacher assisting the child with that weaving.

What we have learned about child development is abstracted and reformed into theories. Theories seek to explain phenomena. Theories change: they have to be opened up, modified, or discarded in the face of new evidence. The grand theorists in child development changed their ideas over their lifetimes as a result of further research. Conflicting theories thrive in opposition, for it is the role of researchers to propose and test out different hypotheses in their search for better explanations.

A contender for a new theoretical position has been the idea that there is or could be "a natural way to learn." As the complexity of what was being learned about literacy was explored, this idea gained advocates. Research showed how, in the "natural environment," children learn many things about literacy from informal interactions, parent modeling of reading and writing, and staged opportunities to explore literacy materials—all in the child's home. There are social interactions in story reading, with a clear expert role played by adults; and higher psychological functions are developed in the negotiations of meaning between child and adult. However, for many children on this planet that is not a description of their "natural environments"! The argument is convincing when it is expressed in the abstract, but it assumes that something like a rich, literate, middle-class, Western environment is available to all. Published accounts describe the positive instances; there is nothing exciting about the millions of children who are not getting the opportunities to do these things.

Back to Learning

So when I am in the United States and a question from the audience is "What do children have to know when they come to school?" I have to say that is not a valid question. Individual differences, contexts, learning opportunities, and culture all create the inevitability of different knowings, known in different ways, with different highs and different lows. Valid questions for the teacher who recognizes the need to work with, and build on, what the child already knows are "What does this child already control?" "What can this child do?" "How does he or she understand the task?" Teachers are supported by their understanding of the nature of literacy and the fact that it is complex. They observe the students for signs of what they understand and what they are grappling with. It is important for teachers to recognize small gains in control even when there is clearly still much to learn.

The "environment" of learning includes the context, the expectations, the adult model, and the existence of novice-expert differences displayed at an appropriate level. Dyson encourages educators to work harder to understand and develop examples of teachers building on the diverse kinds of child resources, "particularly the resources of children whom schools traditionally have not served well" (1990, p. 17).

Since the path along which the child has come will be in some respects individual and unusual, lacking learning opportunities in key areas, one approach is to proffer many opportunities and observe how he or she engages with them. I see no reason to make the child discover these alone. I agree with Dyson that we should "share the task by doing what he cannot do . . . at least he knows that there is more to learn and you provide a model of doing rather than a model of what to learn" (1990, p. 17). If no one gave the three-year-old the opportunity to discover the delights of book sharing, then as a four-year-old that child is long overdue for this engagement, and I would interfere to give extra time and attention, supporting the child's tentative moves into involvement with books enthusiastically. Support means sharing the task for as long as it takes. I would also share the construction of primitive writing, leaving the child to be as independent as his or her own competencies would allow.

Perhaps the tenet of developmental learning that I feel most comfortable with is the one that says "The new entrant is where he or she is and can be nowhere else." My program must go to where that learner is and take him or her somewhere else. If my program can take different Johnnies and Janes by different paths to similar outcomes, I may be addressing individual differences and cultural differences within the abstracted theoretical research descriptions of progressions in the literature. I can interact with each learner at that learner's specific level of ability, as literacy tasks come under that child's control, woven in unknowable patterns into complex processing, which will produce ever-expanding control over literacy tasks.

The understanding of a single teacher trying to work alone can be expanded by discussion with colleagues who bring their pooled experience to the problem of complex processes being learned by individuals. Where does a developmental description of progressions fit into this? It is not the map of the sequence through which children will, should, or can pass. It is a body of knowledge in the heads of teachers that guides their interactions with pupils. Whether this knowledge helps or hinders children's learning depends on the tentativeness and reflective practice of the teachers.

References

Baltes, P. B. 1983. Lifespan Developmental Psychology: Observations on History and Theory Revisited. In R. M. Lerner, ed., *Developmental Psychology: Historical and Philosophical Perspectives,* pp. 79–111. Hillsdale, NJ: Lawrence Erlbaum.

Bloom, L., and M. Lahey. 1978. *Language Development and Language Disorders.* New York: Wiley.

Brailsford, A. 1985. Kindergarten Children's Literacy Experiences. Ph.D. diss., University of Alberta.

Brown, R. 1973. *A First Language: The Early Stages.* Great Britain: Allen & Unwin.

Cazden, C. B. 1991. Active Learners and Active Teachers. In J. F. Flood, J. Jensen, D. Lapp, and J. R. Squire, eds., *Handbook of Research on Teaching the English Language Arts.* New York: Macmillan.

Cazden, C. B., and H. Mehan. 1989. Principles from Sociology and Anthropology: Context, Code, Classroom, and Culture. In M. C. Reynolds, ed., *Knowledge Base for the Beginning Teacher.* Oxford: Pergamon.

Clay, M. M. 1975. *What Did I Write?* Auckland, NZ: Heinemann.

———. 1987. *Writing Begins at Home: Preparing Children for Writing Before They Go to School.* Auckland, NZ: Heinemann.

———. 1991. *Becoming Literate: The Construction of Inner Control.* Auckland, NZ: Heinemann.

Donaldson, M. 1979. *Children's Minds.* New York: Norton.

Duckworth, E. 1984. Teaching as Research. *Harvard Educational Review* 56, 4: 273–274.

Dyson, A. H. 1987. Individual Differences in Beginning Composing: An Orchestral Vision of Learning to Compose. *Written Communication* 4: 411–442.

———. 1990. *Weaving Possibilities: Rethinking Metaphors for Early Literacy Development.* Occasional Paper 19. Berkeley: University of California, Center for the Study of Writing.

Ferreiro, E., and A. Teberosky. 1982. *Literacy Before Schooling.* Portsmouth, NH: Heinemann.

Ilg, F. L., and L. B. Ames. 1950. Developmental Trends in Reading Behavior. *Journal of Genetic Psychology* 76: 291–312.

Juel, C. 1988. Learning to Read and Write: A Longitudinal Study of 54 Children from First Through Fourth Grades. *Journal of Educational Psychology* 80: 437–447.

Karmiloff-Smith, A. 1979. *A Functional Approach to Child Language.* Cambridge, UK: Cambridge University Press.

Lindfors, J. W. 1987. *Children's Language and Learning.* 2nd ed. Englewood Cliffs, NJ: Prentice-Hall.

Paley, V. G. 1981. *Wally's Stories.* Cambridge, MA: Harvard University Press.

Pintrich, P. R., D. R. Cross, R. B. Kozma, and W. J. McGeachie. 1986. Instructional Psychology. In M. R. Rozenweig and L. W. Porter, eds., *Annual Review of Psychology,* pp. 611–654. Palo Alto, CA: Annual Reviews.

Read, C. 1975. *Children's Categorization of Speech Sounds in English.* Urbana, IL: National Council of Teachers of English.

Robinson, S. E. 1973. Predicting Early Reading Progress. Master's thesis, University of Auckland.

Senn, M. J. E. 1975. Insights on the Child Development Movement in the United States. Monograph. *Society of Research and Child Development* 40, 3–4: 1–107.

Vygotsky, L. S. 1962. *Thought and Language.* Cambridge, MA: MIT Press.

———. 1978. *Mind in Society.* Cambridge, MA: Harvard University Press.

Wertsch, J. V. 1985. *Vygotsky and the Social Formation of Mind.* Cambridge, MA: Harvard University Press.

6 A Fable

TMANY YEARS AGO THERE LIVED a developmental psychologist named Xxfldmn, who drew up a plan for having all the children in the land ready to learn when they came to school. He reviewed the research, read all the books, and spoke to all the important people. Like the governors of yesteryear he decreed the idea viable.

Xxfldmn was dedicated to science. He collected together all the knowledge about how children grow and learn, and then he would have them ready to reach their highest potential for learning when they entered school. Unfortunately, nobody could tell him how to estimate that potential before they actually got the opportunity to learn. Nature, said the experts, had deliberately introduced an element of random chance into children's genetic makeup to make humans adaptive.

At that time nobody could tell Xxfldmn how to engineer the overall quality of that genetic makeup, and society had already put a ban on cloning. Xxfldmn had considered cloning young school entrants primed with high potential, thus saving parents the bother of childbirth and the preschool years. In fact, he heard of one man in history who did try to purify a country's genetic stock, but ended up doing grossly inhuman things without succeeding in his aim. So genetic variation would have to remain. And what is more, perhaps parents would have to be allowed to bring their preschool children up any way they liked. It would have been

My apologies to all who work at this level of education. This fable and the caricatures are intended to stimulate thought, not to criticize.

convenient if Xxfldmn could have controlled the nine months of growth and development that occur in utero, because there are known influences that help or hurt the development of the growing fetus. For instance, smoking, drugs, and poor diet may stunt development, and being one of a multiple conception is sure to result in lower birth weight.

Furthermore, it is known that low birth weight can go along with various developmental risks for boys but not for girls. However, even if it could be done, there is no point in breeding a race of only girls. So once again Xxfldmn was faced with the issue of individual differences.

The Home Experience

Once in society, children are surrounded by people. Some of them have strange beliefs, such as thinking it is useless to talk to children because they cannot talk to you. Other families do talk to babies and even read books to them, but many people believe that these are foolish activities. Such beliefs and associated practices are known as culture, and some cultures emphasize school readiness more than others.

Yet the education system respects cultural background more in the abstract than in practice. If Xxfldmn insisted on having all children ready for literacy learning at five or six years of age, he would ignore respect for cultures that value talking but not literacy; it was an inconsistency that should not exist.

In addition, preschool children have a widely varied set of opportunities and challenges. Some are born addicted to drugs. Others are born into homeless families. Still others are born with the AIDS virus. These things and others like them occurred in Xxfldmn's country and not only in distant lands. Indeed, they occurred in most groupings of people in his land and not only to those who didn't know any better.

Xxfldmn was obsessed by the notion that children should be ready to learn when they arrived at school. It seemed to him from his reading that in most countries and cultures of the world, now and throughout history, children usually talked when they were toddlers.

In fact, children seemed to talk like their parents, act like their parents, and do things they had seen done in their homes. If this were all genetic, then new responses that children produced could be unfolding on a prearranged time schedule, he concluded. He could tick them off on a developmental scale that his science would dictate. That was a convenient theory for his purposes.

Once Xxfldmn visited a preschool where six different languages were spoken. Different staff members were hired to suit the speaking needs of each child. Xxfldmn wasn't sure whether he approved of this or not, but he wondered if home language might have something to do with being ready for school.

It was confusing that consistent similarities appeared among children in particular locations—so that this group of children was compliant, that group was centered on being with people and interacting with adults, and another group was managed and cared for by other children. Xxfldmn could not believe that these differences had anything to do with learning because he hypothesized that learning began when children entered school. He concluded that genetics and human makeup had the most influence on these early years of development.

Expectations, Preparations

Sure of his ground on these preschool issues, Xxfldmn next turned to study the schools that children went to. Some children, even as babies, spent the day with other children in crèches. Children from poor families were given extra preschool opportunities to give them an even start with other youngsters.

Children whose families were not poor could attend preschool centers where their parents paid fees. At one university Xxfldmn counted seven or perhaps eleven different programs for preschool children. Each pushed this or that emphasis—language, thinking, personality, friendliness, competitive motivation for money-making, sporting prowess, and so on. Strange, he thought, that these emphases amounted to a push for particular kinds of learning even before children went to school!

At some time dictated by the sun and the time of year and not at all by the stars under which the child was born, things changed dramatically. It was time to go to the Garden for Children, but this was a euphemism because the "Garden" was actually a room in a huge two-story building called school where children spent half a day. They walked up and down stairs in long lines under the commanding eye of a teacher, learning to go to the toilet or the lunchroom at timetabled breaks in a quiet and obedient manner.

In the Garden for Children classrooms, one could always find curious decorations such as friezes of alphabets and numbers. Somewhere on the chalkboards would be symbols like 2/4/93 that magically signified days, months, and years. These numbers changed every day.

There were books in the Garden for Children, too, but the teacher read them aloud because the children were unable to read. There were also desks, chairs, routines, activities, and a general air of getting ready for something to come while engaging in something rather like adult trivia games.

Parents were overjoyed that their cherubs were marking books with circles, learning to recognize a square, drawing lines from this to that and emitting strange staccato noises whenever the teacher pointed to a particular letter among the mess of marks. There were great expectations, great preparations. The philosophy of the place was "Let's get ready for something in the future that will be really worthwhile."

Xxfldmn began to feel uncomfortable, for the anticipation of traveling necessary routes without really arriving was gripping at times. Therefore, he was glad to find some children who were moving on to that "something in the future." With high expectations, he followed them through the Greenstone Door into the Perfumed Garden (or up another flight of stairs to the Grade 1 classroom).

A Strange New World

Aha! Xxfldmn had the distinct sense that nothing had preceded this. This was first base, Grade 1, a new beginning with no real connections to anything that had gone before. Here were reading books containing a new language, and real work was now done—in workbooks. The language of the books was strange, the language of the teacher was strange, and only a few links could be made to what had occurred in the Garden for Children.

So here was the challenge. This was a new beginning. In this strange new world what you already knew and what you could already do were banned as wasteful of learning time. What was important was not what the child already knew but what the teacher knew was waiting over the horizon, tomorrow and the next year.

"Chop, chop, change!" thought Xxfldmn. From home to crèche to preschool to kindergarten—these were like holding pens, places to wait before being chosen to enter Grade 1.

If what had gone before was unimportant, then how could he, Xxfldmn, have children ready for this totally new experience that could not be prepared for?

Still puzzled, Xxfldmn spoke to some of the new Grade 1 children, whose answers reflected their struggle to adjust:

- I go everywhere but everywhere is different.
- It's not like kindergarten here. We do real work. We used to only play, but now we do sounds and letters, and I write the date, and I read my reading book. Not a storybook, Mr. Xxfldmn, 'cause that's not a reading book.
- And I write books, and I can publish books, and do math and play in the playground. I make friends and sometimes Grade 1 is fun.

Seeking Continuity

Then Xxfldmn had a brilliant idea. He knew what he would tell all the people who were concerned about having children ready for school. Educators should visit the Children's Garden, the preschool, and the crèche to see what those children could do. They should consider how individual children make their personal traverse through these special environments, each with their own philosophies and routines.

If educators could bring continuity to the transitions between the various institutions, perhaps on arrival in Grade 1 children would show competence instead of bewilderment. They would know how to use what they already knew in the new setting. If you replace the "chop, chop, change" with a sense of "Here we are again, let's see how can we go on from what we know already," then children in Grade 1 may look as though they are ready for the school.

Xxfldmn talked at conferences and wrote in journals, and people applauded his brilliant idea about how educators could change things if they really wanted to have children ready for school. But nothing changed. The crèche, the preschool, the Children's Garden, and Grade 1 each had a well-thought-out philosophy, closed at the edges and creating walls that only some children could negotiate alone.

Yet what one already knows is important in determining what one will come to know.

PART TWO

Understanding What Children Know

THIS SECTION TURNS TO LOOKING and seeing in the classroom, which is much better understood today than when I first began writing about it. Being sensitive observers is not enough for supporting learning. Teachers will have to observe closely, holding their own prior assumptions in limbo, and find out where individual children are before embarking on new learning. To have constructive learners, teachers must look for strengths and forget the notion that what testing provides is a catalogue of what is not known. Testing does that, but that does not lead to appropriate teaching. To discover the constructiveness in learners we must look at the things they can do, and how these are achieved, and then build on that foundation. Many beginning school programs acknowledge this starting point in their goals, but most school curricula and testing for accountability stress expected outcomes. I have long known that I cannot board the bus by concentrating on its destination.

In this section I consider children's entry to formal literacy instruction. Children come to this phase of learning with very different preparations. What they know is governed by what they have and have not attended to in their preschool years. Concepts of what one can find in books, and how messages are laid out, and what things one can attend to on a page of print, and in what order, have to become "second nature" if children are going to be able to move on to other features of the literacy code. Literacy learning is something like road signs used by drivers: there are rules that tell one where to look next. Research is pointing to "print awareness" as an early phase of literacy learning that is probably a prerequisite for applying phonemic awareness to reading and writing.

Writing is easier to attend to than reading when you are little. In the act of writing, somehow, what you look at, and how you do it, and what people around you do, are more apparent to preschoolers than the more mystical act of reading, silently or even reading aloud from a book. We pay early writing far too little attention. Reading to children is treated lightly in what follows only because its value is much better understood. The last chapter in this section is a plea for widening, rather than narrowing, the lens on literacy learning, accepting that storytelling (return to Tomai for the example), acting out stories (read Vivian Paley for the quintessential exemplars), and creating art and craft products (read Elwyn Richardson for the roots of this emphasis), are all ways for children to test what they have learned and understood.

7 Looking and Seeing in the Classroom

IT MAY SEEM STRANGE TO suggest that teachers should look more closely at language behaviors. Surely, we assume, we need only look at the answers to comprehension questions or at essays and exercises in written expression. A recent emphasis in research, however, has been to go beyond these products to observe the process of producing them.

My research began with a dissatisfaction with theories of reading acquisition. With a background in normal child development research and the study of atypical children, I became interested in the prevention of problem behaviors, social and academic. I wanted to find out how early one could see the process of learning to read moving off course. The obvious way to approach this problem was to use the strategy of biological science in studying unplotted territory, and that was to observe and record exactly what occurred in the natural setting. I found ways of observing the first steps into reading, became fascinated with early progressions in writing, and began to attend with new interest to changes in oral language acquisition in the older child. As a developmental psychologist, I already knew about methodologies for child study, and I was particularly concerned with the changes that occurred. How could yesterday's behaviors evolve into tomorrow's?

Over the years, the procedures I designed have been adapted for classroom teachers who want to ask questions about particular children. What processes is this reader or writer using? Knowing what the pupil does leads to more significant teaching because the teacher poses a question designed to bring a new aspect of the process into prominence for a particular pupil.

Achievement levels, grades, and competency scores may be used to equalize groups of students, but how they get their scores can still be vastly different.

To become observers, we have to decide on language units to be studied, and we need to define conditions for recording the behavior. There will be a task, a process of working toward a solution, and a product. Task and product may be open in nature or closely specified. A piece of creative writing would be an open task with an open product. The writing vocabulary task I have used with six-year-olds is a constrained task. They are asked to write down all the words they know. The word lists differ from child to child, and so are open products. For a year or two this is a very discriminating indicator of who is becoming a writer; it is a good way of capturing changes occurring at this stage.

Two examples of observing oral language activities for young children would be a sentence repetition task and a request to retell a story. A carefully graded series of sentences of increasing syntactic complexity can reveal different levels of control over the structures of the mother tongue. Both the task and the product are constrained. The child is told, "Be sure to say exactly what I say." Any deviation suggests the child is not able to group the language delivered in the linguistic forms given, but rather reassembles the message within more familiar and comfortable sets of linguistic usage. The required task with a required product leaves room for children to process the sentence through their own sets of linguistic learning. The task reveals to the observer something that might never have been noticed without the setting up of those constraints.

A more open task is retelling a story. Any appropriate story can be used. The task is required, but it leaves children free to reveal strengths and strategies, and any two children will proceed in different ways to produce different results. It is easy to find examples of the child's language through which a traditional story is told.

> One day Cinderella was doing all the work when the ugly sisters said, "Do me up." So she did . . . ; And the fairy said, "Yes, I'll change your dress." And it was a lovely yellow—a really, really nice dress.

I have had surprised students who found children, apparently well prepared for school, unable to retell a simple tale. "How would they read their reading books?" the students asked.

Many reading behaviors I observed were discovered about the same time by Ken and Yetta Goodman. We all set out to record what children said and did as they read aloud. The task is constrained by the author's text. An accurate rendering is a constrained product; but, as in sentence repetition, there is scope for work done to reveal something of the processes by which children learn. One thing readers do is to correct themselves without any prompting or sign from others that an error has occurred. To explain this "error behavior," one has to begin to ask what children could have been responding to. Was the sense destroyed? Was it *un-English?* Was there something inconsistent in the letter-sound pattern of the word readers uttered with that of the text word? Was the reading fine within the sense of the sentence but nonsense in terms of a previous page? Such questions begin a train of thought that leads to ideas about complex cognitive and perceptual processes going on inside the head as the active reader reconstructs the author's message.

An interesting change occurs in teachers who observe closely. They begin to question educational assumptions. My students in a summer course assured me that local United States children of five years would not be able to write anything. I insisted they check on that, and they were delighted with the products they brought back—attempts on the part of preschoolers to make sense of the print world around them, recording logo-like forms, sprinklings of initials, and their own names written like confetti anywhere on the page. They also found children willing to read what had been produced. Seeing how far the kindergarten children had moved into the world of print in terms of the concepts they understood, if not in extensive control over the medium, my students asked, "Why do schools seem to assume that children will not be able to write before they can read?"

Such observations can lead to other important questions: "When is it appropriate to demand accuracy?" or "Does one really learn from one perfect performance followed by another perfect performance?" It is shattering to one's theory of of importance of learning correct responses to record the conversational speech of competent adults and find that many of their sentences are ungrammatical. The place of error or miscue or estimate or approximation in language learning becomes an interesting discussion topic for observers. Studies that record change over time in the same individuals will show in reading, and in writing, the same phenomena that have been recorded in language acquisition: children generate errors according to the rules they formulate to guide creative or productive or generative behaviors, and those errors change as they are seen by the child to conflict with other evidence. In their place come new errors occurring at the point where the new theories are not yet refined enough to cope with further evidence. So the early theories or hypotheses of the child serve to sustain a level of productivity needed to continue a learning process, and by means of these hypotheses language activities widen to include more and more options, fitting more and more closely with the permissible usages of the language.

A kind of learning occurs in natural language tasks that is rarely thought about. Proceeding by rough and ready theories but using self-correction processes, children practice old learning, giving it minimum attention, while new learning is laboriously worked over until it has found a place in the system. Every time a child reads a sentence or writes a story, each letter sequence and language form in that sentence is, by its use, moving from somewhere on the novel language dimension toward being used with minimum attention. The hard-to-spell new word seems to be the one that requires processing, but every other word in the sentence profits by being used, moving the child further towards fluency, automatic responding, and flexibility of use. High-frequency words move most rapidly to this state. So when we record a series of correct responses for the child reader we do not really notice these processes of learning and overlearning.

Observations should be made under conditions that reduce the error of personal bias in the observer to a minimum. If this is not so and observations are carried out to confirm our assumptions, there would be nothing in the results to surprise us. The observer has to become objective in data collection, analysis, and interpretation. An observer can easily influence the observations and must take all precautions not to. Other things can distort the value of the record. The child's behavior today may not be a good indicator of behavior tomorrow, so the record we have may not be a reliable one. Then the program the child has been exposed to will have acted like an experimental treatment. It will have trained the child in some behaviors and will have overlooked others, or it may have attended to the parts of the activity while failing to provide opportunities for the child to learn how to orchestrate the parts in a continuous, productive activity. So along with the influence of the program on what we may be able to observe, we have the problem of the lack of opportunity to learn, or the effects of the restrictions imposed by the program.

Observant teachers not only discover new behaviors and changes in behaviors but also think about children's learning in new ways. Sometimes readers who are accurate by the teacher's standard nevertheless go back, repeating themselves, rerunning the message. Is this immaturity, uncertainty, incompetence, or error? Could it be they have been surprised by what they read, and have rerun it to ensure that it is correct? Monitoring one's language activities and correcting error when it occurs has a great deal of relevance in formal and informal educational experience. It is important and needs to be encouraged. Teachers who are not good observers could well punish the very behaviors that would make their pupils more accurate.

It is helpful to become detached observers of children at work, seeing how they go about the tasks we set them. If we keep today's record as a baseline and on several occasions observe children again, we can, from a short series of observations, record change over time, capturing progress.

References

Clay, M. M. 1975. *What Did I Write?* Auckland, NZ: Heinemann.

———. 1993. *An Observation Survey of Early Literacy Achievement.* Auckland, NZ: Heinemann.

Clay, M. M., M. Gill, T. Glynn, T. McNaughton, and K. Salmon. 1983. *Record of Oral Language* and *Biks and Gutches.* Auckland, NZ: Heinemann.

8 Using the Concepts About Print Task with School Entrants

THE NEW ZEALAND MINISTRY OF Education has selected several assessments for use with children at school entry, one of which is called "Concepts About Print." That assessment, which I designed and published to help teachers observe what young children know about printed language (Clay [1972] 1993), is now used by many teachers as part of a survey of observations made after children have been at school for a year. This chapter deals with some questions that are commonly asked about this assessment, specifically:

- What is the Concepts About Print task, and what are its origins?
- Is it important to give this task to school entrants?
- What do we know about this task from research studies?
- How might teachers use the information it provides to help children?

What Is the Concepts About Print Task?

A recent Ministry publication, *The Learner as a Reader* (1996), states that "the concepts that children need to learn about print include directional movement, one-to-one matching (of spoken words to printed words) and book conventions" (p. 38) and that "skillful teaching is required to focus the student's attention on the details of print while ensuring that the message of the text and the enjoyment of the story are not lost" (p. 39). (See also Chapter 7.)

For a 1963 research project I watched five-year-old children trying to read simple introductory reading books, and I devised some tasks that children of this age might do with such books. The new tasks looked promising for showing teachers what I had been able to observe.

As an educational psychologist I could draw on my experience with preschool children and my knowledge of what makes for good and bad items in tests used with them. I began to refine my pilot tasks. I was trying to capture awareness of print *before* children had been taught to read so the children could not be asked to read, write, or name any print. If the observer read a simple story to them, and the assessment involved asking them to act in some way, like turning a page or pointing to something on request, then the children could show what they knew rather than have to tell what they knew.[1]

After trials and test development procedures this task became one of six parts of a larger observation survey (the original name was "a diagnostic survey") to be used by *classroom teachers* for the systematic observation of young children's progress at any time during the first two years of school, but in practice the survey was usually given after one year at school and became known as the "six-year-old (safety) net." The challenge in the 1960s was to convince teachers to be systematic about locating children who were making much slower progress with literacy learning than their classmates. The balancing act was to allow children who had entered school with different kinds of awareness of print some time to engage with the school's program but to avoid having them drop too far behind their faster-learning classmates. Research had reported how children, one by one, become readers and writers under the careful tutelage of their teachers in their first year of school, but it was obvious that some took a long time and fell further and further behind their faster classmates.

So the Concepts About Print task (C.A.P.), designed at first as a means of observing the early progress of five-year-old school entrants in a research study, became part of a survey that could quantify the progress of high-, middle-, and low-progress children after one year at school. By 1978 this survey was also used to select children for Reading Recovery, children who needed more assistance than they could get in their classrooms and who would receive a period of individual instruction to boost their progress. The survey was a way to observe all beginners, and any child's progress in the following two years, including a few children selected for individual help after a year at school. Recently the Kia Ata Mai Educational Trust, whose Maori Observation Survey is almost ready for publication, has developed and trialed Concepts About Print in Maori as Ngā Tīkanga o Te Tuhi Kōrero (in close consultation with the author and with permission of the publisher).[2]

Is It Important to Make These Observations?

If C.A.P. was a subtest of the survey used after one year at school, why is it now being recommended for school entrants? Recent research has opened our eyes to how much preschool children notice about "language in print" before they come to school. The flip side of that understanding is that we also know that some children have little opportunity for such learning or, despite opportunities, they have taken little notice of it. This happens even when they are moving around in a print-saturated environment. Some adults believe that literacy is "school territory" and best left until children go to school, so they do not attend to this kind of learning. Because of such varied opportunities new entrants have vastly different levels of interest in print. Teachers know this, and they also know that those who are more aware of print move into reading and writing before those who do not. Children bring different amounts of prior knowledge to the new school challenges.

Child development theories have taught us how healthy children, with many learning opportunities, sound emotional development, good motor control, and good language use tend to be more successful in school. In addition, research in the last two decades has convinced most educators that what preschoolers learn about books and written messages can make school literacy learning a little easier. Teachers need to observe literacy behaviors as well as the more general indicators of individual differences over the first few months of school.

There is a particular reason why learners need to grasp book and print orientation skills early in the first year at school. The conventions of written language control how readers direct their attention and what they attend to. The order of letters and words is of vital importance when trying to read and write. Like traffic conventions, which vary from country to country, the conventions of print vary from one script to another, but invariably they direct the order in which the reader attends to the print. Wonderful knowledge about letter shapes, or letter sounds, or words cannot serve a reader well if he or she is traveling the wrong way down a one-way street! Learning about the arbitrary ways in which we write down what we say is necessary in every language, it seems. Educators in countries like Germany, Denmark, and Israel have reported on how concepts about print are learned in other languages and scripts.

When young children who are just becoming familiar with books are handed a storybook, what do they attend to? Do they turn the book the right way up? Start at the front? Look for the first page of text? Attend to the picture? Or to the print? Turn pages in sequence one at a time? One of the first code-breaking activities in reading is to discover something about these arbitrary conventions of how books, or any printed messages, are presented. I demonstrated this to my undergraduate classes by distributing children's storybooks from Japan and Israel and letting them observe their own confusions.

Once children have some idea about how books are presented and can look at a storybook in sequence there is still more to learn. In what order does one attend to the bits of print? Where does one start? In what direction does one move? How does one move through a word? These things are features of any message written in continuous text; they may not seem so important if we are only thinking of single letters or words. Parents and teachers who see children fall easily into appropriate ways of surveying print often overlook this important learning and fail to notice other children who are very confused, who take a very long time to "get it all together" or frankly ignore these things altogether. C.A.P. can reliably select out children who have such learning under control from those who do not, either at school entry or throughout the first year at school. It uncovers those who need more of the teacher's attention and intensive make-up opportunities in order to learn what many preschoolers have already mastered. The group requiring extra help may in some schools include up to half an intake class. Research on different cultural groups in New Zealand over several decades has shown that what is known about letters, sounds, and words begins to expand rapidly once these orientation tasks no longer need the learner's attention. That is the teaching goal: to do away with the need to give close attention to "the rules of the road."

Some Research That Has Explored C.A.P.

Extensive evidence has helped us to understand how, and how fast, children's knowledge of the written code changes throughout their first year at school, once they meet up with expectations that they will learn to read and write.

In my original research the C.A.P. scores of the 100 children studied weekly increased over the first year of school. The performance of both the high- and the low-progress groups changed significantly during that year, showing that teachers were reaching both groups at their own levels, which was good; but the low group was about nine months behind the high group. That study provided evidence that responding successfully to the left-to-right rule in written English was not dependent on hand preference or verbal concepts of left and right. A mere sensory-postural awareness of movement in the correct direction, no more than a feeling for a consistent way of approaching certain experiences, was all that was required. Yet a few children became confused about this, and their confusion persisted for months.

Directional learning is more likely to be related to learning than maturing. This was supported by a research study of identical quadruplets that showed how individual differences can be created even when genetic and environmental histories are close to identical. For four same-age sisters from the same home, kindergarten, and new-entrant class experiences, directional movements across a text took different amounts of time to settle down to a consistent sequence of attention to a text, ranging across 12, 26, 38, and 46 weeks for the four, or from three to twelve months at school! Other evidence in this study showed that all four children were teachable once teachers noticed what specifically each child needed to learn.

From 1967 to 1991 many studies of early literacy progress in New Zealand classrooms contributed similar evidence, although they used different research theories and methods. Space only allows for two to be reviewed here. A detailed observation study based on fifteen-second intervals was made throughout the morning of eight children in new entrant rooms in ten Auckland primary schools (Watson 1980)—that is, 80 of the newest of new entrants. Throughout the whole morning 53 percent of teacher moves were related to reading instruction, 20 percent were related to writing instruction, and only 27 percent were related neither to reading nor writing. Whatever the timetable activity, teachers understood that these children were beginners in literacy learning and took opportunities to get the children attending to printed messages in appropriate ways.

My study of how children engaged with the program of instruction in the first term of school (Clay 1985) showed how quickly they got their heads down to academic matters. Early reading and writing behaviors were being learned. Teachers achieved this progress with very few controlling moves and kept their children on task more than 90 percent of the time. They were adept at getting to children for individual teaching, and they distributed their attention positively and equally across all subgroups studied (European, Maori, and Pacific Island groups). Results showed that C.A.P. scores distinguished between those children who knew a great deal about printed language on entry to school at five years and those who knew very little. The scores provided a baseline for all children against which subsequent progress could be judged. In each school new entrants on the average shifted from low C.A.P. on entry to school to knowing half the items tested after only one term. This was a time of rapid change for most children (including subgroups of pakeha, Maori, and Pacific Island children), and any remaining low scorers were clearly in need of extra time, extra attention, and extra ingenuity if they were not to be left behind.

C.A.P. caught the attention of researchers overseas, like Helen Robinson at the University of Chicago. In the late 1960s she espoused a renewed emphasis on the observation of children's behaviors in the United States. She used one item from C.A.P. as an example. It showed that many beginning readers do not know the boundaries of printed words. This, Robinson reported, led to experimental research by others, confirming the results and extending them to spoken words, letters, and sounds. She cautioned, however, that the fact that a C.A.P. score might be a good predictor of progress should not be as important as its implications for teaching.[3] She emphasized that children need to learn the direction of English print; that children have to learn what a letter is and what a word is; that this is uncertain knowledge at the end of one year at school; that finger pointing to words and staccato pronunciation may be an important stage in matching printed words to spoken words; and that pupils must be given time to respond and must not be harassed if they search at length or fail to respond.

Reading Research Quarterly published an independent evaluation of C.A.P. in 1980. Other researchers had shown it to be a reliable and valid test for American children before Jerry Johns studied how it worked with 60 first-grade children who were above-average, average, and below-average readers. He grouped the items according to four patterns under the headings

- book orientation
- print direction
- letter-word concepts, and
- advanced print concepts.

All his (six-year-old) Grade 1 children obtained perfect scores on book orientation after their year in (U.S.) kindergarten, but his above-average readers were superior to below-average readers in the other three categories. His conclusion was that awareness of concepts about print may exist both as a consequence of what has occurred in a child's life so far and as a cause of further progress in reading (a conclusion also drawn from the original New Zealand correlation data). Teachers may wonder why this is even questioned because it seems so obvious, but in the academic hunt for causes of literacy difficulties that might explain reading progress the concept of reciprocity—that one competency helps and extends a different competency—is very hard to control and has only recently appeared in theoretical discussions.[4]

Research that follows children over time shows that learning about book orientation and print direction begins early, but mastery (in the sense that no slips occur) takes longer. The situation is very different for letter-word concepts. Below-average readers confuse the concepts of letter and word for a longer time than teachers think. There is a mystery hurdle in here that could only be sorted out in an elegant, developmental research study. The problem is not simple or obvious, and it occurs despite a great deal of teacher talk about it. Some children who are reading and writing well still confuse these concepts on a test.

The other advanced print concepts are mastered cumulatively over time under the influence of reciprocal learning—that is, children master more concepts through reading more, and become better readers as more concepts are mastered.

New Zealand studies of school entrants over more than twenty years show small increases in entry to school scores, and increasing average scores on C.A.P. after entry to school, with most children acquiring the critical concepts before they have been at school for six months and mastering the advanced concepts gradually over the next eighteen months. This is an appropriate foundation for progress. In research studies, scores should for a period correlate well with progress, but once mastered these concepts should not be highly related to later progress. Other variables take over as important. For example, the mastery of a set of "visual icons" (letters), to use a modern metaphor, and an understanding of how they represent the sounds of oral language, plus an increasing mastery of words one can write and read correctly, become effective markers of later progress. C.A.P. plays an important role early in reading acquisition.

How Might New-Entrant Teachers Use This Information?

So are there benefits to be had from using C.A.P. within a month or two of a child's arriving at school? Many teachers have explored this already. For those who have not, and for new readers, may I claim an author's right to express my opinion?

C.A.P. should not be used to predict who will learn to read and write and who might have difficulty. To have all children become successful readers and writers, teachers must aim to make such a prediction false by making *all* children knowledgeable about these essential concepts and opening the door to literacy.

New-entrant teachers in New Zealand appear to have a good understanding of the importance of concepts about print among their students. Their activities introduce children early to how to approach written texts. Children expand this learning throughout their first year at school but have more advanced concepts to learn in the second year at school.

However, scores would be higher and more concepts would be known by more children earlier if the lowest-achieving children could receive help and careful monitoring in their first six months of school. Those who take a long time are likely to be children with a variety of characteristics—for instance, children who

- turn away from focused and sedentary activities
- have not yet discovered a liking for book browsing, story reading, and storytelling
- find it difficult to pull ideas together in a focused way
- miss too many days at school to make links between the things they do
- have been immersed in an oral culture in homes where written texts are rare
- are afraid to write or do not like to write, and
- do not give this learning their attention for many other reasons.

If new-entrant teachers knew where each child was starting from in this orientation to print area they would be better prepared to observe gradual change as it takes place. Giving more focused help to the least prepared more quickly in the first year of school will lead to greater earlier success for that group. This might well mean that children reach a second-year test scoring better in this particular aspect of literacy learning (but of course letter identification, early writing, and hearing sounds in words would also need teacher attention).

Would this perhaps mean that the number of children who reach their sixth birthday and need to be referred to Reading Recovery would drop? Well, actually, no. Contrary to some ill-informed opinion, children who go into Reading Recovery have not yet failed anything. They have been learning, but not fast enough to keep up with classmates who are racing ahead. So if teachers lift the speed at which these children orient to text and learn to find their way around it, and even lift their C.A.P. scores by the time they are six years of age, that would not necessarily reduce the number entering Reading Recovery.

First, orienting to texts is only one of the steps needed for constructing a reading and writing process: there are other important things to learn about letters, words, sounds, and meanings, and how we put language things together. Teachers work on all these factors, too.

Second, and more important, what Reading Recovery represents is insurance that the scores of the lowest 20 percent of our children will not drag down the average performance overall. So if we were to lift literacy achievement in our schools to higher average levels we would still need to take out about a 20 percent insurance on our lowest achievers to support that lift in general achievement. Do critics of Reading Recovery miss that obvious point about relativity? Individual help is given not to overcome failure but, to use a different metaphor, to provide extra fertilizer to bring the crop on a little faster before the winter of failure sets in.

So, for teachers of new entrants and those who lead their professional development, my current favorite question is this: When you review your program, have you considered carefully whether there are rungs at the bottom of the ladder for the short kids when they enter school? Hopefully school entry assessments will help us ensure that there are.

Endnotes

[1] Teachers find it relatively easy to see and hear what children know about letters, sounds, and words in the daily activities of the classroom and can be good observers of where children are in their knowledge of literacy, but the knowledge tapped by C.A.P. requires a well-designed task to uncover what children know.

[2] A report celebrating Maori achievements (*Kokiri Paetae,* Issue 3, July 1996) told of how the Ministry of Maori Development in Hamilton established a trust after teachers identified the need for better teaching resources for Maori immersion programs. The trust have been responsible for increasing the available books for beginning readers and have developed an appropriate assessment for learners in Maori immersion classes, in consultation with the author and publisher of the original material. The assessment is based on the English-language observation survey and includes the Concepts About Print task in Maori. The trust have trained teachers in administration of the observation tasks and have also produced a training video.

[3] A close relationship existed between C.A.P. scores at 5:0 and reading success at 6:0, as close as intelligence on an individual test ($r = 0.60$), but when both were tested at 6:0 the relationship was even stronger ($r = 0.79$). This implies that knowing the concepts was helping children progress in reading and that the reading progress was helping the children to learn the advanced concepts. C.A.P. gets better at discriminating good and poor readers during this year and at the same time indicates some of the things that the lowest scorers need to learn.

[4] An interesting feature of these results appears when they are compared with those of children in a different education system where this age group is only "in preparation for real reading." When there is no expectation that children will become readers although they become familiar with the ways of books, the distinction between a short orientation period and progress as a reader, between prior knowledge and reciprocity in learning, does not appear. As soon as there is an expectation that children will read, then changes in the patterns of scores occur. New Zealand children were about a year ahead of Johns's Grade 1 children except in the book orientation cluster. This points up the effect of society's expectations about literacy achievements for five-year-olds in New Zealand, England, and Scotland, but not in the United States, Canada, or Denmark, for example. It is expectation rather than age that determines what is to be learned.

This raises a question for New Zealand. Are we in too much of a hurry to rush children along the path of literacy learning? If we eased up a little on pushing hard to get children further into literacy learning in the first six months of school, to what else could we profitably direct our energies? We could schedule more time to encourage children to initiate learning opportunities in oral language—invite them to talk, to question, to explain to other children, and to talk to the teacher as he or she moves among them extending their expression of ideas into oral or written statements. We could identify classroom situations that create opportunities for learning to talk with teachers and with peers. Storytelling and acting out the stories of one's peers have a place in a balanced program. For this reason, it will be interesting to see what teachers learn from the story retelling task in the Ministry's assessment battery. Literacy would still be introduced, but time might be shared more equitably across all language activities. Slowing down our demands overall would be one way of having more children described as successful, of course! I am not advocating this switch in emphasis; I am only recommending we start a discussion about the oral language foundation of literacy learning.

References

Clay, M. M. 1967. The Reading Behaviour of Five-Year-Old Children: A Research Report. *New Zealand Journal of Educational Studies* 2: 11–31.

———. 1974. Orientation to the Spatial Characteristics of the Open Book. *Visible Language* 8, 3: 275–282.

———. 1985. Engaging with the School System: A Study of New Entrant Classrooms. *New Zealand Journal of Educational Studies* 20, 1: 20–30.

———. 1989. Concepts About Print: In English and Other languages. *The Reading Teacher* 42, 4: 268–276.

———. 1991. *Becoming Literate: The Construction of Inner Control.* Auckland, NZ: Heinemann.

———. [1972] 1993. *An Observation Survey of Early Literacy Achievement.* Auckland, NZ: Heinemann.

Day, K. C., H. D. Day, R. Spicola, and M. Griffin. 1981. The Development of Orthographic Linguistic Awareness in Kindergarten Children and the Relationship of This Awareness to Later Reading Achievement. *Reading Psychology* 2, 2: 76–87.

Gough, P. B. 1972. One Second of Reading. *Visible Language* 6, 4: 291–320. Republished in R. B. Ruddell, M. R. Ruddell, and H. Singer, eds. 1985. *Theoretical Models and Processes of Reading,* 3rd ed., pp. 661–686. Newark, DE: International Reading Association.

Johns, J. L. 1980. First Graders' Concepts About Print. *Reading Research Quarterly* 15, 4: 529–549.

New Zealand Ministry of Education. 1985. *Reading in the Junior Classes.* Wellington, NZ: Learning Media.

———. 1996. *The Learner as a Reader: Developing Reading Programs.* Wellington, NZ: Learning Media.

Robinson, H. M. 1967. Insights from Research: Children's Behavior While Reading. In W. D. Page, ed., *Help for the Reading Reacher: New Directions in Research.* National Conference on Research in English.

Watson, B. 1980. Teaching Beginning Reading: An Observation Study. Master's thesis, University of Auckland.

9 Concepts About Print in English and Other Languages

WHAT IS C.A.P.? I WAS watching a five-year-old try to read a simple caption book. It was 1963 and I was doing the pretests for a research project. I wrote down everything the child did and said. After thinking a great deal about what I saw, I took three caption books of identical format, devised some tasks that children of this age might do with such a book, and even undid the staples and turned some text and pictures upside down.

I tried the tasks on other five-year-olds and refined them, using my extensive background of testing preschool children and a knowledge of what makes good and bad items in test construction as a guide. The collection of tasks looked promising. Educators in the United States, Brazil, Germany, Denmark, and Israel have explored this instrument in a number of ways, and authors have sent me copies of their plans and reports from which this chapter has been prepared.

The Concepts About Print task, or C.A.P. (Clay 1982; Goodman 1981), consists of twenty-four items administered individually in about five to ten minutes. The test booklet is a little story told with a picture on one page and a text on the other. The story is read to the child (a fact some educators overlook), and the child is asked to help the tester. Some of the concepts C.A.P. explores are whether the child knows the front of the book, that print and not pictures tells the story, what a letter is, what a word is, where the first letter in a word is, and whether pairs of upper- and lowercase letters and some of the punctuation marks can be found.

Five- and six-year-old children have some fun and little difficulty with the form of this observation instrument. It can be used with new entrants and non-readers. It can show individual differences and how well prepared children are for a particular instructional program. It points the way to instruction for particular children, and it is a way of recording progress in the first year of instruction. After that first year it is of less use, except for problem readers. Their confusions about these arbitrary conventions of our written language code need early attention.

There are two forms of C.A.P. If a child is to be assessed over short intervals of time, memory for what happened in the previous testing period may determine later responses, so good measurement procedures require parallel forms of a test to overcome this. The first story, "Sand," written for children in an island country, was about a little boy digging holes in the sand and watching the sea flow in. This story proved highly inappropriate for children who lived inland in remote parts of continents and in large cities and who had never seen the sea. I searched for a more universal theme to meet this problem. "Stones" was the result; in that story the little girl climbs a hill, kicks a stone, and watches it roll into a pool of water.

Construction of that parallel form was the first adaptation of C.A.P. I had to write a new text that was, item by item, able to test precisely the same things as "Sand." As the text contains the tasks, this was a challenge.

What C.A.P. Captures

Conventions for recording languages differ. Some languages use other scripts (Chinese or Hebrew), some use other signals (like the question mark upside down in Spanish), and some use different directional conventions (moving right to left, or from the back of the book to the front). There always are recording conventions that determine what follows what, so the temporal sequencing of attention is always important.

My theory is one of visual and mental attention centered on two questions: "What is the child attending to?" and "In what order?" If the child's visual and mental attention is on the wrong page, or on the wrong part of the page, or on a word instead of a letter, or on the back end of a word, it will be difficult for that child to profit from teaching. These behaviors are what psychologists call *orienting behaviors,* and children learn them over a period of time. When teachers explain things to children, they cannot assume that their words have taught the child's eyes and brain to locate, recognize, or use this information.

There may be many reasons why children find these orienting behaviors difficult—they may lack the conceptual or linguistic tools, or the opportunity to learn—but if children are not able to stay with the constraints of the printer's code, they will be impeded from making progress in reading. The emergence of children's control over attention is what C.A.P. tries to capture.

The orienting behaviors have:

- a movement, or motor component;
- a visual perception, or looking component; and
- a mental, or cognitive component.

The important question is, to what is the brain tuned? When children are young and printed language is new to them, they are only vaguely aware of some features in print, and they shift from vague awareness to clear understanding and even verbal manipulation as their control over print is strengthened. Not only do children increasingly get the items right, but they come to know why they are right and can check their decisions in more than one way. They have verbal, visual, motor, and order information about C.A.P. items. When asked how they know they are right, competent children after a year or more of learning may be able to give several correct answers. School entrants will test low on these tasks and will increase their scores to near perfect performance as they become readers and writers.

C.A.P. works well as an observation instrument for teachers to find out what children are attending to, whether progress in an appropriate direction is occurring, and what action they should take to try to change the child's responses or to change their way of teaching that child. C.A.P. was not intended as a test of readiness; it was only one of several observation tasks recommended to teachers. It was also not designed to predict reading progress or to measure metalinguistic awareness.

Visual attention is hard to observe, and C.A.P. gives teachers information about this aspect of learning to read at the important time when formal school instruction tries to create links between oral language and reading. In the United Kingdom teachers have used it most often to monitor progress and guide teaching.

C.A.P. in Braille

An innovative modification of C.A.P. was the development of a Concepts About Braille test (Tompkins and McGee 1986). Sighted children are immersed in a world of written language as preschoolers, but visually impaired children may have little experience with Braille prior to schooling and may begin formal reading instruction without awareness of the functions and processes of reading. How could blind children be tested? The Braille version was constructed to match closely C.A.P.'s twenty-four items, with four items added for concepts specific to reading Braille—three related to hand movement and one to identifying a whole word sign.

Pictures were replaced with common household objects that had strong tactile qualities, and a new text was written around these objects. The order of the items was changed, but special care was taken to retain the type and difficulty of the psychological tasks involved. It was necessary to avoid Braille words with abbreviations within them, and to choose reversible Braille characters in place of reversible print letters. The reconstructed test was typed in Grade 2 Standard English Braille.

The progress of visually impaired children was compared with that of sighted children. Low scores at the end of kindergarten increased over first and second grade with the largest gains occurring in first grade. The visually impaired children took longer than the sighted children to learn to perform the items and continued to improve their scores up through the primary grades. The pattern of overall development seemed to be similar in the two groups; the lag in learning could be related to lack of prior experience on entry to school (Tompkins and McGee 1986).

Using C.A.P. with Preschoolers

In a two-year longitudinal study of concepts about print in 95 Black, Mexican American, and American Indian (reservation and urban) children in U.S. Headstart programs (aged 3 years 7 months to 5 years 9 months), Griffin et al. (1985) found that the children had few concepts about print at the beginning of the study (mean score 2.05–3.72), but that they had many concepts two years later (mean score 9.07–14.36). The groups were not significantly different in scores either at the beginning or the end of the study. All of the nonmainstream minority children were developing concepts about print. Their print awareness was similar to that of mainstream groups.

Changes for Different Cultures

The stories "Sand" and "Stones" work fairly well in most English-speaking Commonwealth countries and in the United States, although I have heard of attempts to produce other versions, such as one written for New York City in which the child kicked a can along the street until it disappeared down a drain.

C.A.P. has been used with very different cultural groups. It was used for research in Papua–New Guinea with non-English-speaking children who were learning English at school. Most of the trials of C.A.P. have been with children raised in literate and print-rich environments, and most were taught in school in their home language. Neither of these things was true in Papua–New Guinea, and one would expect slower acquisition of print concepts by these pupils.

Delightful redrawing of the illustrations for "Stones" ensured that the children engaged with the task, and the story worked quite well in cultural translation, although the text was still in English. These children, however, did not learn some of the concepts about print in their first two years of school (Moore 1981).

Even at the beginning of the sixth grade a proportion of these pupils continued to produce errors in their understanding of first and last, and letter and word. In the years between first and sixth grade, some of the instruction must have seemed very puzzling to those pupils.

This is a clear example of where the use of C.A.P. as a test may be culturally inappropriate, but its value for observing mismatches between children's understanding and instructional procedures, with the goal of guiding instruction, could be great.

Another trial in a very different culture was in one of the many Australian aboriginal languages, Walpiri. To readers of English the long Walpiri words look difficult. Cataldi, Dixon Napanangkarlu, and Watson translated "Stones" into the children's home language and used it for three years with all children of appropriate age at Lajaman School in Katherine, in the Northern Territory of Australia, where Walpiri is the instructional language up to Grade 4. These researcher-teachers made the following changes:

1. The illustrations of the main character were changed to look more like a Walpiri child (the background landscape did not need redrawing).
2. As the Walpiri language does not depend on word order for subject-object definition, substitutes were designed for items that used reordering of words.

Cataldi wrote, "The children come from an oral culture and their difficulties are often precisely explicable. If the school does not teach reading precisely (and avoid confusing the children) nothing in the environment will make up for it. A Walpiri child at Lajaman cannot learn to read outside the school" (personal communication, May 13, 1986).

Although this version used a translation of C.A.P. (see next section), it is useful to place it alongside the Papua–New Guinea material. The common factor for these very disparate groups from Papua–New Guinea and Northern Australia is that the children were growing up in an oral society with little opportunity to read outside of school. The use of C.A.P. to monitor early learning is very appropriate, either in the native tongue or in the second language, so that both teachers and children can learn what concepts are required and when they have been learned.

Translations of C.A.P.

Translating C.A.P. means translating the tasks, the texts, and the instructions. If some of the items do not seem to measure well in translation, one must examine these three aspects of the instrument. For example, Rodriguez (1983) used a panel of experts to assess her Spanish version of C.A.P. for Mexican American children based on the following criteria:

- the accuracy of the language translation,
- the accuracy of the re-design of the C.A.P. tasks, and
- the appropriateness of the instructions and texts for the culture group studied.

Iturrondo (1985) of the University of Puerto Rico used "Sand" *(Arena)* as the pretest and "Stones" *(Piedras)* as the posttest in a study that explored the possible relationship between story reading and the emerging knowledge of printed Spanish for a group of 124 lower-class preschool children. She matched two groups of children on C.A.P. scores, and then exposed one group to story reading at least three times a week. After four months, she found a significant difference in C.A.P. scores in favor of the children who had heard the stories.

Rodriguez's Spanish version of C.A.P. was produced to allow for dialect differences in the southwest region of Texas. She evaluated four variants with Mexican American children, using English directions with English print, Spanish directions with English print, Spanish directions with Spanish print, and English directions with Spanish print. Her results showed the importance of having the instructions in the language children understand best. The children with the lowest English-language scores scored higher on C.A.P. when the instructions were in Spanish, *whether the text of the story was in English or Spanish,* and lower when the tasks were given with English instructions. Children whose English was average or better performed equally well in any of the four conditions. I conclude that the concepts may be the same in English or Spanish versions once children understand the instructions.

Only minor changes to the texts were necessary for both these Spanish versions, and no changes to the pictures were made. The books were easy to use with preschoolers, and the instruments seemed to be excellent for the intended purpose of assessing children's learning needs. If the two authors of the Spanish C.A.P.s are correct in their judgments for their own populations and linguists agree with them, then the production of different dialect versions for some language groups may be appropriate.

Using a Portuguese translation, de Antrade (personal communication) piloted the C.A.P. in Brazil. She used children aged 6 to 6 years 4 months, 7 to 7 years 4 months, and 8 to 8 years 4 months and found mean scores increasing through three grades.

Children in the United States and Denmark were studied in a cross-cultural study by Schmidt (1982). C.A.P. was used in its designed form in translation. As preschoolers and after one year at school, Danish and U.S. children scored in similar ways. However, at ages six to seven, U.S. children were in school and Danish children were not. Marked differences emerged at that time as a consequence of instruction. The differences disappeared after the Danish children had completed their first year of school.

Changes to Theory, Tasks, Items, and Script

Theories tend to change as the current questions for education or psychology in a particular society change, and C.A.P. has occasionally been adapted accordingly, with radical shifts from its original rationale and nature.

Brugelmann (1986) used a C.A.P.-like assessment in research aimed at understanding the concepts of reading and writing that children bring to school and helping teachers better match their activities and learning tasks to children's knowledge. A shorter story was used and items were deleted, because several text features and questions relating to them were too difficult or frustrating for German school beginners. Items excluded were those involving the changes in order of lines, words, and letters, items important for monitoring visual attention to print detail as children learn to read. (They are also highly discriminating items in an item analysis of this test and the ones that present a steep gradient of difficulty.)

Brugelmann's purpose was not to monitor the progress of children learning to read nor to try to capture visual attention. His aim, like several others who have used something like C.A.P., was to pretest children before they began to read.

New items in Brugelmann's test reflected recent research findings about preschool children's ability to distinguish words from nonwords and their knowledge of the use of space to separate words. His new instrument was to be tried out with school beginners in the autumn of 1987.

If this instrument aims only to inform the teacher at the time when the child enters school and is not intended to be used to detect and facilitate progress during the first year of learning to read and write, then perhaps the more difficult items about temporal order in print will not be missed. Those items would be needed to show up differences between average- and high-progress children during their first year's progress. In the original C.A.P., if a child failed a couple of those items, the other difficult ones were not administered, although to keep the story intact the pages were read by the observer.

Wohl used C.A.P. in Israel as one of several measures to evaluate a new reading scheme. "Sand" was judged to be culturally inappropriate (personal communication, July 8, 1987). A different story, written in Hebrew script, used almost the same instructions for some items of the original C.A.P. The researcher substituted items about Hebrew letters that had two orthographic alternatives for the upper-/lowercase question in English. This Hebrew version of C.A.P. was piloted with 150 children entering first grade, and they were retested to see whether their concepts about print had changed as a result of tuition. A second Hebrew version of C.A.P. has been developed and published with a guide for parents (Ministry of Education 1995).

Reliable, Valid Observations

One problem with understanding what C.A.P. scores tell us is that it turned out to be a rather good test. A reliable and valid observation technique that teachers could use to monitor children's progress in their first year of school would need to have the characteristics of a good measurement instrument. If the instrument is a "good test," it gives a score that does not change much in a short period of time, reflects important changes over time, and relates closely to the thing we are trying to measure.

C.A.P., designed as an observation instrument, was shown in research studies to have the qualities of a good test. First, it captured shifts in book behavior that change rather rapidly over the first year or two at school (Clay 1966; Perkins 1978); second, the items used discriminated quite well between low and high performers (Day et al. 1981; Johns 1980); and third, it had a good range for use with preschool children through high-progress readers after a year at school. Reliability coefficients have ranged from 0.73 to 0.95 (Clay 1985; Day and Day 1980; Johns 1980), and correlations with reading progress have ranged from 0.63 to 0.69.

Johns found significant differences among above-average, average, and below-average first graders in the United States, and analyses of individual items revealed above-average readers to be superior to below-average readers on print-direction concepts, letter-word concepts, and advanced print concepts.

What Theories Does C.A.P. Support?

READINESS THEORY

When a strong relationship of C.A.P. with the Metropolitan Readiness Test was found (Day and Day 1980), C.A.P. was tagged with the label "a readiness measure," although those authors concluded that C.A.P. involved knowledge that could be acquired while learning to read. I had found this to be true of the Metropolitan Readiness Test also (Clay 1966).

Day and Day showed that kindergarten children in the United States had widely differing scores on concepts about print at the beginning of the school year and changed markedly over that year in a program without reading instruction. They concluded in a conference paper presented on this study, "One could suppose that when they enter first grade and begin formal reading instruction these children will be on different cognitive levels."

LINGUISTIC AWARENESS

A theory of linguistic awareness was used by Mattingly (1972, 1978, 1979) to describe the process by which children develop knowledge about the nature of their own language. Others (Weaver and Shonkoff 1979) have added that this includes knowing what reading is. Authors have used or discussed concepts about print as if it measured metacognitive awareness.

COGNITIVE CLARITY

Downing (1979) proposed a state of cognitive confusion for young readers who had not yet reached cognitive clarity. (This seems a negative way to describe preschoolers' competence.) He maintained that learning to read consists of rediscovering the functions and the coding rules of the writing system. The rediscovery depends on linguistic awareness of features of communication and language.

Children approach reading instruction in a normal state of confusion, and under reasonable conditions of instruction work their way out of confusion into cognitive clarity. According to Downing's theory, cognitive confusion continues to arise throughout later stages of education as new subskills are added to the student's repertoire.

Crucial for Text Reading

Those who have explored what children know about books by verbal means, asking questions like "What is reading?" and "What is a word?" (Dalgren and Olsson 1986; Downing 1971–72; Reid 1966), have placed considerable emphasis on whether the child can comment on the code and discuss it with the teacher. That state, in my opinion, is reached at the end of a long set of learning about print, not the beginning.

When a theorist studies readiness, or linguistic awareness, or cognitive clarity, or metacognition, or verbal discussion, or reading, and uses C.A.P. or some similar test of print awareness with strong measurement qualities in his or her research, it may appear to confirm several different theoretical formulations. C.A.P. cannot satisfy all the theories for which it has been used as a test unless there is some rationale that links them.

Perhaps it is the visual attention process directed to features of print before the child can read that is the common factor in several different theories. The child may have come to these attentional processes by a number of different routes. If that is so, the information to be gained from C.A.P. relates to some starting points in the slow process of shifting from vague awareness to conscious manipulation of concepts about print.

Full understanding of the language of instruction or cognitive clarity about written language is a long way down the track. Literacy awareness is a much more complicated variable than C.A.P. can measure, and print awareness does not imply the conceptual depth of this early learning. It is, however, important for educators to get some control over the starting point in such an elusive process. Attending to features of print and discovering the rules of order and sequence are two such starting points.

References

Brugelmann, H. J. 1986. Discovering Print: A Process Approach to Initial Reading and Writing in West Germany. *The Reading Teacher* 40, 3: 294–298.

Clay, M. M. 1966. Emergent Reading Behaviour. Ph.D. diss., University of Auckland.

———. 1982. *Observing Young Readers: Selected Papers.* Portsmouth, NH: Heinemann.

———. 1985. *The Early Detection of Reading Difficulties.* 3rd ed. Auckland, NZ: Heinemann. (Includes test booklets "Sand" and "Stones.")

———. 1993. *An Observation Survey of Early Literacy Achievement.* Auckland, NZ: Heinemann.

Dalgren, G., and L. E. Olsson. 1986. The Child's Conception of Reading. Paper presented to the American Education Research Association, San Francisco, CA, April.

Day, H. D., and K. C. Day. 1980. The Reliability and Validity of the Concepts About Print and Record of Oral Language. *Resources in Education,* ED 179–932. Arlington, VA: ERIC Document Reproduction Service.

Day, K. C., H. D. Day, R. Spicola, and M. Griffin. 1981. The Development of Orthographic Linguistic Awareness in Kindergarten Children and the Relationship of This Awareness to Later Reading Achievement. *Reading Psychology* 2, 2: 76–87.

Downing, J. 1971–72. Children's Developing Concepts of Spoken and Written Language. *Journal of Reading Behavior* 4, 1: 1–19.

———. 1979. *Reading and Reasoning.* New York: Springer.

Goodman, Y. M. 1981. Test Review: Concepts About Print. *The Reading Teacher* 34, 4: 445–448.

Griffin, M., R. Spicola, A. Banks, and E. Reyes. 1985. *A Comparison of Developmental Patterns in Print Awareness in Indian, Mexican-American, and Black Children, Ages 3 to 7.* Denton, TX: College of Education, Texas Woman's University.

Iturrondo, A. M. 1985. *Story Reading and the Knowledge of Printed Spanish: Exploring Their Relationship in the Preschool Classroom.* Research Report. Rio Piedras: University of Puerto Rico.

Johns, J. L. 1980. First Graders' Concepts About Print. *Reading Research Quarterly* 15, 4: 529–549.

Mattingly, I. G. 1972. Reading, the Linguistic Process, and Linguistic Awareness. In J. F. Kavanagh and I. G. Mattingly, eds., *Language by Ear and Eye,* pp. 133–147. Cambridge, MA: MIT Press.

———. 1978. The Psycholinguistic Basis of Linguistic Awareness. Paper presented at the annual meeting of the National Reading Conference, St. Petersburg, FL.

———. 1979. Reading, Linguistic Awareness and Language Acquisition. Paper presented at the International Reading Association–University of Victoria International Research Seminar on Linguistic Awareness and Learning to Read, Victoria, BC.

Ministry of Education, Israel. 1995. *Concepts About Print: A Tool for Assessing the Buds of Knowledge.* Jerusalem: Ministry of Education.

Moore, D. W. 1981. First and Last, One and Two, Letter and Word: Concept Formation in Papua–New Guinean Community Schools. Paper presented to the Fourth National Conference on Mathematics, Lae, Papua–New Guinea.

Perkins, K. C. 1978. *Developmental Observations of Kindergarten Children's Understanding in Regard to Concepts About Print, Language Development, and Reading Behavior.* Denton, TX: College of Education, Texas Woman's University.

Reid, J. 1966. Learning to Think About Reading. *Educational Research* 9, 1: 56–62.

Rodriguez, I. 1983. Administration of the Concepts About Print SAND Test to Kindergarten Children of Limited English Proficiency Utilizing Four Test Conditions. Ph.D. diss., Texas Woman's University, Denton, TX.

Schmidt, E. 1982. A Comparison of United States and Danish Children's Emerging Learnings of Written Language. Reading by All Means: Selected Proceedings, 12th New Zealand Conference of IRA. (Hvad ved skolebegyndere om bøgernes sprog? Serien Laese Rapport, 6. *Laesning.* Copenhagen: Danish Reading Association.)

Tompkins, G. E., and L. M. McGee. 1986. Visually Impaired and Sighted Children's Emerging Concepts About Written Language. In D. Yaden, ed., *Metalinguistic Awareness: Findings, Problems, and Classroom Applications.* Portsmouth, NH: Heinemann.

Weaver, P., and F. Shonkoff. 1979. *Research Within Reach: A Research-Guided Response to the Concerns of Reading Educators.* Newark, DE: International Reading Association.

10 The Power of Writing in Early Literacy

It is not my intent to suggest any changes to the ways in which teachers in the first years of school teach their pupils to write. Rather, in this chapter I put forward some ideas about the common ground between reading and writing for children in the first years of school. It might be called "Thoughts About the Common Ground" and implies nothing directly about how writing should be taught. My position on good teaching is that it arises out of the understanding teachers have of their craft and never out of prescriptive programs. The first years of school are crucial, because they lay the foundation in literacy learning of all the verbal learning that follows in an individual's school career. That foundation needs to be sound.

Writing can contribute to the building of almost every kind of inner control of literacy learning that is needed by the successful reader. And yet there is no predictable sequence in which the shifts will occur! We can be sure that as children write they do some but not all of the following:

- They attend closely to some features of letters.
- They learn about letters, distinguishing one from another.
- They access this letter knowledge in several different ways.
- They work with letter clusters, as sequences or chunks.
- They work with words, constructing them from letters, letter clusters, or patterns.

- They work with syntactic knowledge of what is likely to occur in the language and what does not happen.
- They use their knowledge of the world to compose the message and anticipate upcoming content.
- They direct attention to page placement of text, directional rules, serial order, and spaces.
- They work with some sense of the sequence rules and probability status of any part of the print.
- They break down the task to its smallest segments while at the same time synthesizing them into words and sentences.

That list describes a large agenda for learning but it does *not* indicate what a teacher's instructional plan should look like. We should better understand what is going on before our eyes because better understanding results in better-quality teaching interactions, whatever your teaching approach.

Teaching practices today engage the child in authentic reading and writing tasks of wide variety presented with some sort of management over the gradient of difficulty. Every writing opportunity should be rich enough to give the child a chance to expand competence in any one of the areas listed above. As learners write using what they already know how to do, they should also have opportunities to discover some characterisitics about print that they have not attended to before.

That may sound complex. It is. Those who think that you can teach children to read and write by either teaching them to see words, or teaching them to sound out words, and any politicians, journalists, or critics who speak and write as though that is what successful teachers do, have definitely got it wrong. It is immeasurably more complex than that!

Dyson (1994) argues that "a broader and more complex vision of written language and its development is critical if educators are to build on the resources of all our children" (p. 298). This chapter explores one aspect of Dyson's broad charge by examining the reciprocities between *early* reading and *early* writing (Ferreiro and Teberosky 1982; Dyson 1982, 1983; Sulzby 1985a, 1985b; Teale and Sulzby 1986; Tierney 1991; Shanahan 1990). In writing, text is broken down to its smallest features—letters—and these letters are then built into words and sentences. Clearly, these activities have relevance for learning to read. Writing reveals the taking-apart and building-up potential of the code to young children who are trying to write and read.

Early school writing gives many new opportunities for learning about how languages are written down; how letters, sounds, and spellings are formed; how some words resemble other words; and how sentences, narratives, and reports are constructed. By the middle years of primary (elementary) school it is more or less accepted that speaking, reading, and writing complement each other in literacy learning, and they are often taught within language arts classes or English curricula.

The reading and writing achievements of the upper primary school are delicately balanced on the foundation created during early literacy learning. Trying to understand the common ground between reading and writing in the first years of school opens up a small window on the processing of printed messages at a time when children work slowly, and when they spontaneously externalize some of their decision-making.

The construction of this liaison begins in literate cultures somewhere between two and six years, when children become aware that people put marks on paper. Before long the child makes a primitive and usually untutored separation of "writing" from "drawing." The child begins the shift from representing objects in speech (what Vygotsky [1978] called the first-level symbol system) to representing that oral speech code with symbols in print (the second-level symbol system). Provided with opportunities, and in imitation of people who write, children produce scribbles, mock writing, or mock letters. Their linear scribble is a gross approximation of adult writing, and children think adults understand it.

Research has demonstrated fascinating shifts in children's understanding of what writing represents (Ferreiro and Teberosky 1982; Goodman 1990), and by the time they enter school they will usually have explored some aspects of print while neglecting others (Bissex 1980). At the same time they have spent their entire lives constructing an understanding of the world and control over oral language, two sets of knowledge that support literacy learning. Each school curriculum for literacy learning selects which aspects of the written code to bring to children's attention. Some encourage attempts to write messages; some begin with learning letters; and some stress learning to read before learning to write. The most practical approach in terms of managing classroom learning is to have children learning to read and write at the same time.

The interactive liaison between composing and constructing a written message and reading it back provides opportunities for noticing some of the ways in which language works, while forming letters calls attention to perceptual forms and critical features. But in school practice the teacher's emphasis tends to be on writing *or* reading rather than on what one activity can do for the other, that is, their reciprocity. Both activities introduce the novice to printed language, but how are the interactions that occur between these two activities conceptualized? What, for example, do curricula, or research studies, or theories have to say about the reciprocity of what is learned in one area for assisting new learning in the other? Few theorists have addressed this question.

What Do Children Do?

New entrants to school, aged five to seven years, write in idiosyncratic ways using whatever knowledge they have learned as preschoolers. The list of things they learn to do, as mentioned earlier, is impressive and the potential for reciprocity across reading and writing is high.

Changes come rapidly in the behaviors listed. New entrants to school apply any prior learning about print they have to some of what they produce (but not to all of it, and not all of the time). They expand their understanding in a supportive classroom with an observant teacher, so they know much more by the end of their first year in school. Children learn how to work on different reading and writing activities, and begin to form connections, pathways, or neural networks from reading to writing and vice versa. All this occurs *long before any one set of learning in a particular area (such as letters or sounds) is completely mastered;* mastery of one type of knowledge before attending to a second or third set of knowledge is not usual in early childhood learning. Tentative, immature forms of responding are the precursors of later refined, correct responses (see Chapter 4).

In a longitudinal study of 100 children in their first year in school I observed children as they changed their performances along different paths and at different rates. The shifts were individually paced as children moved from idiosyncratic starting points, ranging from scribble and discovery to tracing or copying a model, through a period of dependent appeals for help when they knew they did not know, to self-initiated, self-organized sequences of behavior carried out with a minimum of outside support (Clay 1967, 1975).

Children's writing begins with attention to external models in the culture, but becomes controlled by the learners themselves, who generate the messages, break them up, and code them into written language. Inevitably attention to the fine detail in print to distinguish shapes and forms from one another is sharpened by participation in writing activities. Children learn ways of checking for accuracy and learn when to use teachers as a resource and when and how to work alone. This is precisely the kind of shift predicted by Vygotsky's theory of teacher support leading to inner control (Clay and Cazden 1990). When teaching supports self-initiated writing, more child-generated learning results. Like children learning to speak, writers who wish to be understood learn to put messages on the page in ways that comply with the adult reader's assumptions about written messages.

No one—author, theorist, publisher, administrator, politician, or teacher—can write a sequenced curriculum to teach in one or two years the array of learning discussed above, nor can any such list of learning indicate what the teachers' instructional plans should look like. When individual progress is recorded in longitudinal research studies, curriculum sequences do not match well with much of the learning that is occurring, and every time teachers move on in a curriculum sequence they leave some children behind. (We like to think this is not so.) What a sequenced curriculum ignores is the deeper and broader orchestration of "knowing about print" that is being constructed by any single learner. How can we achieve what Vygotsky (1978, p. 119) recommended: "that children should be taught written language, not just the writing of letters"?

A Research Problem

Detailed recordings of what individual children are learning produce very different descriptions of change over time from research that seeks to capture the dominant features in the averaged scores of groups at a particular stage of progress (Bissex 1980; Frith 1985; Ehri 1991). Studies of individual children's writing show an early isolating of known letters or features (as opposed to logographic responses); use of a few letters of the alphabet as signs that govern responses; single-letter analysis; some clusters recognized, and one or two words known, probably at least one orthographically complex word; and changes occurring on all fronts. Daily or weekly records in longitudinal studies show *a gradual buildup in each of these areas* as more letters, more words, more segmented clusters, and more links between these knowledge sources are acquired. The cumulative nature of learning *concurrently in a range of areas* makes nonsense of stage-wise descriptions as a guide for teachers interacting with individual children.

Yet controlled experimental studies of groups have tended to report that alphabetic, phonological, and orthographic stages in letter learning seem to occur sequentially. Average scores give rise to stage-wise descriptions of progress; the design of the research determines the outcome description. Such descriptions of stages derived from research are then used by practitioners to construct curriculum sequences that drive the instruction delivered to groups in classrooms (too often in grossly simplified versions). Practices driven by averages rarely explain how individual children use what they can do today as a basis for moving on to the next stage, which is what teachers need to know about. It is not helpful to have stage theories define new, emergent strategies unless the theory also shows how the reader/writer works within the previous stage to bring about the emergent processes or strategies that are the key to the next level of operating.

The scripted curricula sequences often used in schools are also determined by historical tradition, cultural values, orthodoxy, or political expediency rather than how young children actually learn, and they have negative effects when they close out certain learning opportunities for individuals by rigid adherence to "the lesson being taught today." Some individuals need to take a different route, but are kept from doing so by the demands of the classroom sequence. What teachers attend to, because of requirements, adoptions, ease, or personal assumptions, determines where children are required to direct their attention, and this may interfere with what a child might be able to achieve in another program.

Timetabling and the demands of school organization divide learning into subject compartments, which often divorce writing and reading. If such a divorce is avoided, young school learners can work within and across their limited knowledge of both reading and writing, discovering where to place the new knowledge they have just attended to. Many school practices block such serendipitous learning. In the extreme case, whole school systems institutionalize the assumption that children can learn to write only after they have learned to read. The assumption produces results that confirm the assumption. Research studies in classrooms are only able to capture evidence heavily invested with the emphases of the current line of instruction.

A Theoretical Problem

Juel (1991) illustrated stage theories for reading in which "each stage reflects an additional (and usually more efficient) way to identify printed words." Advances in reading ability occur *as new processes or strategies can be employed.* She described, as one example, selecting specific cues at stage 1, mapping a string of phonemes onto a string of letters at stage 2, and reaching an automatic stage 3 when word analysis strategies are replaced by either automatic recognition of many well-rehearsed high-frequency words and orthographic patterns or automatic phonological processing. Other theorists label these stages as alphabetic, phonological, and orthographic.

Dyson, however, issues an important warning, arguing that "differences in the contexts in which children encounter and use the written language system may well result in differences in the specific behaviors they display, thus making a linear description of writing development problematic" (1994, p. 301). The researchers get to record and analyze behaviors that have been massively influenced by the activities selected for attention in communities, preschools, and school.

What is being learned in beginning reading overlaps with, and informs, what is being learned in beginning writing *if it is allowed to do so.* When a new entrant "finds" the two letters he or she knows how to write are in his new reading book, the construction of common knowledge resources about print for literacy learning is already under way.

Perhaps it is because of some of these intermingled constraints of curricula, research methods, and theory that reading theorists have neglected writing as integral to their explanations of beginning reading, but the neglect reduces the utility of their theories for practice, because learning to write contributes to the building of almost every new kind of inner control needed to become a successful reader, although the knowledge and skills acquired may be used in early reading in ways that differ from their use in early writing. Although the connections between reading and writing are simple enough for children to utilize (just as they worked on the intricacies of oral language by testing, every minute of their waking days, what they had already heard in their conversations with others), these connections are more complex than theorists and program designers have imagined. That was also the finding of researchers in the 1960s who studied how preschool children construct the adult grammar of the language (Brown 1973; Cazden 1972; Lindfors 1987; Genishi and Dyson 1984).

The conclusion that we have only to teach children to see words, "sound out" words, copy words, or memorize words to make them readers and writers is a gross simplification of the learning that children do. That explanation of learning to read ignores the fact that children have already taught themselves to speak, and are contemporaneously learning to write the code that they are being taught to read.

What Is Meant by Reciprocal Gains?

My attention was drawn to reciprocal gains when I began to record the behavior of five-year-old school entrants learning to read in New Zealand (Clay 1967). Every child was invited every day to draw a picture and write about it, but only some were thought to be ready to begin to read from books (a view that has since been modified). Daily writing gave teachers evidence of how children's knowledge of print was changing. When children reread their writing, teachers had further evidence of how children's understanding of the new language symbol system was changing. Children were encouraged to write whatever they could independently and to ask for help whenever they wanted it. Teachers supported the activity by sharing the task and writing for children what was too complex for them to do alone. *Learners attended to any kind of information in the language* of which they had knowledge as they recorded simple statements in writing; attention was not directed to one level (such as word learning) or a particular set of features in the language hierarchy (such as letter-sound relationships) to the exclusion of the others. Additionally, early writing was seen as an opportunity for reading (in this case one's own work) and it was not secondary to reading or done in the service of reading or to be learned after reading. One activity provided a context for the other. Teachers had opportunities to see from day to day what new print awareness was demonstrated by individual children.

A second source of knowledge about reciprocity came from my clinical experience of teaching children who were having extreme difficulty learning to read. Children with limited control in writing and in reading have more responses to work with if they can be encouraged to search for information in the knowledge they already have in either reading or writing. When a teacher helps the learner to use either activity to support the other, establishing reciprocity between these two ways of learning about the printed word, the learner's literacy repertoire is enlarged. It is very easy for teachers who know their students well to help students use what they know in writing in the service of reading and vice versa. The following example illustrates how economical the teaching interaction can be if the teacher knows the child's current challenge. The child was reading to the teacher.

(*Text:* My mother likes me.)

Child (reading): "My mother cooks me." (*Looking at the teacher*) I don't know that word.

Teacher (recalling the child's writing from the day before): Yes, you do. Write it.

Child (starts to writes l-i . . .): Oh! *Likes.*

From a few clear examples the child can gain a sense that knowledge can flow in either direction, from writing to reading or from reading to writing. The result is that two meager bodies of tentative knowledge can combine as a larger resource for problem-solving. Perhaps there is also a cognitive advantage of knowing something in more than one way.

What Can Writing Offer to Learning to Read?

The discussion that follows in no sense advocates that writing should be used in some instrumental way in the service of learning to read. To the contrary, the analysis is not intended to shape or drive instruction. Rather, I wish simply to explore the processing connections that must arise in the learner who is being taught to read texts of many kinds and to write texts of many kinds by the best instruction currently advocated. That is the surface situation; but beneath the surface, within individual learners, a rich network of connections is being constructed. To establish a case for such reciprocity of learning and the use of common sources of information in both reading and writing, my discussion must go beyond what is needed to support quality instruction. Rationale and explanation are needed to argue the case for reciprocity, so theories must be examined.

Close observations of young writers show no fixed sequence in what individual children attend to. Most preschool children begin to write using visual information and not attending to the phonological components that represent sounds in words. As they interact with young writers teachers should support children's personal analyses, for it takes time for different details to catch the learner's attention (Clay 1993b, p. 31).

Consider these four advantages of learning to write as one becomes a reader:

1. *Writing fosters slow analysis.* Writing is the slowest of the language activities. Speaking can be very fast; reading can be fast or slow and provides the luxury of immediate reviewing. Writing, in contrast, is slowed by the motor, muscular, or movement nature of the task and by the need to construct every detail of the words, not just in forming letters but also in juxtaposing one against another. Beginning writers explore many of these relationships in their own names.

We do not find it easy to examine our own speaking, and the ability to make language forms opaque so we can attend to them, of and for themselves, is a special kind of language performance (Cazden 1974). The act of writing provides one with the means of making one's own language somewhat opaque, revealing things about oral language to young writers. Read (1975) and Treiman (1993) showed how young writers discover some of the intricacies of the phoneme system of oral English when they try to write down their own language using what they already know about print and the names of the English alphabet. Writing words forces attention to detail, which can easily be overlooked in the quick visual perception of a word that is read, for in writing the attention is directed by the act of producing letter forms and sequences. The slow production of writing provides the young learner with time and opportunity to observe visual things about printed language that were not previously noticed, and to observe organizational and sequential features of printed language. This could be critical experience at a time when learners are constructing fundamental and fast visual perception processes for recognizing print forms.

2. *Writing highlights letter forms, letter sequences, and letter clusters.* Writing forces attention to the features of letters that distinguish one from another (Smith 1978; Haber 1978; Rumelhart 1994). In writing one must write a letter at a time, scanning and rescanning the sequence: this is an authentic task *that makes the reader/writer analyze print at the letter level and analyze letters at the feature level.* Teachers of reading (and those who make workbooks) devise ways of helping readers to "see" letters and letter order within words; in a free writing task that analysis is *detailed and unavoidable!*

Writing induces pressure to group letters into sequences and clusters because there is an imperative to get the message down before you forget it. Control over a cluster of letters frees attention for other things. Mastery over writing one's own name begins the clustering of letters.

3. *Writing seduces the learner into switching between different sources of knowledge (that is, levels in the hierarchy of information in print).* If I have a message to transmit I begin to compose it in my head, think of the first words, and start with the first letter in the first word. Letter by letter I write, and my letters build up into words, my words into phrases, my phrases into sentences, paragraphs, stories, or nonfictional discourse. I know that letters make up words and words make up phrases, and I know without a formal analysis that language can be thought of as organized on several levels, a hierarchy of different kinds of information in print. The starting point for my writing is tutored by my vast experience; the beginner enters the task with control over the few particular segments of knowledge he or she controls.

Any feature within the language hierarchy (texts, sentences, phrases, words, sounds) may capture the learner's attention as he or she builds letters into words, words into phrases, and phrases into sentences and stories (Clay 1975; Teale and Sulzby 1986). Some issues alluded to in theories of beginning reading (like seeing shapes without attending to letters, or not scanning all features of every word on every reading, or not attending to letter sequences), things that suggest a neglectful visual perception of necessary features in print in appropriate order, must be conceptualized differently if the learner is concurrently reading and writing, because of the analytic nature of the act of writing.

Writing can foster reading competence and vice versa if the learner becomes aware of the reciprocal nature of these acts. Reading and writing can be learned concurrently and interrelatedly.

4. *Cognitive advantages can be predicted.* Being able to bounce one kind of knowing off the other—to link, compare, contrast, and self-correct in writing (analogous to what happens in self-correction during reading)—is necessary for monitoring performance. Duckworth (1979) provided a Piagetian explanation of how children build their own primitive theories out of their experiences. If the child already has a theory (hunch, suspicion, hypothesis, or fixed idea), just one new example can contribute to further understanding. With a personal theory the learner can pay attention to the results that confirm or contradict that theory. Noticing a new feature in print may lead the child to some awareness of a contradiction between the print and his or her theory and a need to take the new feature into account. In this way a few examples can raise the child's understanding to a more complex level.

In short, writing allows a slow analysis of detail in print; both reading and writing draw on the same sources of knowledge about letters, sounds, chunks, clusters, words, syntax (or grammar and sentence construction), the rules of discourse, and narrative structures and genre differences; gains in reading may enrich writing and vice versa; and dipping into a large pool of both reading and writing knowledge will help those with limited knowledge of the language, and may have cognitive advantages.

What Is the Child Attending to in Print?

ENTERING COMPLEXITY FROM DIFFERENT STARTING POINTS

A guiding question for teachers and researchers who study children's writing is "What part of the writing task is this child attending to or working on, and how does this fit into what we know of his or her total view of written language at this moment?" (Ferreiro and Teberosky 1982). There is a great deal of information in print, and the learner has to direct attention to different sources of information—to the letter codes, spelling patterns, words, and common chunks and clusters found in words. All these are also attended to in reading; *writing involves learning some of the same things as reading, but in somewhat different ways.* The novice becomes in some sense aware of the various aspects of printed information and builds a rich (often tacit) knowledge of many features, units, sequences, probabilities of occurrence, and possibilities of combining all these things in what is known as the English language.

Three authors from the University of Sheffield (Weinberger, Hannon, and Nutbrown 1990), working with parents, asked them to record on blank jigsaw-puzzle pieces their observations of literacy events to which young children attended (Figure 10). This task captures and illustrates the many ways in which children can begin to approach writing and makes it clear that different children might begin their exploration of written language in different ways. But the jigsaw metaphor is still a thing of fixed connections, each piece having only one place to

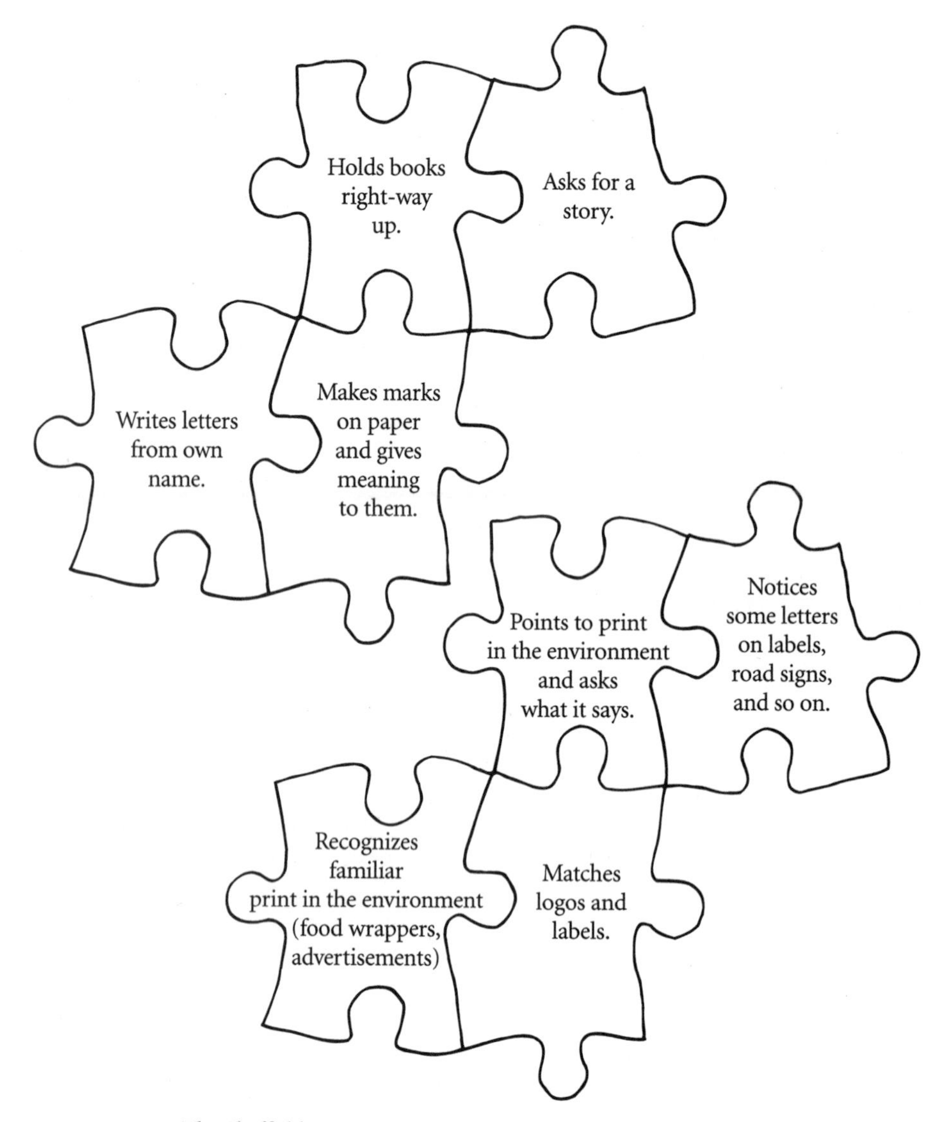

FIGURE 10 *The Sheffield jigsaw.*

go, and I fear that it might be used to justify teaching children all their letters or single-letter sounds, or having them read a hundred words or ten books before allowing them to start on another part of the puzzle. Children create multiple connections between aspects of writing and reading with a flexibility that cannot be represented in two dimensions. Constraints exist and have to be learned, since both oral and written languages have their rules; but the alternatives and exceptions to rules are legion, so flexibility must be a feature of the developing system.

The emphasis in literacy instruction has been on "What shall I make the learner attend to in my teaching sequence?" and adults have been highly selective when answering that question. Reading or writing is analyzed into sets of letters, sounds, and words, and scant attention is paid to how embedded and interconnected this knowledge must become in the expert reader/writer. An alternative approach is for teachers to observe daily the changes occurring as individual children become writers and to help them make connections between their new experiences and their existing competencies in reading and writing.

Different children entering school will have learned to attend to quite different parts of the complex whole, as the jigsaw metaphor implies. Their preschool contexts provided different opportunities, and children have preferred activities that they attend to. Consequently, individual children have vastly different responses to the invitations to learn offered to them in school. In a period of open exploration "children may need teachers to help them build from and orchestrate their diverse experiences with words and symbolic worlds" (Dyson 1994, p. 317). When we begin in formal ways to encourage children to attend to writing in school their response repertoires are already diverse. While expecting children to differ in abilities, or to have had different kinds of opportunities to learn, educators have been less likely to think about children having taken hold of different aspects of a complex task—as the jigsaw metaphor makes clear.

Despite the diversity that exists between children, what any one child knows at any one time has been described as "an organized set of knowledge," a totality. From this set of knowledge the child produces writing responses. This is similar to what happens in oral language in the preschool years; then the grammar the child uses to produce oral language is a child's grammar with its own rules, not matching well with an adult's grammar. To express their thoughts children must stay within the grammar and vocabulary that make up their own repertoire, but after hearing the replies of the people they are talking to, children gradually change their grammar to resemble adult grammar. Emilia Ferreiro is an authority who sees this clearly. Development, she says, is a progression of totalities. When a child attends to some new feature of print, he or she must incorporate it into an organized whole, reorganizing what he or she already knows. A teacher sees only glimpses of what the child knows. A primitive totality is transformed as new concepts are learned and new pieces of information are added to the design in a kind of kaleidoscopic reshuffle.

DIFFERENCES AMONG WRITERS WHEN THEY FIRST COME TO SCHOOL

School curricula often address some of the things in the jigsaw puzzle in a prescribed way for convenience in classroom teaching. An easier transition for children is to have teachers who do not ignore what they already know but who observe what they are attending to when they are given opportunities to draw pictures, produce writing, dictate something for the teacher to write, copy something written, retell what their scribbles were meant to be, point to text and parts of text, or put messages down in writing. Children's products allow us to know something of what they are attending to (Clay 1987, 1991), and this can guide personalized instruction during a transitional period. The teachers' observations may arise from classroom activities, or they may arise from a standard task (Clay 1993a).

Beginning writers switch their attention slowly and laboriously. Teachers will recognize the adjectives "slow and laborious" as descriptive of both early writing and early reading. Children's attention goes to features of letters, to letters, to clusters of letters, and to sentence production in both writing and reading. When Samuels (1994) wrote his article "Toward a Theory of Automatic Information Processing in Reading, Revisited," he explored how *readers* might direct their attention and how their reading becomes faster until they can perform reading tasks with less effort and attention. This concept of a response becoming (almost) automatic so that it requires little attention can be extended to any form of competence in reading or in writing. It fits very well with a child becoming more accurate and speedier at forming letters as well as recognizing them, using less effort and attention. For an act's being (almost) automatic we require accuracy combined with speed. Being (almost) automatic is not a place to begin complex learning; it is a place to arrive at. Being *wholly* automatic is not to have parts of the response sequence available for solving new print problems; access to slow analysis remains a necessity.

In reading, information in print comes to be *processed* rapidly with minimum attention; in writing, information in print comes to be *produced* with minimum attention.

TWO ESSENTIAL FEATURES

Two essential features that emerged in the research samples I collected of young children's writing (Clay 1975) are very important for the forward thrust of learning about writing. Even limited and tacit awareness of either may take the writer a large leap forward in understanding literacy.

The Flexibility Principle. Children experiment with letter forms, creating a variety of new symbols by repositioning them. They explore the limits within which each letter form may be varied and still retain its identity. When is a sign not a language sign? When is a sign a new sign? Can you turn this letter around, or begin on the right-hand side of the page or at the bottom? Sometimes it seems as though old, established learning must regain some flexibility to admit new learning before it settles into a new organization. Flexibility may be of critical importance for the early stages of complex learning; too early and rigid patterning might prevent later modification. Written English requires learners to be particularly flexible when estimating how new words might be spelled.

The Generating Principle. From the alphabet you can generate the dictionary. From the grammar you can construct all sentences in the language. From the morphophonemics and spellings of the language you can generate all the words and create new words. By analogy you can get to possible spellings. At first the learner does not understand the principle of generating new from known. It is easy to extend one's repertoire if one knows some elements and knows some rules for combining or arranging these elements. One can then produce many new statements in an inventive way. Generating statements seems to suit the young learner better than the more laborious task of copying (see Tomai in Chapter 3). I have heard anecdotal accounts of children who seem to rapidly reorganize their knowledge after gaining "generative insight," but I know of no scientific account of this.

We are moving slowly toward understanding what the writing and reading knowledge of school entrants can look like and how to help each child build the processes needed to work on print. Teachers have personal preferences for introducing children to the vagaries of printed English, but essential learning that is rarely taught but always learned by the competent reader and writer includes how to use the structures of the language, what are the probable letter sequences in English, which of the highly likely spelling patterns to use, and how to group variant letter forms and different fonts.

Sources of Knowledge Common to Reading and Writing

The theory of reading most accommodating to "the reciprocity case" is Rumelhart's (1994) interactive theory, which asserts that the knowledge sources available to the reader are not constrained by top-to-bottom functional sequencing or a specific learning sequence. Additionally, Haber's (1978) and Smith's (1978) discussions of the redundancy of printed language, the work on visual perception of print by developmental psychologists Zaporozhets (1965) and Zinchencko and Lomov (1960) and by Gibson and Levin (1975), and research on competent readers (Haber 1978; Kolers 1970) point to a need to have multivariate theories of learning to read and write as well as single, "main cause," or "stage" theories because these latter theories, while providing explanations of what seems to occur, can in practice lead to poor teaching. Typically they result in this-before-that models of learning sequences or this-above-all models of what is important (Gough 1972; Stanovich 1986; Bryant and Bradley 1985; Meek 1982). Rumelhart's (1994) version of an interacting processing model allows one to argue that writing and reading draw on common sources of knowledge, that multiple sources of information are used at what appears to be one and the same time.

In considering how beginners get to be the mature readers described in an interactive processing model, I need to be able to assume that highly interactive processing can start from anywhere (in the top-down, bottom-up hierarchy) and proceed in either direction, and I find this in beginning readers and writers. What looks like parallel processing in the skilled reader may begin as somewhat deliberate attention shifting and somewhat separated "work" across different sources of knowledge (or kinds of information). More flexibility is available if we avoid the concept of a hierarchy altogether, especially when thinking of beginning readers and writers. A brief review of some of the sources of knowledge shared by reading and writing activities from the beginning shows clearly that every source of knowledge discussed by Rumelhart is a source of information common to both reading and writing. How one gets to a particular source of knowledge, or files away new information into that resource, may of course involve different processing.

How young children get and use information from print is captured in evidence from several languages about children's knowledge of concepts about print when they enter school, a source of knowledge closely related to progress in learning to read two years later. "Concepts about print" was first described as learning that arose when books or environmental print were read to children, but studies of early writing led to a broader theory. Children construct theories about print from diverse experiences—seeing print in the environment; putting pencil to paper; thumbing through magazines; and receiving birthday cards, invitations, and mail from friends. This broader concept of literacy knowledge accounts for the high scores obtained by a minority, immigrant group of Samoan school entrants in New Zealand on concepts about print. They came from Samoan-speaking homes and did not have children's storybooks in their own language, yet they knew as much about print when they entered school as children with a rich story-sharing background. This was probably the case because their parents wrote letters to Samoa and received replies, and because of the strong church affiliations of this group, with Bible reading a family activity. Children can attain awareness of the importance of print by different routes before or after school entry (Clay 1977; McNaughton 1995), sometimes via writing and sometimes via reading.

One must assume that the potential for common knowledge sources to be used in both reading and writing is increased if teachers believe that experiences in reading and writing provide a powerful resource the one for the other, and decreased if they do not.

LETTER KNOWLEDGE

Attending Closely to the Features of Letters. The distinctive features that distinguish one letter from another can be considered the "lowest" level of processing written language (Rumelhart 1994; Smith 1978; Gibson 1969). Beginning writers attend closely to some features of some letters, and use that knowledge to recognize known letters and explore new letters. Writing forces visual attention to critical features, and attending to differences in features also leads to the discovery of new letters. The movements of writing help with learning the response to visual forms. *S* is distinct; *E* and *F* catch the attention; *a* is often confused with *e, m* with *n, n* with *u;* the *k* and *y* confusion is not uncommon; and *I, l, L* are a confusing set. Letter features are one type of selective cue that children attend to, and their writing shows us some of the features they are noticing. Visual features can be the selective cue that triggers a response (Ehri 1987; Gough and Hillinger 1988). Rumelhart (1994) cautions that the perception of letters in mature readers often depends on the surrounding letters, so that no model that supposes that readers first perceive letters in a stimulus and then put them together into higher-order units can be correct (p. 872). Gough would probably not agree.

When visual perception of print received more attention in the 1960s than it does today, the effect of pretraining of visual perception skills was explored, along with the question "Does writing experience facilitate perception of letter forms?" Kephart (1960) advocated training children with special needs to produce single letters as an aid to recognition of forms because the visual data "come to have meaning in terms of movement patterns made" (p. 212). Vernon (1960) wrote that

> when children begin to read they may notice the length of a word and certain letters in it. But they may not perceive or remember correctly the exact shapes of any letter, nor all the letters in the word, nor the relationship or order in which the letters occur. (p. 5)

The pattern in all its detail is acquired with further encounters; more and more detail is added until the letter is organized as a unit and continues until all the variant but acceptable forms of the pattern are known. Diack (1960) severely criticized the practice of allowing children to think they were reading when they were achieving "false success" discriminating between words deliberately chosen for gross differences in forms. He argued that the important skill in reading is to be able to discriminate between two similar words. *We should remember that this is an outcome and not necessarily a place to begin one's learning.* If difference makes learning easier, we can work towards similarity tasks as soon as control over the "difference" tasks are established. Undoubtedly when children *write* two similar words we have clear evidence of the discrimination made by the child in the similarities and the differences of the products.

Learning About Letters. Children continue learning about letters until each is distinct from the others. Close observations of children over short periods of time record their steady differentiation of letters one from another as each child moves from unknown to known, to known in different ways and forms, to being almost error-free in letter recognition. High-progress writers can access letter knowledge in more than one way—by the feel of how you "make it," by sight, by sound, by name, or by recalling a word that begins with it. Shown some cards with single letters on them, Louise, aged five, surprised me with her nonverbal responses. As I removed each letter from sight she spontaneously but silently wrote it in the air. When she came to a familiar letter she could verbalize what she knew: "That is Delwyn's little *d*." High-progress six-year-olds in my early research had little trouble giving 54 letter sounds, names, and words beginning with each lower- and upper-case letter. *Knowing the symbols in several different ways allows a writer to utilize whichever kind of access route is reached first in a search of the knowledge base.*

In reading, undue attention to letters has been reported as a stage when print-governed attempts occur (Sulzby 1985b), when increasing use is made of graphic information (Biemiller 1970) and the child seems to be glued to print (Chall 1979). This may be a necessary precursor to more rapid recognition.

While discrimination of the set of symbols of the language continues, access to the identity of letters speeds up for frequently occurring letters, followed by less frequently occurring ones. The learner moves from slow responding to fast production in writing or fast recognition in reading of letter forms.

DIRECTIONAL RULES AND OTHER ARBITRARY FEATURES OF THE PRINTER'S CODE

Directional rules for the linear ordering of print, the placement of text on the page, the serial order of letters and words, and the function of spaces all have to be learned if the reader is to pick up information in the correct sequence. They seem to be learned effortlessly by children until one looks closely at their earliest encounters with print, or at children who are having great difficulty. Then one becomes aware of how important directional conventions are and how they "direct" the brain's attention. (The set of rules learned for English will work for several, but not all languages.)

Young writers cannot avoid attending to these factors when they give attention to words or texts. Writers are forced by their need to communicate to organize their productions in a time/space coordination; and directional rules are important—where to start, which way to go, and where to go next, letter by letter, word by word, line by line, and page by page—just as they are in reading. When allowed to write freely on a blank page young children write in unorthodox ways, sometimes favoring economical use of limited space over directional necessities (Clay 1975).

KNOWLEDGE ABOUT CONSTRUCTING WORDS

Phonemes. Linguists call the smallest units of information transmitted in oral language *phonemes.* They do not have any written form. Some authors use the term *phonological awareness* to refer to the ability to hear a broad range of sound components of speech, going beyond single phonemes to clusters of sounds or clusters of sound features, as when children spontaneously play with rhyming. *Phonemic awareness* is what children are learning when they become aware of the sounds that make up the words they *speak,* and can attend to them.

Writing forces learners to search their speech for the acoustic units that count in printed language so that they can represent them in writing. A child trying to write an unknown word or literate adults trying to write down names they have never seen in writing find ways of analyzing the flow of sounds in the words. A second step in the process is to search for and find letters that might represent those sounds. Associating letter forms with sounds is *not* part of phonemic awareness, but letter-sound relationships are impossible to learn if you cannot hear the sounds in the words you speak.

Beyond initial phonemic awareness and letter-sound relationship learning there is another hidden task: it involves learning the probabilities of certain letter sequences that represent certain phonemic sequences (Dewey 1970).

Children easily break up the words they speak into syllables, finding the rhymes of songs and nursery rhymes easy to learn. They also find it easy to inflect words with appropriate endings governed by preceding phonemes, showing great skill in this kind of auditory analysis by about five or six years (Clay et al. 1983). The sequential phonemic analysis needed in reading and writing is apparently a more difficult task, and particularly so for some children. They have to attend to the smallest units of sound that make a difference between two words, and in the English language speakers run those sounds together in ways that make the medial sounds hard to hear. If we used the wrong phoneme in speech we would transmit a different message, and children seldom do that, but their pronunciations do puzzle us at times. One type of activity that is helpful for children who find phonemic distinctions difficult to hear is to articulate the word or phrase slowly. The articulation helps them distinguish closely linked or very similar sounds. This requires little more than an encouragement to "say it slowly—drag it out . . ."

When Reading Recovery was being developed we paid particular attention to a subgroup of children who could not hear the sounds in the words they were trying to write. Linking this to Elkonin's (1971, 1973) observation of Russian children beginning to learn to read, we benefited from his suggestion that children would develop their phonemic awareness by writing, hearing the sounds in the words they needed to write. Hearing the sounds was the hard part of the task. Since then, experimental research has documented phonemic awareness as a critical variable at an early stage of reading. The increase of the child's control is gradual. Cazden (1992) described the Reading Recovery task of hearing sounds in words as one example of what she calls teachers "revealing" important things to children without "teaching through telling"; the task of hearing sounds in words probably reveals some things about the phonemic system of the language to many teachers.

Teachers can help children learn more about phonemic awareness in simple writing tasks, watching the increase of the child's control over (1) hearing the sounds and (2) learning letter-sound relationships. They can call for the use of that knowledge during writing simply by saying, "What can you hear? What else can you hear?" as they interact with children who are writing. Carried over into the reading lesson this becomes "What would you expect to see?" or "What would that sound like?"

Over time children encounter all the sounds and how they might be recorded as letters and letter clusters—the regular, the alternatives, and the outright exceptional. They become somewhat aware of orthographic peculiarities, such as one letter with many sounds, or one sound represented by more than one spelling pattern, or letters that are not sounded.

Read (1975, 1986) did not say that children will invent the capricious orthography of English all by themselves, without teacher interaction; he showed how they used a knowledge of the alphabet systematically to represent the sounds they could hear in their own speech. He showed how and why spelling errors occur because it is hard to hear some parts of English words, like the *n* in *bent*. Treiman (1993) provides a more recent and extended study of beginning spelling.

As they learn oral language children have thousands of conversations with expert speakers, who fail to understand them when they get too far away from standard forms of English. There is no finer tutorial for learning oral language than not being understood when talking to someone. The shaping is done in every interchange, in every attempt that the child makes to convey a message. The feedback is a naturally occurring event, but it is tutorial.

Something akin to the preschool child's conversations occurs during writing in the classroom when teacher and child interact, as the teacher keeps the child on the task as an active participant, shares the writing task by writing difficult words for the child, interacts with the child over the taking of risks, but calls on the child for both analysis of the phonemic sequence and the search for the probable letters to record. This knowledge of letter-sound relationships used to write words from an analysis of their phonemes does not shape up the precise process needed to write new words in English because of the irregular nature of English orthography. Writing contributes to reading because it enlarges the pool of knowledge about how words are constructed in many alternative ways, and it is easy for teachers to draw on specific knowledge from the learner's recent writing when the child is also reading (see the example on page 136).

Letter-Cluster Knowledge. The young speaker may not necessarily identify a word as a word because words are run together in speech, so we should expect young writers to run words together in the texts they write, as in "brannew" (brand new) and "apastate" (half past eight).

They quickly learn how to find words in speech, though they become confused for a while by syllables and inflected endings, and they learn to work with subword units in reading. In their earliest writings a familiar cluster of letters (spelling pattern) with either a same-sound rendering (*come* and *some*), or competing sound renderings (*some* and *home*) can be handled in writing or reading, earlier than phonics programs can introduce the writer to all the single letter-sound relationships (see Juel 1991, pp. 764–765, reviewing Gibson 1965).

The novice writer trying to put a message into print soon learns that the English language is not highly predictable, but learning about the spelling system of English is not difficult for young learners who act as if to say, "If it's not like this word then it might be like that word." Acting with this flexibility and awareness of analogy and the generative nature of language establishes a tacit awareness of the probabilities of occurrence and pronouncability. In contrast, groups of words that rhyme and that have common spellings are what many teachers focus upon, calling them "word families," which is strange when you think about the term. What do children find helpful about this task? The idea of word "families" produces misconceptions like "All words belong to a few families" or "This is a memory game" (as distinct from a constructing game) and "English words are regular," which is a limiting conclusion for children to arrive at.

Learning to get to new words by making an analogy to words you know is one useful strategy, but generating words is not about building word families. It is about constructing a word you can say *by any means at your disposal* and getting as close as you can to the way it is probably written in English. In contrast to learning a word family, adding one or two words with the *-tion* pattern to one's writing vocabulary by actively working on the words in some way could anchor that pattern for a multitude of future uses. An approach used in some older literacy programs was to construct groups of words around anchor words or teaching exemplars.

Knowing many different words enlarges your chances of getting to the new words you want. Children who can write many words that are different one from another can generate more words than those who know the spelling patterns of only a few simple and regular words, or of three and four letters in word families.

Competent writers seem to break the task into as large a unit as they are familiar with, matching a cluster to the sound sequence heard and synthesizing a word using a medley of single letters, letter clusters, syllables, and an unusual sequence segment (like *deo* in *videotape*). As children act on information about the orthographic structure of the language, including tacit knowledge of the probability of various strings of characters, they reveal to themselves more about such sequences and probabilities. In a contrived curriculum of phonics or spelling, sequenced by an adult who "thought it up," what opportunity has the learner to build a sense of the probabilities of English spelling?

Individual writers engage in their own forms of segmenting words in order to write, and there seems to me to be no predictable sequence in which any of this learning will occur! The construction is idiosyncratic, derived from an individual repertoire of experiences; but data are available to show that by the end of a year of daily writing even hard-to-teach children control a large repertoire of known letter clusters, which they use in flexible ways.

THE WORD, OR LEXICAL, LEVEL OF KNOWLEDGE: A WRITING VOCABULARY

"Readers' eyes come to favor words as the units that are most easily processed" (Ehri 1994; see also Rayner and Pollatsek 1987), but it is increasing proficiency in reading and writing that brings this about.

As successful children write they build a writing vocabulary that continually expands the body of words they know how to write and the features and sequences they know in every detail; and knowing forty to fifty words will cover almost all the letters, many high-frequency words, many common-letter clusters, and some orthographic or spelling patterns useful for getting to other words by analogy, in either reading or writing. This small writing vocabulary plays host to almost all letter knowledge and quite a variety of the letter-cluster knowledge. The words can be constructed or remembered, or taken apart and used in analogies. Children have little difficulty reading them or very quickly learning to do so. Mark's spontaneous and independent listing of his writing vocabulary ("All the words I know") contained these words:

> I am and a It is in on No you mum Dad Mark Denise car cat of for Mother to too He me Mr/ look zoo dog cow Ann I'll uq come go Book so bell ball at bat hat sat fat mat rat the Here doll we we nt where five

Knowing many words makes it easier to write stories, because the writer will need to pay little attention to a choice of letter or its formation, so the word goes down quickly, freeing attention for the new words that must be constructed. Knowing many *different* words in reading *and* in writing enlarges your chances of getting to the new words you want, while knowing only short words, regular spellings, and teachers' lists of word families like *cut, but, nut,* and *shut* restricts the options.

Writing vocabulary is made up of the words the child is currently able to construct, and in scanning a list of "all the words you can write" one looks for evidence of the child's generating new words. If word families are important in the classroom program the list of words produced by the children will be constrained in various ways. But if, in response to the invitation "Write all the words you know" a child suddenly breaks out of a varied list and produces several words with the same ending, or several words with the same root but different endings, the child is demonstrating a range of things he or she can do to construct words and a flexibility with accessing new words. King (1980) wrote of this as tacit learning, intuitive knowing, something learned but not articulated. She provided this example from a child who wrote about a witch in almost correct English, but included the witch's magic words:

> diggety
> dawgety ziddle dee
> zump ka lumpityo
> mumbo junbo ka
> jellaphant zum zum
> zaroot zilly zop &
> skaroodle dee doo
> ker snickety snaff

The words are phonemically and orthographically possible in English, (with the possible exception of *-tyo*) and display the writer's tacit knowledge of the rules for word construction in that language, word construction that rivals Lewis Carroll's.

Children trying to write a new word for the first time will have some visual information about its form and will make some analysis of the sound, by saying the word slowly and listening to what they are saying, by remembering something like this word that they have met with before, or by linking up with some sense of the story so far. As children learn to write some words correctly with little effort, they are freed to pay attention to other things—new words and new writing challenges. Teaching word families has to be contrasted with teaching children to use the process of analogy, starting with something they already control, and being aware that many knowledge sources will assist them to construct something new from something already known.

The more words you already know that are different one from the other, the easier it becomes to generate something new by using something you know. Exposing children to writing, which encourages them to try to construct a wide range of words, allows them to begin to sense something about the rules and the vagaries of English orthography. Learning that writing words works in this way greatly helps children read new words in texts.

Words gather information around them—information from speaking, writing, and reading; quantitative knowledge about approximate frequency and probability of occurrence; knowledge of sound clusters and spelling patterns; and personal knowledge. A network of knowledge around each word the child knows explains how that child can access a particular word with different types of processing or from different sources of knowledge.

WORKING WITH SYNTACTIC KNOWLEDGE

In literacy activities we work with syntactic knowledge of what is likely to occur in the language and what does not happen. First-grade research studies show that most errors in reading are grammatically consistent with the sentence up to the point of the error (Clay 1968; Kolers 1970; Weber 1970; Stevens and Rumelhart 1975). Rumelhart concluded that this "higher level of processing determines the perceptibility of units at a lower level" and makes this phenomenon difficult to explain in a linear model of processing in reading (Gough 1972). But Rumelhart (1994) also writes that "this knowledge source is designed to operate in both a bottom-up and top-down mode" (p. 888). Words to be written are structured by the composing of the message into syntactic contexts. Studies of the syntax of reading errors demonstrated that sequences of words are anticipated in reading; and as well as creating the risk of producing error, such tacit awareness of syntax contributes one kind of information to the selection of a response.

Writing forces an analysis of word sequence. The words we speak, write, and read are organized into grammatical units, and readers and writers consider the relationships of meanings within and between grammatical units. Children have been making use of syntactic knowledge in speaking since they began putting two words together, and this strong source of oral language knowledge influences their production of print.

SEMANTIC-LEVEL KNOWLEDGE AND COMPOSING TEXTS

Rumelhart (1994, p. 873) reminded us that our perception of words depends on the semantic environment in which we encounter the words. Higher-level processing apparently affects our ability to process at a lower level; lower-level processing enables us to check our decision at the higher level. Even our perception of syntax has been shown to be dependent on the semantic content in which the string appears so that semantics can determine which of two alternative syntactic structures we use (as in "they are eating apples." The sentence as written hides two possible readings of the same four words in the same order.)

Helping children to compose texts as they write their stories is *not* about having them mimic the texts in storybooks or paraphrase the teacher's model; it is about having them move from ideas to spoken structures and then to printed messages. Letter learning, exploring the phonology of clusters, and word construction will occur *concurrently* embedded within the production of written messages.

The child is already composing utterances in conversation, so the first steps in writing may be an utterance that teacher and child write down together. Talking to a reluctant writer, engaging the child in conversation and capturing a promising utterance with "Let's write that down," is one way to start, providing the teacher gives sufficient help to make the task easy by writing the hard parts for the child. If the teacher has to take it down as dictation, acting as a scribe, the next lesson should include some calls for the child to contribute something he or she knows, making the effort collaborative and allowing the child to work as a writer does. Teachers help children learn to compose and write stories, reports, or messages by going from ideas to spoken words to printed messages. Contrast that with merely teaching children to spell little words that they then use for "building blocks" for sentences.

Composing has to be learned; *Wally's Stories* (Paley 1981) enables us to observe children learning to compose oral narratives that will become classroom dramas. Children's individual differences in such compositions are vast when they first enter school. For all children it is important learning; for some it takes time. Writing is a personal activity in which we compose messages that we could speak, but that we put down to be read. Some beginning writers make notes intended to jog their memories, like

> DoWnt Givv Me-Me Evvr Evvr Eniy FreNch fris NUN
> (Don't give Mei-Mei ever, ever, any french fries, *none*)

written by a five-year-old who shared his french fries with a sister who took more than he expected (Goodnow 1977, p. 29). Written messages may also be used to control the behavior of others, rather like Paul's note above his workbench

> DO NAT DSTRB GNYS AT WORK
> (Do not disturb. Genius at work.)
> (Bissex 1980, p. 23)

Information from the current contextual situation and from one's cultural experience of literacy is also part of what we bring to our semantic interpretations of text, and they influence how we process an individual letter, cluster, word, or text at any given time.

Using the Knowledge Sources

The mature reading process is explained by Rumelhart (1994) as the product of the simultaneous joint application of all knowledge sources.

> [O]ur apprehension of information at one level of analysis can often depend on our apprehension of information at a higher level. How can this be? . . . The answer, I suspect, comes by presuming that all these knowledge sources apply simultaneously and that our perceptions are the product of the simultaneous interactions among all of them . . .
>
> Each knowledge source contains specialized knowledge about some aspect of the reading process . . . Each knowledge source constantly scans the message center for the appearance of hypotheses relevant to its own sphere of knowledge . . . (pp. 887, 889)

A series of important questions could be asked about how links between these knowledge sources are created so that they come to operate in parallel processing. Yet the study of young children writing captures in slow motion the form of interactive processing that occurs between the sources of knowledge (information): this slow processing provides, first, a methodological opportunity for researchers or teachers to analyze parallel processing not available from reading only, and, second, evidence that is readily available to teachers who are trying to become responsive to individual learning needs.

Three concepts are necessary for my argument that reading and writing can share common knowledge sources and the learner can use what he or she learns in one activity in another activity.

1. *Children construct their literacy knowledge.* The developmental view is that children are cognitively constructive and build a knowledge of the world, a control of language, a reading process, and a writing process through interactions with the external world. They construct solutions helped by teachers who scaffold the interactions, allowing the scaffold to self-destruct gradually as the need lessens (Cazden 1992) until the child can conduct the activity independently (Teale in Teale and Sulzby 1986, p. 15).

2. *The system is self-extending.* Constructive learners can generate novel reading and writing responses out of previous knowledge by processes like analogy and self-correction, but they learn how to do this best on texts and in interaction with an expert, using new knowledge different from that used to enter the task,

and using reading or writing experience flexibly. In this way a possible novel response is generated and tested against what is already experienced and remembered. By middle primary (elementary) school, silent readers and frequent writers add to their competencies as a result of using them, and the processing systems not only work more effectively but also, hypothetically, change to take in more complex kinds of texts.

3. *Frequency of occurrence is a factor.* The frequency principle operates at all levels in all languages: some units—letters, letter sequences, words, spelling patterns, sentence patterns and writing forms—occur more frequently than others at every level of the written language hierarchy. Herdan (1956) regarded the occurrence frequency of a word as only a makeshift device of the roughest kind for grading the order in which words would be learned. However, frequency usually ensures repeated exposure and thus repeated encounters. Repeated opportunities facilitate learning in speaking, reading, and writing over both items and processes. Control over content and process is continually expanded. If the child speaks, reads, and writes language that retains at first the frequencies that occur in child speech, the knowledge and processing alters under the influence of the frequencies of language use in reading texts that come to the child's attention. Usage continues to be confirmed until mastered, or known in every respect, or until the response is (almost) automatic. Such (almost) automatic learning supports and provides context for new learning. The frequency principle in common language sequences supports a child's attempts to read and write. The often-encountered requires less attention and the newly noticed requires more attention. This is especially so for the young child when his or her oral language knowledge can be used as a resource. Contrived texts in reading and contrived tasks in writing tend to destroy the richer learning opportunities provided by the naturally occurring frequencies of language units.

Reading and writing have in common knowledge resources and a repertoire of implicit, nonconscious strategies that learners can use to access these resources on demand. Learners control serial order, draw on stored information, act on stored information, problem-solve with more than one kind of information, use phonological information together with the meaning of what was composed and the language of what was composed, and all the while the learner searches, checks and corrects, and works with language categories, rules, and probabilities.

There are many ways in which readers and writers work strategically with these knowledge sources as these sources increase in size, and most researchers underestimate the variety of strategies used by beginning readers and writers. Discussions on self-monitoring and self-correcting or getting to new words by analogy have begun this exploration.

Writing induces learners to check the language they use in speech and find in books. The network of fast and effective ways of working with knowledge sources involving letters, sounds, clusters, words, groups of words, syntax, sentence making, world knowledge, task knowledge, and meanings are common to both reading and writing. Actions that a young reader might initiate while reading are using background experience, using information in print, using the conventions of print, using words and letters, searching for meaning, taking risks, confirming checks, rerunning, self-correcting, cross-checking, using word endings and letter clusters, and reading words. Precisely the same list would apply to writing simply by changing the last item to read "writing words."

A research study of the *teaching moves made by the teacher while hearing one child read* (see Chapter 12) uncovered the following moves:

bringing the topic into the conversation
maintaining interactive ease
prompting constructive activity
accepting partially correct responses
playing with anticipation
asking the child to "learn" something
lifting the difficulty level
increasing accessibility of the ideas
supporting performance
asking the child to work with new knowledge
accepting child involvement
developing attention to . . .
praising strategic behavior
revisiting the familiar

The subject of the report was creating opportunities for children to read familiar books, but *any of those teaching moves could be used to support children's writing.*

These Things Are Not So Obvious

A child's being unable to do much writing on entry to school is not a problem because society is rather indifferent to writing as an area of preschool development. Children who do not explore print in their preschool years *can* become good writers in school; they can make up the difference quickly if given opportunities and help to do so. They can learn at accelerated rates to make up for not having had extensive preschool opportunities. Dyson (1994) is reassuring on this issue:

> [T]here is no need to assume that the onus for children's written language progress lies in particular kinds of "natural" language experiences in the home, given a rich, flexible literacy program in school, one that allows children to make use of the tremendous resources they all bring. There is however a great need to understand how educators might build from these diverse resources. (pp. 315–316)

Once children are in school, three problems mask the obvious relationships between reading and writing:

> *Problem one* is that it is very easy for the less able student to keep reading and writing separate from each other.
>
> *Problem two* is that any students are likely to keep them separate when teachers make them separate, particularly in the early years of literacy learning.
>
> *Problem three* is that parents, schools, and society usually treat reading and writing as different achievements with different explanations for each.

Through reading and writing young children quickly learn many things about written language:

- the aspects of print to which they can attend
- the visual structure of some letters, clusters, and words
- phonological links to letters, clusters, and words
- the aspects of oral language that can be related to print
- ways to explore detail
- ways to detect and correct errors
- feedback mechanisms that keep reading and writing on track
- feed-forward mechanisms (such as anticipation) that keep information-processing efficient

—to name only a few. Progress depends on children being active processors of information and constructive learners. Starting from some known feature, the search for information among the different sources of information includes checking on any other level; in the beginning this searching appears sequential. (Rumelhart conceptualizes most of it as simultaneous in the adept reader.)

Anything a child can write—a letter; an easy word, such as his or her name or a pet's name; or a hard word, such as *friend*—has to take *three* journeys:

> *the first journey* is from unknown to partially known to just known, to easily produced, to never wrong in any context and in many variant forms;
>
> *the second journey* is from very slow to labored production to fast execution of the writing (often too fast for the teacher to stop the flow, even when an error occurs);
>
> *the third journey* is finding and continually adjusting its placement in the orchestration of the whole system of written language as understood by the learner at any particular time (see Dyson 1994, p. 302).

Teachers should ask themselves, "Is my way of teaching facilitating all three journeys? What activities allow for the increase in knowing? the increase in speed? the exploration, the orchestration, the cross-referencing, and the extending or expansion of the system that the learner uses for literacy tasks?"

As children write messages they come face to face with most of the regularities and some of the exceptions of English orthography, and they use what they know to generate new words by analogy. Writing texts provides a varied, rich, meaningful, and quick way to learn about the letter-sound and letter cluster-sound combinations in written English, and teachers can discuss challenges with learners as they occur. Writing introduces the complexities of the orthography very well and very early. It involves an authentic task, an active child, scope to notice new things serendipitously, repetitive practice because of the frequency principle, and a gradual withdrawal of teacher support as independence asserts itself. Independence has the advantage of the child's being able to get the task done more quickly than waiting for teacher interaction!

Learning about the phonemes of the language and how they link to letters and letter clusters in the context of trying to write a message, and trying to get down a new word that is in your own story but that you have not tried to write before—that is a meaningful analytic task that quickly gets you working on the rules and exceptions of spelling in the English language and using them generatively—to reach new words or phrases. I am impressed with the potential of early writing as a highly satisfying experience for young children, one that complements an early reading program—providing that teachers are available for interacting. The more the learning can be organized by the learner the greater its value; the more the teacher feels compelled to direct, sequence, correct, and oversee this learning the less value for reading it will have.

Teale (Teale and Sulzby 1986, p. 24) proposed three general types of experience that are of critical importance for good progress in reading and writing:

1. Children should interact with adults in speaking, reading, and writing situations.
2. Children should explore print independently, initially through pretend reading and "scribbling" and later through rereading familiar storybooks and composing messages.
3. Adults should model use of language and literacy.

With teacher support, children build on each source of knowledge as they work on texts. The reciprocity of reading and writing is seen in checking on something uncertain and confirming a response. When eyes, ears, hands, and speech articulation are jointly involved in the management of a task, each may provide an opportunity to check on another way of knowing. Writing can make learners aware of new ways to check the language they have been speaking and are finding in the environment and in books (Clay 1991). Writing is a natural place to decompose words, and the process is not unlike the decomposing that sometimes is needed for new words in reading. How can so many theorists studying reading proceed as if the learner were not at the same time learning to write?

I have not discussed how one might teach reading, only that it has to help to be learning writing at the same time. Checking on your knowledge, going beyond it to new experiences on your own, building a literacy system that extends itself by its own effective operation calls for children, as part of their school's program, to compose their own utterances, to write sentences much as they would speak them, to construct words in addition to knowing how to spell, to develop a large writing vocabulary containing very different words as the host to phonemes or spelling clusters already under control, to attempt longer sentences with more complex structures, to be challenged to attempt new words for themselves, and to know when to ask for help. This brings about, as one child wrote, "*.nc.nt.rs*" of the constructive kind.

References

Biemiller, A. 1970. The Development of the Use of Graphic and Contextual Information as Children Learn to Read. *Reading Research Quarterly,* 6: 75–96.

Bissex, G. L. 1980. *Gnys At Wrk: A Child Learns to Write and Read.* Cambridge, MA: Harvard University Press.

Brown, R. 1973. *A First Language: The Early Stages.* Great Britain: Allen & Unwin.

Bryant, P. E., and L. Bradley. 1985. *Children's Reading Problems.* Oxford: Blackwell.

Cazden, C. B. 1972. *Child Language and Education.* New York: Holt, Rinehart & Winston.

———. 1974. Play with Language and Meta-Linguistic Awareness: One Dimension of Language Experience. *Organization Mondiale Pour l' Education Prescolaire* 6: 12–24.

———. 1992. *Whole Language Plus: Essays on Literacy in the United States and New Zealand.* New York: Teachers College Press.

Chall, J. 1979. *Stages of Reading Development.* New York: McGraw-Hill.

Clay, M. M. 1967. The Reading Behaviour of Five-Year-Old Children: A Research Report. *New Zealand Journal of Educational Studies* 2, 1: 11–31.

———. 1968. A Syntactic Analysis of Reading Errors. *Journal of Verbal Learning and Verbal Behavior* 7: 434–438.

———. 1975. *What Did I Write?* Auckland, NZ: Heinemann.

———. 1977. *Write Now: Read Later.* Auckland, NZ: Auckland Council of the International Reading Association.

———. 1987. *Writing Begins at Home: Preparing Children for Writing Before They Go to School.* Auckland, NZ: Heinemann.

———. 1991. *Becoming Literate: The Construction of Inner Control.* Auckland, NZ: Heinemann.

———. 1993a. *An Observation Survey of Early Literacy Achievement.* Auckland, NZ: Heinemann.

———. 1993b. *Reading Recovery: A Guidebook for Teachers in Training.* Auckland, NZ: Heinemann.

Clay, M. M., and C. B. Cazden. 1990. A Vygotskyan Interpretation of Reading Recovery. In L. Moll, ed., *Vygotsky and Education: Instructional Implications and Applications of Sociohistorical Psychology,* pp. 206–222. Cambridge, UK: Cambridge University Press.

Clay, M. M., M. Gill, T. Glynn, T. McNaughton, and K. Salmon. 1983. *Record of Oral Language* and *Biks and Gutches.* Auckland, NZ: Heinemann.

Dewey, G. 1970. *English Spelling: Roadblock to Reading.* New York: Teachers College Press, Columbia University.

Diack, H. 1960. *Reading and the Psychology of Perception.* Nottingham, England: Peter Skinner.

Duckworth, E. 1979. Either We're Too Early and They Can't Learn It or We're Too Late and They Know It Already: The Dilemma of "Applying Piaget." *Harvard Educational Review* 49, 3: 297–312.

Dyson, A. H. 1982. The Emergence of Visible Language: Interrelationships Between Drawing and Early Writing. *Visible Language* 6: 360–381.

———. 1983. The Role of Oral Language in Early Writing Processes. *Research in the Teaching of English* 17: 1–30.

———. 1994. Viewpoints: The Word and the World Reconceptualizing Written Language Development or Do Rainbows Mean a Lot to Little Girls? In R. B. Ruddell, M. R. Ruddell, and H. Singer, eds., *Theoretical Models and Processes of Reading.* 3rd ed. Newark, DE: International Reading Association.

Ehri, L. C. 1987. Learning to Read and Spell Words. *Journal of Reading Behavior* 19: 5–31.

———. 1991. Development of the Ability to Read Words. In R. Barr, M. L. Kamil, P. Mosenthal, and P. D. Pearson, eds., *Handbook of Reading Research,* Vol. 2, pp. 383–417. White Plains, NY: Longman.

———. 1994. Development of the Ability to Read Words: Update. In R. B. Ruddell, M. R. Ruddell, and H. Singer, eds., *Theoretical Models and Processes of Reading.* 4th ed. Newark, DE: International Reading Association.

Elkonin, D. B. 1971. The Development of Speech. In A. V. Zaporozhets and D. B. Elkonin, eds., *The Psychology of Preschool Children,* pp. 111–185. Cambridge, MA: MIT Press.

———. 1973. Reading in the USSR. In J. Downing, ed., *Comparative Reading,* pp. 551–580. New York: Macmillan.

Ferreiro, E., and A. Teberosky. 1982. *Literacy Before Schooling.* Portsmouth, NH: Heinemann.

Frith, U. 1985. Beneath the Surface of Developmental Dyslexia. In K. E. Patterson, J. C. Marshall, and M. Coltheart, eds., *Surface Dyslexia,* pp. 301–330. London: Erlbaum.

Genishi, C., and A. Dyson. 1984. *Language Assessment in the Early Years.* Norwood, NJ: Ablex Publishing.

Gibson, E. J. 1965. Learning to Read. *Science* 148: 1066–1072.

———. 1969. *Principles of Perceptual Learning and Development.* New York: Appleton-Century-Crofts.

Gibson, E. J., and H. Levin. 1975. *The Psychology of Reading.* Cambridge, MA: MIT Press.

Goodman, Y. M., ed. 1990. *How Children Construct Literacy: Piagetian Perspectives.* Newark, DE: International Reading Association.

Goodnow, J. 1977. *Children's Drawing.* Glasgow, Scotland: Fontana.

Gough, P. B. 1972. One Second of Reading. *Visible Language* 6, 4: 291–320. Republished in R. B. Ruddell, M. R. Ruddell, and H. Singer, eds. 1985. *Theoretical Models and Processes of Reading,* 3rd ed., pp. 661–686. Newark, DE: International Reading Association.

Gough, P. B., and M. L. Hillinger. 1988. Learning to Read: An Unnatural Act. *Bulletin of the Orton Society* 30: 179–196.

Haber, R. N. 1978. Visual Perception. *Annual Review of Psychology* 29: 31–59.

Herdan, G. 1956. *Language as Choice and Chance.* Growingen: P. Noordhof.

Hobsbaum, A., S. Peters, and K. Sylva. 1996. Scaffolding in Reading Recovery. *Oxford Review of Education* 22, 1: 17–35.

Juel, C. 1991. Beginning Reading. In R. Barr, M. L. Kamil, P. Mosenthal, and P. D. Pearson, eds., *Handbook of Reading Research,* Vol. 2, pp. 759–788. White Plains, NY: Longman.

Kephart, N. C. 1960. *The Slow Learner in the Classroom.* Columbus, OH: Charles E. Merrill.

King, M. L. 1980. Learning How to Mean in Written Language. *Theory into Practice* 19, 3: 163–169.

Kolers, P. 1970. Three Stages of Reading. In H. Levin and J. Williams, eds., *Basic Studies on Reading,* pp. 90–118. New York: Basic Books.

Lindfors, J. W. 1987. *Children's Language and Learning.* 2nd. ed. Englewood Cliffs, NJ: Prentice-Hall.

McNaughton, S. 1995. *Patterns of Emergent Literacy: Development and Transition.* Auckland, NZ: Oxford University Press.

Meek, M. 1982. *Learning to Read.* London: Bodley Head.

Paley, V. G. 1981. *Wally's Stories.* Cambridge, MA: Harvard University Press.

Rayner, K., and A. Pollatsek. 1987. Eye Movements in Reading: A Tutorial Review. In M. Coltheart, ed., *Attention and Performance 12: The Psychology of Reading.* Hillsdale, NJ: Lawrence Erlbaum.

Read, C. 1975. *Children's Categorization of Speech Sounds in English.* Urbana, IL: National Council of Teachers of English.

———. 1986. *Children's Creative Spelling.* London: Routledge and Kegan Paul.

Ruddell, R. B., M. R. Ruddell, and H. Singer, eds. 1994. *Theoretical Models and Processes of Reading.* 4th ed. Newark, DE: International Reading Association.

Rumelhart, D. E. 1994. Toward an Interactive Model of Reading. In R. B. Ruddell, M. R. Ruddell, and H. Singer, eds., *Theoretical Models and Processes of Reading,* 4th ed., pp. 864–894. Newark, DE: International Reading Association.

Samuels, S. J. 1994. Toward a Theory of Automatic Information Processing in Reading, Revisited. In R. B. Ruddell, M. R. Ruddell, and H. Singer, eds., *Theoretical Models and Processes of Reading,* 4th ed., pp. 816–837. Newark, DE: International Reading Association.

Shanahan, T., ed. 1990. *Reading and Writing Together: New Perspectives for the Classroom.* Norwood, MA: Christopher-Gordon.

Smith, F. 1978. *Understanding Reading: A Psycholinguistic Analysis of Reading and Learning to Read.* 2d ed. New York: Holt, Rinehart & Winston.

Stanovich, K. E. 1986. Matthew Effects in Reading: Some Consequences of Individual Differences in the Acquisition of Literacy. *Reading Research Quarterly* 21, 4: 360–407.

Stevens, A. L., and D. E. Rumelhart. 1975. Errors in Reading: Analysis Using an Augmented

Network Model of Grammar. In D. A. Norman, D. E. Rumelhart, and the NLR research group. *Explorations in Cognition.* San Francisco: Freeman.

Sulzby, E. 1985a. Children's Emergent Reading of Favorite Storybooks: A Developmental Study. *Reading Research Quarterly* 20: 458–481.

———. 1985b. Kindergartners as Writers and Readers. In M. Farr, ed., *Advances in Writing Research,* Vol. 1, *Children's Early Writing Development,* pp. 127–199. Norwood, NJ: Ablex.

Sulzby, E., and W. H. Teale. 1991 Emergent Literacy. In R. Barr, M. L. Kamil, P. Mosenthal, and P. D. Pearson, eds., *Handbook of Reading Research,* Vol. 11, pp. 727–757. White Plains, NY: Longman.

Teale, W. H., and E. Sulzby, eds. 1986. *Emergent Literacy: Writing and Reading.* Norwood, NJ: Ablex.

Tierney, R. J. 1991. Studies of Reading and Writing Growth: Longitudinal Research on Literacy Development. In J. Flood, J. M. Jensen, D. Lapp, and J. S. Squire, eds., *Handbook of Research on Teaching the English Language Arts,* pp. 176–194. New York: Macmillan.

Treiman, R. 1993. *Beginning to Spell: A Study of First-Grade Children.* New York: Oxford University Press.

Vernon, M. 1960. The Development of Perception in Children. *Educational Research* 3: 2–11.

Vygotsky, L. S. 1978. *Mind in Society.* Cambridge, MA: Harvard University Press.

Weber, R. 1968. The Study of Oral Reading Errors: A Survey of the Literature. *Reading Research Quarterly* 4: 96–119.

———. 1970. A Linguistic Analysis of First Grade Reading Errors. *Reading Research Quarterly* 5: 427–451.

Weinberger, J., P. Hannon, and C. Nutbrown. 1990. *Ways of Working with Parents to Promote Early Literacy Development.* Sheffield, UK: University of Sheffield Educational Research Unit.

Yendovitskaya, T. V., V. P. Zinchenko, and A. G. Ruzskaya. 1971. Development of Sensation and Perception. In A. V. Zaporozhets and D. B. Elkonin, eds., *The Psychology of Preschool Children,* pp. 1–65. Cambridge, MA: MIT Press.

Zaporozhets, A. V. 1965. The Development of Perception in the Preschool Child. *Monographs of the Society for Research in Child Development* 30, 2: 82–101.

Zinchencko, V. P., and B. F. Lomov. 1960. The Functions of Hand and Eye Movements in the Process of Perception. *Problems of Psychology* 1 and 2: 102–116.

11 Fostering Independence in Writing

IN THIS CHAPTER, CO-AUTHORS WENDY GIRLING-BUTCHER, a classroom teacher, and Gwenneth Phillips, a graduate research student, discuss with the author their observations and reflections on the writing development of very young authors in Wendy's classroom. A close look at the progress of one of Wendy's students, Tania, reveals how a skillful and perceptive teacher makes use of the child as informant to support continuing learner independence.

Wendy Girling-Butcher's classroom is in a working-class district of a large city in New Zealand. The five-year-old school entrants are beginning formal literacy instruction. When Wendy's children are writing, the class is organized in small groups—some are painting, others read or look at books, some dress up, and one group draws and writes on unlined sheets of paper. Gwenneth, a university research student, recorded the ways in which the children and teacher worked at writing in the first three months of school.

Typically, each child first drew a picture about a personal experience and then wrote about the same experience. The message was central to the task, and it was the child's own message. At times it was such an effort to write the words that the story was momentarily lost, but rereading what was written or glancing at the picture reinstated the message.

Wendy moved among the young authors and expressed delight at any show of independence. Her help was always given in the context of the child writing a whole message. She did not hesitate to sit with those who needed help, writing a letter, word, or occasionally the whole story for a child. She highlighted the sounds children were trying to identify to spell a word. She drew their attention to things they already knew. She helped others locate a model of the letter or word they were trying to write. To maintain attention on the message, children were consistently encouraged to reread. Wendy was helping them become active participants in literacy learning.

During Gwenneth's observations in the classroom, she recorded the behavior of both teacher and learner during writing tasks. Three of these records of one child's writing behaviors are shown on the next page. These particular records were selected because Tania's records were relatively easy to read. More complex teaching/learning interactions occurred.

The first sample was taken during Tania's second week of school, the second and third during the fourth and tenth week respectively. The sentences are recorded on the line marked "Text" for the reader's information; they did not appear on Tania's paper. For example, in the first sample, Tania wanted to write *I played with Amy at kindergarten.* The actual text written by Tania appears on the line marked "Child." The legend at the bottom of the figure explains that the underlined letters are ones the child copied. Above the line marked CHILD the angular marks (⌉) indicate each time some rereading occurred. Rereadings that were prompted by the teacher are marked *T;* and those initiated by the child are marked *C.* Rereading from the beginning of the story was encouraged. Letters the child wrote without help are recorded without underlining on the line labeled "Child."

Tania's growing knowledge of writing can be observed by comparing the three samples. Sample 3 shows many signs of Tania's development: (1) the teacher's prompts to reread disappear and Tania independently rereads for herself as necessary; (2) many letters are unmarked, indicating that the child is independently identifying the speech sound to be written and finding the letter needed in the writing; (3) Wendy gives very little help in articulating or stressing sounds; (4) Tania knows how to write most of the letters she needs without copying; (5) Wendy withdraws her support as Tania is able to write more and more for herself. Only in Sample 1 did Wendy think it necessary to write words for Tania; she wrote no words in Samples 2 and 3.

In the writing samples, much attention to letter forms and to hearing sounds within words can be seen. There are many examples that Courtney Cazden and Jerome Bruner would call scaffolding, where the teacher helped in the completing of the whole task by doing some of the work, withdrawing as the child learned more about the task. The theory of Vygotsky could explain what was occurring as teacher and child achieved together something that the child would later be seen to do alone. The writing records captured some of these shifts, and the emphasis seemed to be on letters and sounds.

Tania's Records of Writing from School Entry

Sample 1 **Week 2**
(Friends had been the topic of an earlier class discussion.)

Text: I played with Amy at kindergarten.

Child: I ⌉T p ⌉T w ith ⌉C A ⌉T my ⌉T at ⌉T k ⌉T

Teacher support:

to hear: ø ø ø øø

to write: *layed * *** * y * *indergarten.

Sample 2 **Week 4**
(Trees were the theme for science at the time of this writing.)

Text: I have fruit trees in my garden and I have roses.

Child: I ⌉T hv ⌉T f t ⌉T t s ⌉T in ⌉C my ⌉T g d ⌉T and I ⌉C av ⌉C e ⌉T

Teacher support:

to hear: ø ø ø ø ø

to write: * ** * ***

Sample 3 **Week 10**
(The class was about to have a "bring and buy" stall.)

Text: I will buy a drink and I will buy a sausage.

Child: I ⌉C wol ⌉C bie a drink ⌉C And I wol ⌉C die a sausage. ⌉T

Teacher support:

to hear: ø ø ø ø

to write: *** ** * *

LEGEND:

Text:	This line records the "story" the child told.
Child:	This line records letters and words the child wrote.
⌉T	Teacher reread or prompted rereading from beginning.
⌉C	Child initiated rereading.
	Child wrote unmarked letter or word without copying.
____	Child copied letter(s) or word.
Teacher Support:	
ø	Teacher helped child hear speech sounds in words.
*	Teacher helped child find a letter form.
layed	Teacher wrote letter(s) for child.

FIGURE 11 *Three records capturing change in teacher-child interactions in first ten weeks of school.*

An Interview with Wendy

Gwenneth and Marie were interested in knowing how the recorded behaviors matched with Wendy's view about what she was doing as a teacher. Gwenneth interviewed Wendy, trying not to ask leading questions about what we had seen in the records. The interview provided Wendy with opportunities to talk about her writing program. The interview uncovered an interesting paradox. Wendy did not talk about attending to letters and sounds, but she gave them a great deal of attention!

The transcript of the interview that follows retains the conversational language. It has been shortened in places, requiring explanatory comments from time to time. These comments are in brackets.

WENDY DESCRIBES HER CLASSROOM PROCEDURES

Gwenneth: Wendy, what could a child like Tania do when she entered school?

Wendy: When she came to school, she sat with her little group and she was involved with what they were reading. She was highly motivated and very on-task, and I thought that was more important than anything else. She knew some letters [thirteen lowercase letters, according to Gwenneth's test records, but Wendy did not know this]. She knew a message could be written; she knew things had to go a certain way; and she knew how to behave in school. Other children write strings of letters or copy my model.

Gwenneth: What do you expect children like Tania to do by the end of three to six months at school?

Wendy: Well, by that time I like them to have moved out of the emergent stage to where they can read and write independently from beginning to end and have some awareness of spelling conventions, too . . . You can give them suitable material knowing that without support they can write a story. They have enough strategies to work on words, take risks, or look for ways of confirming something, and they read it back as they work on it, making sure it said what they wanted to write . . . The thing I didn't mention is that they would be enthusiastic about it. They are self-winding. They've learned to learn more. They get more of their writing correct. It's like steps on the ladder. They've got a foot on the ladder and enough momentum to swing the other foot up. They have a special grasp of things . . . and they just keep moving up the ladder.

Gwenneth: What are some of the things you do that make these changes occur?

Wendy: I don't think they just happen. The classroom environment does facilitate them. The child must feel secure . . . and free to take some risks. I think the aim of most teachers is to empower children to take over the task of learning for themselves. So that's the aim . . . and I try to give each child support. If a child takes the next step by himself or herself, you gradually move away and let the child take more and more responsibility.

In writing, I get them to write about their own experiences. I get them to talk about them and relive them. There's a lot of natural flow of oral language about things that are near and dear to them. Then they do some sort of art, so they put their ideas into some other form. I will have modeled how we write a story with the children and with their help. When they write their stories I give them whatever support they need.

Gwenneth: What sorts of support do you see yourself giving?

Wendy: A huge range. For those who can barely hold a pencil, you actually have to hold their hand and hold the pencil in it. Anna's been tracing over the top of my writing of the story she told me. She's at the most basic level. The next step is when they start getting a little bit of letter knowledge, like Tania [in Sample 1]. She can write what she knows, and I fill in the gaps and that just becomes more and more of her taking over and me withdrawing. When they write the whole thing for themselves, though, it might look incorrect, but it is their own message and they have done it independently [Sample 3].

Gwenneth: What about supporting the composing of the message?

Wendy: I get them to tell me the story, and if they find it difficult I refer them to their picture. I suppose it is the extreme support if you have to generate the story for them. I find it doesn't take too long before they are generating their own. Some children write and write and don't stop to think how to write . . . some children will write the same stories day after day, going back to something they know. I think it is valid to do that, but you've got to know when to draw them away from that. I like to publish their stories. I also like to have the children read them to each other, but I don't often get sufficient time for that.

Gwenneth: How do you move the Tanias of this world from where they were at the beginning to where they've got this independence? [The interviewer is trying to get Wendy to talk about what was observed in Tania's records.]

Wendy: I don't think I do it. I think they do it. It's like an evolution, but I work with them for quite a long time.

Gwenneth: But what are you doing with them as you work with them?

Wendy: I'm trying to get them to the idea that if they write what they hear and leave spaces between words, you've more or less got a story you can read back. I sit with them and help them do some of it, and I write the rest. They become more adept at putting down what they hear and what they know and at reading back what they've written.

When they can write for themselves, then I think my task is to come in every now and again with "Don't forget to leave spaces" or "Read the story again" or ask a question to extend the story. I might give them some vocabulary. Sometimes I say to the more advanced ones, "Can you find that word on the card?" so they check on themselves to see if they've spelled it correctly. I try to build the idea of correct spelling.

Gwenneth: You suggested you don't do too much to push the kids because they take over and do things for themselves.

Wendy: Actually I probably do quite a lot, especially at the beginning up until they get a bit of fluency in their writing. But when they are ready they're almost saying, "I want to do this by myself—go away." Like Tim said, "Don't look at me; I want to do this for myself." There's no rudeness about it. They seem to know they've got the ability.

GWENNETH DISCUSSES TANIA'S WRITING RECORDS WITH WENDY

Wendy: This is interesting [looking at Sample 2], isn't it—that I didn't actually fill in the gaps there whereas there [in Sample 1] everything was filled in to make it conventionally correct? So that's where I stand back and let her go on her own. That allows children to get the idea they can put it down without help.

Look at the rereading [in Sample 3]. When I prompt this, she has taken it on for herself. That strategy [rereading from the beginning of the sentence] has been successful! When they get to that point, they are no longer making staggering attempts at hearing sounds. There's a fluency to it.

Gwenneth: Why do you think that is so effective?

Wendy: Probably because when she'd get stuck, she wouldn't know how to proceed, so you'd take her back to the beginning. Then she's pushing the message through herself and invariably when she does that . . . she gets the next word because she's got the sense of it.

Gwenneth: Why do you think the child gets stuck? What makes the rereading necessary?

Wendy: I suppose it's a bit like what Marie Clay says about changing gears in reading. [Marie's interpretation here is that the writer struggling in one gear at the letter level has to have a way of changing gears and getting back to the message level.]

Gwenneth: What do you think was happening in Sample 3 when you didn't do much correcting?

Wendy: I suspect that my aim was . . . just to get the show on the road. Not to worry too much over details.

Gwenneth: Why did you leave those as they are ["wol *bie*" and "wol *die*" for "will buy"]? When might you move in on those kinds of words?

Wendy: The timing of this is very important. If it were Rosa it would be a good time to rein her in, but with Tania she's always been a bit slow at getting things down, so I think I'd want a bit more momentum in her work before I would come in and attend to those details. I'd rather she wrote more with more fluency . . . I might stop her in her tracks if I intervened at that point.

Gwenneth: Do you see any use in keeping this sort of record [the writing record]?

Wendy: Oh yes, not just in terms of what the child is doing and the progress but in terms of what effect I am having as a teacher. When I look at that [the teacher's participation line] I immediately think, "Why did I bother doing that for her when she was probably capable of doing that for herself?" I suspect I could use another way of getting her to write without so much input.

The more you look at the records, the more questions are thrown up at you about your timing, about what the child was really capable of. It would deepen your self-awareness and refine your decision-making in the middle of an intense and busy writing session. It might be interesting to do a series of observations with a successful child to see what you do that promotes success.

Is Wendy Attending to the Sounds In Words?

In the context of each child writing his or her own story, Wendy gave help according to individual needs rather than a set program sequence. To learn letter names and letter forms, she encouraged children to do a slow articulation of a word they were trying to write so they could hear the sounds in their own speech, and she helped them link sounds to letters so they could write them. This is not traditional phonics instruction because the learning challenge is for the child *to hear the sounds in a sequence of sounds.* This continues to be difficult even after the single letters and their sounds are known, according to Charles Read (1986). During the interview, Gwenneth had tried to get Wendy to talk about these aspects of her work, but Wendy only rarely commented on spelling. It was as if Wendy was not really aware of what she had been doing. Rather, she attended mostly to how children constructed their message and how children become independent but active participants in their writing and rereading. These clearly took precedence among her teaching purposes.

Yet Gwenneth had seen Wendy giving specific forms of help:

- writing a letter or word into a story and encouraging a pupil to write over it.
- prompting a link to something the child knew, such as "It starts like your name."
- saying "Look at my mouth" as she said a word slowly and asking, "What can you hear? What does it start like? What can you hear next?"
- pointing to a small number of letters and asking, "Which of these do you think it is?"
- supporting the child's search of his own repertoire, saying, "You know that word."

When checking our draft Wendy commented that Gwenneth had not asked about these things. Then Wendy supplied another good analogy. She said, "I suppose it is a bit like breathing; I suppose it goes on, but as long as there is nothing wrong you don't notice it."

The paradox is that the behavior record seems to distort the picture of how children were being taught. The teacher's attention was on the holistic features of the task, how she could support the whole enterprise of the child becoming an active participant able to work independently to construct written messages. These were the important learning contexts; letters and letter-sound relationships received expert attention but not focal attention. If the distribution of Wendy's attention was about right, and the progress of her children suggests that it was, it makes an important point about learning phonological awareness. We might propose that to teach letters and letter-sound relationships as a separate skill, giving them focal attention, misrepresents the nature of the writing task to the child. It delays the development of the independence that comes with learning how to incorporate such knowledge into the act of writing messages. Tania had just started school.

There is another point to be made about Tania's records. Wendy's children are learning about sounds in words and the relationships between them. Yet the records describe writing, not reading lessons. It is in reading that teachers have traditionally taught children detached associations of letters and sounds. But no one can write a story without segmenting sounds, forming letters, and combining these parts into whole words. Phonological analysis, segmenting the syllable into its parts, and mastering the (spelling) pattern of a word are natural parts of early writing tasks. They are combined with constructing the syntax of the sentence with care and monitoring all this by rereading the message. Once children discover how to do these kinds of things in writing, literacy learning, as Wendy suggested, may be as simple as breathing!

References

Phillips, G. 1997. An Exploration of the Co-Construction of Context in Beginning Reading Instruction. Ph.D. diss., University of Auckland.
Read, C. 1986. *Children's Creative Spelling.* London: Routledge and Kegan Paul.

12 Introducing Storybooks to Young Readers

I THINK INTRODUCING NEW TEXTS that young schoolchildren are going to read demands great skill. In my student days, my psychology lecturer would have described what I am writing about as "creating a set for the task." Developmental psychologists have written about "orientation to the task." Teachers I have talked to call it motivating the children or getting their interest. If we fine-tune our understanding of what book introductions can achieve, we can become more sensitive to the different needs of individual children.

I take Jim Trelease's (1989) message as a given and assume that parents and teachers will read aloud to children of any age, introducing them to texts that they cannot yet tackle themselves. When a story is read to children, the shape of the story is created, the characters emerge, and the style of discourse and the literary turn of phrase are "heard." As a consequence, prediction and anticipation become easier at a second hearing. When books are read aloud, new language forms are introduced to the ear, making the books a little easier to listen to next time. Meanings can be negotiated in discussion before, during, and after the story reading. Reading to children and allowing interaction provide rich opportunities for new learning about texts.

However, if we want children to learn to read new texts independently, we can facilitate this by providing a rich introduction to the story instead of reading the whole story to them in advance. Children who already enjoy shared reading can be encouraged to become more independent as readers if new stories are introduced before they try to read them for themselves. A good introduction makes a new text more accessible.

Obviously, introductions are not needed before familiar books. If a book does not contain new challenges, a teacher may not use an introduction. When children are able to read the new text without any help or with the help of peers, the additional support of an introduction might be considered unnecessary.

In this chapter I provide some examples of book introductions with individual children to illustrate the many different ways in which teachers can provide readers with help to ensure a successful first reading. Such interactions can also take place within a small reading group. The teacher might use a large book that all the children can see, or each child might have a copy of the new storybook.

Book introductions are regular features of New Zealand teaching practice. They are initiated some time during the first year at school when children need more independence in their reading than shared reading. They are only the first step in a reading lesson. Therefore, they are quite different from a directed reading activity (Tierney, Readence, and Dishner 1990), which provides a scaffold for the whole reading lesson. Storybook introductions are designed to ensure a successful first reading early in the lesson before the teacher develops lesson activities. They are also an important part of a Reading Recovery lesson (Clay 1993; Pinnell, Fried, and Estice 1990) where, in one-to-one teaching, the teacher can take into account the specific performance repertoire of individual children.

What Does a Book Introduction Achieve?

Rich introductions to new stories make these stories easier to read at the first reading. The idea of making the task easier by giving a good introduction calls into question the assumption that "real reading" occurs only when the reader is reading new text without prior preparation (for example, in a testing situation). It also calls into question a second assumption: that children will not be able to read the text until they have been taught the words and the new phonological relationships needed to decode those words (an assumption that fosters dependency on an instructional sequence). Introductions are useful when it is important for children to read a new text with a high degree of successful processing (and I think that should always be a high priority).

The teacher's introduction creates a scaffold within which children can complete a first reading of a whole story. The teacher and children have rehearsed some responses; others are recent and familiar because the teacher modeled them. The children's own background knowledge has been called to mind, and some new knowledge has been introduced in a measured way. This applies only if the teacher's introduction has engaged the children's attention, and they have been encouraged to be active participants in the introduction. This is not a case of telling the children what to expect. It is a process of drawing the children into the activity before passing control to the children and pushing them gently towards problem-solving the whole first reading of the story for themselves.

In these transactions, children quickly learn that they must initiate the reading work needed to get meaning from texts. Even at a first attempt to read a new text, children can be expected to work actively with what little they know. At this early stage, perception, constructive activity, and language all work together with meaning. The child's version of the text will be guided by his or her oral language, by the introduction of the teacher, by the pictures, by what the child can find in print that he or she already knows, by the child's knowledge of the world, and by his or her prior knowledge of the structure of stories. Before long, some details no longer need the teacher's attention because they no longer need the child's attention, and the two people in interacting are freed to move the focus of their attention on to other things.

Anderson and Armbruster (1990) wrote that "the teacher's orientation can be lean if the book is easy for the child. A richer orientation is desirable if the book is likely to be difficult." A well-prepared group that has had many experiences with books might need only a lean introduction, and another group might need a longer and richer introduction, yet both may achieve the same success at a first reading.

Here is a simple book introduction:

Teacher: This is a story about a lion who couldn't find his tail. All his friends come along, and they all help him find his tail. He looks very sad and they ask why he's sad, and he says he can't find his tail. So do you know what they say they'll do?

Child: They'll help him.

Teacher: They'll help him look for it. And at the end of the story who helps him find his tail?

Child: The turtle.

Teacher: He couldn't find his tail because what was he doing? He was . . .

Child: Sitting on it!

A Reading Recovery child from the lowest-achieving group in the class, and early in the program, would need an introduction specially tailored to his or her particular limited set of competencies, although towards the end of the program the child's increasing independence would mean that he or she could carry more of the load with only a brief introduction. The most competent children have more reserves of knowledge to draw on at each and every level of language organization; less well prepared children need more careful anticipation by the teacher of which text features might make problem-solving easier for them.

The Introduction

Suppose a teacher has selected an interesting new storybook suitable for one of his or her reading groups, one that will extend the group's competencies in specific ways. As the children's task will be to read the new book independently, the teacher will not read it to them, but will provide some framework to guide the children through the story. The teacher recognizes the need to prepare for the new story, but the teaching will follow the first successful reading. When previewing the text, the teacher became aware of some parts that could prove difficult for this group of children. As they talk about the story, the teacher works into the discussion some well-planned directing of attention to features of the text.

To the observer, what happens does not sound at all like teaching. All the interactions take place within an easy conversational exchange that does not dismember the story. It is like the negotiations between parent and child in the lap-story situation.

The teacher sets the topic, title, and characters with minimal interaction, as too much talk confuses the purpose and distracts from the focus on the story. Titles are odd texts with little redundancy, and they may contain tricks that trip young readers. The title may be something to come back to. As part of the introduction, the teacher may do the following:

- Invite the children to respond to the new book with the help of its illustrations, and link it to other stories they have shared.
- Draw from the children some of the experiences they could relate to this new text, and in doing so uncover potential confusions that can then be straightened out.
- Perhaps sketch the plot or structure the sequence up to the climax (leaving the surprise untouched). The idea is to create an overview of the story structure, to provide a framework for anticipating what will occur.
- To develop understanding around the theme or topic, encourage children to draw on personal experiences or to remember another story shared previously. There may be a conceptual problem, as some of the children do not understand the ways of stories or of cultures (for example, why the fox is stalking the hen). The discussion explores this facet of the plot.
- Try to anticipate when some language, or an unusual name, or some bookish syntactical sequence will not link easily to the children's own language, and use the novel language features when talking about the story, and enunciating them very deliberately. The teacher may intentionally use one particular sentence pattern two or three times, or get the children to repeat a phrase or sentence, running the difficult language or pronunciation across their tongues. This allows the children to have a model of the language in their heads to support their reading of the text. It is not memorizing the lines of the book, but rather readying the mind and ear to grapple with novelty.

Good book introductions explore, test out, and draw on children's knowledge. In discussion, teachers supply novel information on any of the different levels at which language is organized: discourse, plot and dramatic effect, propositions, sequences of events, repeated components, climax or surprise, semantics, syntax, words, orthographic features, layout, and print features. Occasionally, teachers may even address letter-sound relationships of first or last letters or clusters and the pronunciation of unusual names like *Horopokotchkin.* The teacher anticipates what might trip the children as they read the story; yet *the overview of the story is like a conversational exchange, and the attention to detail should not dismember the flow of the story.*

Book introductions enlarge the range of what children can do with whole stories at a first reading. They highlight a particular kind of support for the reader that teaching practice often ignores. With a whole view of the uninterrupted story, children have a feel for the progression of the story through to its climax, so the story itself provides a support within which the detailed processing of information in the text occurs.

Understanding the structure of the whole story provides a kind of scaffold that allows children to focus attention on many new details about print. It makes reading the book easier when the introduction retains the meaning and intactness of the whole story. Teaching practices that deal with a page of a book a day utterly destroy this kind of support. The emergence of little storybooks has now made whole story reading for beginning readers possible. Book introductions are an authentic social interaction about the new book; but when they provide an orientation to novel features of stories and of texts, they are also a kind of teaching.

Interacting with Learners During Book Introductions

Examples 1 and 2 provide illustrations of the many things teachers might do during book introductions. Readers should remember that although the interaction flows like a conversation and leaves room for the child's input to inform the teacher, it also includes deliberate teaching moves.

Maintaining Interactive Ease. Some of the teacher's moves are merely to maintain the interaction, especially when working with new, shy, or somewhat reticent children who give few responses. (This is clearly seen in Example 3, although I have not labeled it as such because this example is provided so readers can try to analyze the teaching moves for themselves.) To repeat or expand what a child says helps maintain interactive ease, but it also models that discussion is acceptable. It may call up more memories to bolster understanding, add new information, remove ambiguity, and possibly sort out some confusion. It serves more to alert children to new features rather than discuss them extensively.

Increasing Accessibility. The teacher provides information from many sources in the books. He or she anticipates what might be new or strange for the group, and takes care with new or unusual words in the context of the whole story. For instance, in Example 1 the teacher anticipates that *granddaughter* may not be a familiar word and introduces it by saying, "They're asking the granddaughter to help, aren't they?"

EXAMPLE 1: INTRODUCING A STUDENT TO *THE GREAT BIG ENORMOUS TURNIP* (HELEN OXENBURY)

Setting the Topic, Theme, and Characters

Teacher: Let's look at our new book. This story is about a big turnip, isn't it? *The Great Big Enormous Turnip.*

Prompting Constructive Activity

Teacher: Let's see what happened. Here's a little old man and he's . . . *(pausing).* What's he doing?

Child: He's telling it to grow.

Teacher: And then what's he trying to do?

Child: Pull it out.

Teacher: Pull it out! Can he pull it out?

Child: *(Shakes his head.)*

Teacher: No! Who does he ask to help him?

Child: The little old woman.

Increasing Accessibility or Presenting New Knowledge

Teacher (turning the page and rehearsing "granddaughter"): They're asking the granddaughter to help, aren't they?

Accepting a Partially Correct Response

Teacher: Who do they ask next?

Child: The dog.

Teacher: The black dog, that's right.

Providing a Model (of Anticipating the Outcome)

Teacher: And does it come up? Does it? I think it might. And they all . . . *(turns the page).* Oh, no, not yet! Who do they have to ask?

The teacher may deliberately enunciate unusual syntax (for example when the text uses a full form and the children might produce a contraction, like *can't* for *cannot*), or may use a sentence pattern two or three times to help children hold the pattern in mind. Sometimes the model is provided by one of the children spontaneously, and then the teacher confirms and reinforces this by repeating what the child said or altering it to agree with the text, as in the following interchange:

Teacher: And what did they do?

Child: Eat it.

Teacher: That's right. They all ate it.

There is some rehearsal of what is novel within the context of the whole story, but without the children actually hearing the text read. In this way, features of the text receive attention not in isolation but within the context of the text as a whole. Holdaway (1979) has written of how "children not thoroughly familiar with the syntactic patterns, idioms and tunes of written English . . . require the joyful repetition of a rich literature through the ear and across the tongue . . . [so that] the patterns of the book dialect are running through the automatic language system of the child" (p. 194).

Prompting the Child to Constructive Activity. From the first days of beginning reading, teachers should encourage children to actively reconstruct the author's text. There are many ways to do this; only three examples are listed here:

1. *Linking to personal knowledge.* Many of the teacher's moves in introducing a new story urge the children to search actively for links within the story and beyond the book in their own experiences: Have they ever done that? Does that happen in their families? Have they ever felt like that? What would they expect to happen? (See Example 1.) What do they know about how the plots of stories unfold? (See the prompt to constructive activity in Example 2 below.)

2. *Pausing for the children to generate the ending.* The teacher may leave something for the children to complete, much as a mother with a two-year-old leaves a rhyme without the last word because that is the contribution the young child can make. The teacher may also pause so that children can anticipate what will occur next (see Example 1). In one- and two-line pattern books, this pausing to anticipate will often occur before a page is turned. Pausing is a tactic that gains and focuses children's attention. It signals that they are expected to be active and work cooperatively with the teacher. Pausing to anticipate contributes to the feel of where the story is going and how the climax is building up, which is an important source of making meaning support the whole processing effort.

3. *Reflecting.* The teacher asks children to reflect on something and make a judgment. "How did you know that?" is a question designed to reveal to the teacher some of the information that a child is using. Questions like "What do you think will happen?" or "How do you think X felt?" are less important as evaluations but still helpful because they call upon children to interact with the messages of the text (see the end of Examples 1 and 2).

These activities awaken some children to the idea that a reader brings understanding to texts. Such exchanges also signal that we can know how we know and that metacognitive awareness may be a helpful part of learning to read and write. The teacher must be astute in judging which of the many possible questions will make the most contribution for a particular group of children.

Accepting Partially Correct Responses. Rarely does a child's response come out of thin air; rather it is a response to some part of the text or some part of a child's experience. If a response is correct in some respect and if the teacher recognizes this and adds information of some kind he or she builds toward a successful outcome from the child's initial response. A sense of what the whole response feels like is gained (see Examples 1 and 2) and that leads to further interactions. If, on the other hand, the teacher discards the learner's response as wrong and gives the child the answer, the child has gained no sense of how he or she could work on a similar problem the next time.

EXAMPLE 2: INTRODUCING A STUDENT TO *TRUG AND LEAF* (PHILLIS FLOWERDEW)

The teacher in the following example clearly thought the story *Trug and Leaf* might be difficult for this child to understand, so she takes particular care with the introduction.

Setting the Topic, Title, and Characters

Teacher: I've got another book about Trug for you. It's about Trug and Leaf this time, and poor Leaf is ill.

Probing to Find Out What the Child Knows

Teacher: Do you know what it means when you are ill?

Child: (No response.)

Teacher: It means you are sick, and Trug's going to try to look after her. Look, she's in bed.

Asking the Child to Work with New Knowledge

Teacher: Trug's going to get some water for her. What do you think water might start with?

Child: W.

Teacher: I bet you can show what word says *water.*

Accepting Partially Correct Responses

Teacher: That word does start with *w.* It says *will.*

Tightening the Criteria of Acceptability

Teacher: Can you find another?

Child: (Locates "water.")

Teacher: That's got *w,* hasn't it? Right, he's going to get some water.

Prompting Constructive Activity (to Understand the Plot)

Teacher: He's trying to carry it in his hands. Is that working? It drips on the mud, doesn't it? That's not much good. Look, it's still dripping! Has he got any water left? I wonder how he is going to get the water. What does he see? What can he use?

Child: The egg.

Teacher: Where has the baby bird come from?

Child: The egg.

Teacher: He's come out of the egg, hasn't he? What's Trug going to do with the egg?

Child: Put water in it?

Providing a Model (of Reflecting on the Story)

Teacher: He had a good idea, didn't he? And he can take the water to Leaf. She might get better now she's got a drink of water, mightn't she? Do you think so? Because she's ill, isn't she?

EXAMPLE 3: INTRODUCING A STUDENT TO *LITTLE BEAR* (L. C. HOLMLUND MINARIK)

In this transcript, using the book *Little Bear,* a teacher works with a child who was just beginning to produce responses in the book introduction format. What kinds of support is the teacher providing?

Teacher: I've got a new book and it's about someone else going for a walk. It's a little bear going for a walk this time. And he sees lots of things.

Child: (Points, a nonverbal participation.)

Teacher: Yes, he sees an ant, and the story is called "Hello! How are you?" Can you say that? "Hello . . ."

Child: "How are you?"

Teacher: And when he goes for a walk he asks everybody how they are.

Teacher and Child: "Hello . . . How are you?" *(The transcript was shortened by omitting a segment here.)*

Teacher: And here's his momma. He's going to say "Hello, Momma."

Child: "Hello, Mummy."

Teacher: Mmmm, *Momma,* he calls her.

Child: Momma.

Teacher: What's he going to say?

Child: "How are you?"

Teacher: And is she going to answer him? Let's turn over and see. She just says, "What a funny little bear you are." You read that with me.

Teacher and Child: "What a funny little bear you are."

Teacher: And he sees someone else and he says, "Wait! Wait!" I wonder who he's seen? Turn over and see.

Child: Bear!

Teacher: Yes, he's seen Poppa. He calls him Poppa. Let's see what he's going to say to Poppa.

Child (anticipating well): "Hello Poppa, how are you?"

Teacher: Mmm. Do you think Poppa's going to answer him?

Child: Yes.

Teacher: He might too. Let's see what he's saying.

Child: "Hello, little bear."

Teacher: Good. "I'm very well, thank you. How are you?" And do you think little bear is well?

Sometimes teachers may praise children for the use of a particular feature; at other times they may choose to accept a wrong response without comment, judging that instruction would be better left until some later time. Observant teachers rarely reject a child's effort. They find something in the response to commend.

Tightening the Criteria of Acceptability. When teachers accept and reinforce responses that are only partially correct, they accept the process that the child used to get to the answer. The strategy being used is accepted as valid and useful even when the response does not match the text. It is then quite easy to call the reader's attention to some neglected information.

Many teachers are good at accepting partially correct responses and calling for more constructive activity without sounding negative or didactic. One response often heard is "I liked the way you thought about X, but did you notice . . . ?" This occurs in Example 2 when the child is invited to locate the word *water.*

Probing to Find Out What Children Know. Busy teachers are forced to work towards short introductions, leaving children to do as much as possible independently. They cannot teach every new concept, but in their introduction to a new book they can probe to find out whether the children already have some knowledge essential for understanding the text. They might ask children to respond to the new story with some kind of "Show me" demand. Then, to test whether the main content is understood or novel, they might ask "Do you know . . . ?" or "Have you seen . . . ?" or "Do you remember in another book . . . ?" questions. This questioning provides teachers with information about what children know (and therefore what they do not need to teach). It also brings relevant knowledge into the minds of the children. It is then readily accessible for the reading that will take place. The teacher's questions are directed to whether children understand and can demonstrate relevant knowledge (see Example 2).

Presenting New Knowledge. Notice in Example 1 that the teacher slips in the phrase "the black dog." When teachers suspect that children do not have the ideas, words, or usage to read and understand a part of the text, they present the children with that new knowledge. They may use a particular phrase, explain some part of the story, or contrast a feature of the story with something the children have encountered in another book. They may help the children discriminate between things, like a school desk and a large adult-type desk. They may anticipate the problem or respond to signals from the child but they switch the child's attention from an unhelpful association to a more helpful one.

From time to time, teachers will be almost certain that a word is likely to be unfamiliar. When this happens, a common pattern I noticed in my observations is for a teacher to talk towards the meaning of a word, describe some relevant object or use, explain some aspect of the word, and only lastly provide the word. There seemed to be an implicit assumption that children need a mental context as preparation for receiving a new word.

Asking Children to Work with New Knowledge. Because they assume that it is important for children to actively engage with the text, teachers gently push children to be active in linking new knowledge with things they already know (see Example 2). They may tell the children something and ask them to talk more about it. They may ask the children to check the new information with the pictures in the book. They might create some opportunity for children to display comprehension of this new knowledge prior to reading.

Providing a Model. From precise knowledge of what their students already know, teachers anticipate what things in the text will be new to their children. They may say the sentence, provide the intonation, or use a word that the children may never have used before. If the teachers' anticipation is wrong, they will not have affected the children's responding. If they are right, the help they give may enable some children to put the task together and perform successfully and independently. At the end of Example 1, for example, the teacher plays with (or models) the anticipation of climax in the plot of the story.

If learning to read involves bringing many complex behaviors together as the reader problem-solves his or her way through a story, then introductions provide the teacher with many opportunities to model important reading behaviors, such as linking, cross-checking, and monitoring.

Changing the Task Demands

As children read aloud, teachers get feedback on how well the introduction went. They find out how well they anticipated and dealt with new features of text in a particular story. They will also discover how well children are mapping what they know onto this new task. Is a particular child surprised, or are most of the features of this task things the child can deal with? Can the teacher shift attention in the next storybook introduction to some new aspects of text? Should he or she encourage or model some searching or self-correcting behaviors during the introduction to support the range of reading work the child is doing?

As the child maps language onto the text, follows the plot and story with understanding, and somehow begins to deal effectively with several dimensions of this complex task all at the same time, changes occur in behavior. When a child checks the picture, pauses, uses a pointing finger to rerun the text, comments on his or her world experience or on another book or lesson remembered, learning is going on. Observing these behaviors enables teachers to fine-tune the teaching that will follow the first reading; it also helps them make better judgments about what the reader might learn next. This informs teachers' succeeding book selections and introductions.

Beyond the Storybooks of Early Reading

Book introductions can be varied according to children's needs. Some children may try the first reading without help; others need only a lean introduction; yet others need a rich introduction. It depends in part on what the child can do, but it also depends on the difficulty of the text the child has chosen to read or what the teacher wishes to introduce. How flexible teachers can be in working with a small group of children may be limited by class organization and the number of children they have chosen to work with. A key feature of book introductions is their responsiveness to readers' needs, in contrast to a scripted overview prepared by the teacher and presented to the readers.

As children develop more control over first readings of new texts, teachers can change the interactive demands of a book introduction. With an increasing gradient of difficulty in texts comes the use of a wider vocabulary that is more specialized by topic. The balance of participation by student and teacher changes, for a successful first reading is more a result of the child's inner control over the task and is less dependent on the teacher to prompt the child how to carry out the task.

Yet some guidance is still needed because the formal educative intent of much schooling is to challenge the child's current competence. It follows that since the child is constantly being challenged to risk going beyond current competence, teachers need to continue to introduce new texts for selected purposes. At all levels of elementary school performance, teachers support new learning as they

- select tasks,
- negotiate the context for the activity,
- model appropriate behavior,
- prompt constructive activity,
- probe for prior knowledge and understanding,
- introduce new knowledge,
- prompt the child to work with the new knowledge,
- promote emerging skill,
- support and affirm uncertain but correct responses,
- accept partial success but encourage further search,
- tighten the criteria for acceptability,
- push gently for independent problem-solving,
- withhold help,
- pass some control to the learner in every interaction, and eventually,
- put the learner in complete control of the task.

The teacher's role is to keep the learner at the cutting edge of his or her competence (where Vygotsky would have said the learner should be). The teacher is continually interacting with unseen processes—the unseen strategies used by readers to produce overt responses or silent reading responses.

Taking a Piagetian viewpoint, some educators would claim that teachers can only arrange for learning to occur but cannot teach. An alternative position with commonsense validity is for the adult to share the task when text challenges threaten successful processing but to gradually withdraw help as the reader takes over new forms of control. This interactive stance makes good sense because it provides teachers with feedback about the task they have set and how they might change the task demands to make for a better gradient of difficulty for a particular child. Teachers can see when children are ready to reach out beyond current competence.

Introductions to new storybooks could occur with a gradient of teacher involvement, from reading to the children; to rich introductions; to shorter, more focused introductions; to a few moves to increase accessibility of a new text; to making the task an unseen, unshared, and unhelped activity. If a group of competent eleven-year-olds must read a new text containing new concepts and vocabulary, they may learn a great deal more if their teachers take time to introduce this new text to them than if they are left to struggle through it on their own. And that makes one think about high school students' reading of literature from past centuries or other cultures, or reading in the content areas. Something like book introductions are a necessary part of what good teachers do with students much older than those discussed in this chapter. A good introduction, leading to a successful first reading by an active reader, sets the stage for a host of teaching ventures around that text.

References

Anderson, R. C., and B. B. Armbruster. 1990. *Some Maxims for Learning and Instruction.* Technical Report No. 491. Champaign, IL: Center for the Study of Reading, University of Illinois.

Clay, M. M. 1991. *Becoming Literate: The Construction of Inner Control.* Auckland, NZ: Heinemann.

———. 1993. *Reading Recovery: A Guidebook for Teachers in Training.* Auckland, NZ: Heinemann.

Holdaway, D. 1979. *The Foundations of Literacy.* Sydney: Ashton Scholastic.

Pinnell, G. S., M. D. Fried, and R. M. Estice. 1990. Reading Recovery: Learning How to Make a Difference. *The Reading Teacher* 43: 282–295.

Tierney, R. J., J. E. Readence, and E. K. Dishner. 1990. *Reading Strategies and Practices: A Compendium.* 3rd ed. Needham Heights, MA: Allyn & Bacon.

Trelease, J. 1989. *The New Read-Aloud Handbook.* Harmondsworth, UK: Penguin.

13 Constructive Processes: Reading, Writing, Talking, Art, and Crafts

FOR A CHILD TO RESPOND to a teacher, whether by reading, talking, writing, constructing a village, or painting a drama backdrop, the child must relate, remember, relearn, monitor, problem-solve, and do all those other powerful mental activities that help humans adapt and create new solutions. The constructive mode is one we must develop. (Wendy was working on this in Chapter 11.)

We listened with interest to the speaker from America as he talked about many things. He told us of a study about engaged time in school. At one point we in the audience gasped. We were psychologists and administrators, teachers and university students—a diverse group except that we were all New Zealanders. What led to our silent surprise was the fact that the speaker was classifying arts and crafts as *nonacademic*. Perhaps we had not really thought about this point, but the stark reality of the American study faced us with it. Fighting this idea, I could not let go of images of classrooms where arts and crafts were widely used in the pursuit of academic activities, associated with talking, writing, reading, drama, content subjects like science and social studies, and particularly high school English. My aim in this chapter is to provide some examples of the use of art and crafts for academic purposes.

Academic Applications of Art and Crafts

In the 1970s New Zealand high school teachers participated with the Education Department in designing a new English curriculum. There was nothing unusual in that; back then curriculum revisions usually emerged as general guidelines from a central department of education that were molded in many ways by the experience of practicing teachers. The new curriculum recognized the importance of the visual medium of television and the oral modes of language stressed by a wider use of radio, television, and satellite communication. Not that reading and writing were neglected, because New Zealand pupils would still get daily opportunities to read, and to write texts they compose.

The newer media forms—records and audiotapes, films, and video—had captured the interests of youth. My daughter was training to be a high school English teacher, and she was required to take out to her first schools a high-quality tape recorder and camera. These were standard pieces of equipment for trainee teachers of English at that time, tools that would be used to record children's oral work in class and visual displays produced by groups of children following some study of literature.

Alternatively, tape recorder or camera might be used to create a starting point for the introduction of a new unit of work. In the past we might have accepted these as preliminary motivating activities, used to stimulate interest. Since then, the development of theories about the constructive learner (Spiro 1980) has given such activities a much more central role in academic learning.

Many New Zealand children enter school with little knowledge of print. Half may write their name; most will know only a few letters. They are a year younger than American beginners and they do not come to school knowing letters: their society has not taught them that this is necessary for schoolwork. I do not know why this is, but see no reason to advocate any change.

In the first days of school, teachers give children blank pages of paper and invite them to draw. Their first school products are drawings.

Before long the children may sign their names or parts of them, and begin to make letters and symbols. Children are drawing and writing before they are reading. When the process is really under way, each child will have a set of ideas he or she wants to represent. The child will make a drawing and then, with help from his or her neighbor, or the teacher, or from the word-filled environment of the classroom, will get some messages down in print about the story.

Some people have explained these drawings as the children's thinking up of the ideas that will later become sentences. Others have seen them as aides to memory, allowing children to hold the ideas in their mind while struggling to write their messages.

On some days the teacher may start with a craft activity and help the children create a strange creature, a cutout dragon, a collage of colors, or a construction of blocks and then use this to elicit oral language, which in turn leads to writing and reading. Sometimes the task is collectively composed, but more often in the early years the product is individual.

When we ask a child to construct some product to show us what he or she has learned, we imply that the child can bring other knowledge to bear on the new task. In a discussion of the constructive orientation applied to comprehension, Spiro (1980) points out that what one already knows is important in determining what one will come to know. Constructive processes have been demonstrated in studies of the roles of story schema, meaning, and prior knowledge in reading. Pickard (1975) provides an illustration. The teacher asked a class of children aged nine to write; she had only been with them for a week and did not know them well. Poetry was a permitted response. One boy wrote this:

> *The Stars*
>
> On a clear moonlight night,
> The stars shine so bright,
> Really we are seeing them
> Long, long ago.
>
> Scorpion biting Orion's heel,
> Argus with sparkling keel,
> The Greeks looked up and saw them
> Long, long ago.

The teacher had not noticed this boy particularly before, and as far as she could ascertain he had never written a poem before. What she found out was that he and his brother were keenly interested in astronomy, and he could link that knowledge with performing the task she had set.

One eight-year-old's writing (Sutton-Smith 1981), gathered in a classroom in Greenwich Village, New York, provides another illustration of what personal knowledge contributes to the task. The story is called "The Dizzy Pot," and it contains images like this:

> If I were a pot made on a wheel I would get dizzy but it would be fun to be taken out of a pack of clay and wonder what I'm gonna be. The person would smack me down on the wood and I would start spinning around and then I would feel a hand push down on me and start shaping me . . . so I would be a real mean pot, I would start going off center . . . Then it would stop and, if I were real I would probably throw up . . . (p. 246)

In Vivian Paley's *Wally's Stories* (Paley 1981), kindergarten children "speak delightfully and wisely for themselves," according to Cazden in the foreword. The children discuss serious subjects, like whether stones melt when they are boiled. Cazden suggested that teachers might explore the ideas that flow from the children's premises. This is what Paley did, with rich gains in language and behavior in this five-year-old community. As Paley wrote, "My task is to keep inquiry open long enough for the consequences of their ideas to become apparent to them . . . My goal is as much to give children practice in exposition as to improve their stories" (1981, pp. 212, 220).

But, my readers may justly complain, these examples are of writing, not of art or craft. The constraints of space in this article and problems of reproduction make it so, but I will try to retell a fraction of a case study reported by Richardson (1964, pp. 187–190).

> David was walking carefully among his father's roosters and hens, watching them. "For we have to be careful, don't we, when roosters are about?" "Big combs and such floppy wattles, big spurs like spears." These were the roosters he saw.

David wrote four rooster and hawk stories one after the other in the next few days. He didn't value them very much. A play followed about an owl and the roosters. The roosters also turned up in a letter to a friend in London. Then,

> The next morning David came with a large piece of lino, asking if he could do a lino block of the roosters for his craft work that week. This fine block was printed as a front cover for the current magazine. The impact of this block was immense for it was by far the best block that had been done up till then. There was, of course, a definite relationship between the one expression and the other, in that the satisfactions of the first led the craftsman on to make a further statement that is an enlarged and more developed expression.

Finally, when teachers are trying to make their instruction relevant to children from very different cultures, I notice they stress art forms and craft activities as well as local storytelling and the recounting of histories. If we take the culture of the child as a starting point for instruction, we allow him or her to construct a response by using both our teaching and the things the child already knows from his or her own culture to achieve some kind of productive response. The child's cultural knowledge will combine with our instruction.

The child's response can be reading or writing; a piece of art or craft work; a construction, model, or mural; drama, music, or poetry; or a book to be read by classmates. Or it could have been a perfect score on ten multiple-choice questions with the result recorded in the principal's book of tests for the month!

Children as Constructors of Their Own Knowledge

Studies of children's thinking and of language acquisition show that children act on their own theories of how things work and change these theories slowly in the face of conflicting evidence. Duckworth (1979) provided a Piagetian explanation of this. If a child has a theory, no matter how primitive, that child will pay attention to instances that confirm and contradict that theory. Noticing a novel feature in his or her own productions may activate the search. A contradiction *may* lead a child to figure out some other theory that would take that contradiction into account.

In thinking, in oral language, in reading for meaning, and in early writing, children are motivated to make sense of the world. At any moment when we deliver our curriculum item they are already operating on their own theories of the world.

Somewhere in the center of all their learning activities, children judge their present experience in terms of its meaningfulness to them and to their theories of the task. Mild conflicts between assumptions and present experience seem to discourage new discoveries.

If we think of children as constructors of responses who become fast and fluent in reproducing the things they know, we can understand how they can attend to new information, to features that were not noticed before. When you can respond to earlier learning without much attention you are freed to notice some new features of the task and make new links to other things you know. Learning to read and write is not just building up fast responses. It is creating vast networks of links between known features of linguistic and real world events.

Holdaway (1979) linked talking, reading, writing, thinking, drawing, and "making activities" in terms of a semantic drive. We express meanings in speech, in writing, and in constructing. We interpret meanings in speech, in reading, and in art. As Holdaway put it,

> the result of energizing semantic content will be a drive toward symbolization of many kinds displaying individual differences of personal style and current need . . . the effective language learning environment will be both one in which the language arts themselves flow naturally one into the other, and also one in which related arts of many kinds will flourish. (pp. 162–163)

Getting into a Constructive Way of Thinking

Paley exposed children to oral storytelling, and Holdaway suggested that we tap their search for making sense of experience. Bussis, Chittenden, and Amarel (1976) recommended that we break from linear programs and allow multiple entry points to new learning. They argued that human beings learn similar things in different ways and that we derive different understandings from objectively similar experiences. One particular concept might be touched on in very different encounters.

> By divesting subject-matter content of its linear organization and "spreading it out" multiple-entry points into knowledge can be created for children. Understanding of balance and symmetry, for example, might be developed

from a beginning of block construction, of making mobiles, or of exploration with a balance scales. (Bussis, Chittenden, and Amarel 1976, p. 24)

I see every reason to assume that a teacher's call for a child to construct a response, whatever form that response takes, requires the child to relate, link, remember, call up, relearn, monitor, problem-solve, and all those other powerful mental activities that help children and adults adapt and create new solutions.

Discussion of constructive thinking has one other side to it. Many theorists and teachers are wary of activities that make it difficult to shift into the constructive mode—such activities as rote learning, repetitive tasks, repetitive formats of exercises and lessons, short tasks (like finding single words or writing unrelated sentences), tasks that allow a child to select only from given choices or direct him or her to one right answer, tasks that appear so frequently that the child comes to assume that *this is writing* or *that is reading.* To develop constructive processes and to make child learners bold enough to use them, I would guess that teachers have to give children opportunities to construct their own responses to tasks *more than 50 percent of the time.* We must not turn constructive thinking off too often, or we risk our pupils' attempts to learn being dominated by less powerful strategies like rote recall and repetition.

Linking up to Other Learning

The argument I have been building up to in this chapter is not that integrated activities make more sense to the child, or that they are more motivating and stimulating, or that they provide better ways of delivering instruction, or even that they are likely to address individual differences. All those things may be true. My argument is that if our instruction requires each child to shift into a constructive mode of thinking, to link the current task with personal knowledge, then *any competence the child has is allowed to contribute to the output.*

Learning in one area enriches the potential for learning in other areas. I assume that children learn more about talking because they become writers and readers, more about reading because they control more talking options (Clay 1983), more about semantic innuendo because they act out the story, or make a drawing of the climax, or model the characters in clay. There must be room for the child to make discoveries, and there must be opportunities for conflicts to surface and be resolved in the making or the discussion or the presentation to others.

Linking up to other learning does not occur spontaneously. The child has to go in search of the connections. Richardson (1964) documented startling growth in the artistic expression of his pupils in a small rural school. He first introduced his pupils to pottery making, and they grew in skill. Later he introduced them to lino cuts and marveled at how his skilled potters made such primitive errors in this second craft. About this time he asked the children to write about their work, but he gave them no instructions. At the beginning the writing was worse than the first stage of the lino cutting. In each new activity the children had specific things to learn, but as they learned, improvement came more rapidly as they linked up with strengths in lino work, pottery, and painting. In discussion, the children sometimes revealed the connections they were making. From time to time the freedom of the school allowed them to produce exceptional expressions. Richardson (1964) wrote,

> I believe that the final success of most of this work came from the forging of a close association of the child's thinking with some actual experience or observation . . . some were observers of nature and showed a keener observation of scientific detail; others had a feeling for space relationships and noticed, for example, that a bird can fly within the bare branches of a winter tree. I think this awareness is also the basis of learning processes such as those found in arithmetic and spelling. (p. 119)

Assessment and Constructive Thinking

To complete my advocacy of arts and crafts in the classroom, I must address the question of assessment. One test of what a child has learned is a standard set of questions that we produce to check for correctness. Yet sensitive teachers have noticed that when they always ask children to read in order to answer questions, much of the pleasure goes out of reading. It becomes something done in order to answer the teacher's questions. To reduce this bias on reading, and on writing answers to comprehension questions, teacher-student conferences were developed.

It is possible to have a teacher-driven curriculum that allows for individual and different responses in assessment. The common form of assessment is to produce written answers to questions. If I structure my questions tightly, I can induce all pupils who know the material to give the same answers. Alternatively, I can set the questions in such a way that the children have to write all they know about the topic as stated. In the first case the answers are all the same, and in the second they are all different. I will have much more information about the form and quality of the students' learning in the second case.

Story retelling is an interesting development of this type of assessment, asking children to reveal the quality of their comprehension by reconstructing a story. Palincsar and Brown's (1986) reciprocal teaching is another example of open-ended production in which the questions a child poses reveal the quality of his or her processing of text.

It would not seem unreasonable to most teachers if the test of comprehension for an exercise on "instructions for constructing a paper airplane" were to actually make the airplane. In analogous ways it has been seen by some as a test of understanding if the follow-through exercise from reading were a painting, a plan, construction of a model village or building, the making of a mural, a dramatic play, or poems for a class book. What has already gone into the brain in reading is linked to things the child already does and knows, and a new creation is produced. This gives the teacher three kinds of information. An observant teacher who knows his or her pupils well would be able to ask:

1. Are my pupils learning what I am teaching?
2. How are they relating this to what they already know?
3. Are they able to use this knowledge constructively (that is, in other activities)?

This constructive mode can be used in relation to reading, writing, and oral language; it lies at the heart of content area subjects.

Assessment and evaluation can also be turned on the art and craft products. The selection of the ideas, the appropriateness of the media and materials, the control and organization of the product, and the intention of the creator are all factors that can be evaluated. Assessments can be done and teachers can learn to evaluate the progressions children make, as we have recently learned in the field of early writing. Towards the end of his account of art in the curriculum of a rural school, Richardson (1964) discussed evaluation in this way:

> If values go unrecognized among a mass of inferior work there is no growth. As soon as judgment begins, as in the selection of some better pots from the mass of work, the influences of the inferior are no longer felt so much, and there is a need and even an urgency for the individual to order his thinking and working to and beyond the recently established level of experience . . . This is illustrated by Mary's comment in a drama session. "I think we should do the section on the launching of the canoes again. I think we should think about the size and weight of the canoe more and then the play will be better. (pp. 196–197, 205)

When sharing and discussion take place in the classroom, children learn to evaluate their own products.

Classrooms and corridors are galleries of constantly changing, well-presented, high-quality art and craft. Their purpose could be embellishment or colorful illustration. It could have aesthetic and creative aims. If children have a large share in selecting the tasks and creating the responses, such displays would imply that the classroom programs give them opportunities to learn in the constructive mode. Paley's work (1981) provides an excellent guide for the tone of teacher-child exchanges of this kind.

In many classroom activities, the teacher's goal will be to have children link what they are reading or writing to what they already know, within and beyond the subject studies. Opportunities to operate in the constructive mode can spread widely across the curriculum, and especially into art, craft, and other visual presentations.

I want to conclude with one further example of constructive processes at work. A book called *Laura's Poems* was published in New Zealand by Godwit Press in 1995. On the back cover is a short poem about a place I know well, written by a seven-year-old girl named Laura. Laura's interest in writing poetry is another example of children taking different paths to educational achievement.

The Sea

the mist smudges out
Kapiti Island

the hills curve and rise
like loaves of bread

the sun sprinkles glitter
on the sea

the wind is writing
what it knows
in lines along the water

References

Art in New Zealand Schools. 1978. Wellington, NZ: School Publications Department of Education.

Bussis, A. M., E. A. Chittenden, and M. Amarel. 1976. *Beyond the Surface Curriculum.* Boulder, CO: Westerview Press.

Clay, M. M. 1983. Getting a Theory of Writing. In B. M. Kroll and G. Wells, eds., *Explorations in the Development of Writing.* Chichester, UK: Wiley.

Duckworth, E. 1979. Either We're Too Early and They Can't Learn It or We're Too Late and They Know It Already: The Dilemma of "Applying Piaget" *Harvard Educational Review* 49, 3: 297–312.

Holdaway, D. 1979. *The Foundations of Literacy.* Sydney: Ashton Scholastic.

Paley, V. G. 1981. *Wally's Stories.* Cambridge, MA: Harvard University Press.

Palincsar, A. S., and A. L. Brown. 1986. Interactive Teaching to Promote Independent Learning from Text. *The Reading Teacher* 39, 8: 771–777.

Pickard, P. M. 1975. *The Activity of Children.* London: Longmans Green.

Richardson, E. S. 1964. *In the Early World.* Wellington, NZ: New Zealand Council of Educational Research.

Spiro, R. J. 1980. Constructive Processes in Prose Comprehension and Recall. In R. J. Spiro, B. C. Bruce, and W. F. Brewer, eds., *Theoretical Issues in Reading Comprehension,* pp. 453–481. Hillsdale, NJ: Lawrence Erlbaum.

Sutton-Smith, B. 1981. *The Folkstories of Children.* Philadelphia: University of Pennsylvania Press.

PART THREE

The Challenge of Helping All Children to Become Literate

A DISTURBING NEW EMPHASIS HAS appeared in the literacy learning field in the 1990s. It requires schools to have all children able to read and write by about their third or fourth year of school. The call makes no concessions to any limitations in learners and presumes that optimum learning outcomes depend only on teaching. The call is to do what no society has ever managed to do, utterly ignoring (1) the complexity of literacy learning; (2) the varied histories of schooling that individuals have (caused by factors like societal differences, and mobility); (3) the limitations that we all have with some aspects of learning; and (4) the inability of the delivery systems of education to meet the learning needs of many learners. General intelligence is no longer considered an important factor and neither, apparently, are language differences.

The call is supported by an assumption that "the information society" will require people to have higher levels of literacy skills. That assumption may be realistic. However, the call recognizes no range of performance, only a fixed hurdle that all are expected to be able to clear. My analysis of where the current emphases will take us is this: the higher we set the hurdles and the better our classroom programs become, the more efforts and resources we will need to direct to "accommodating diversity" in learners to bring those with checkered histories and personal limitations into the middle range of performance. This call is the most inappropriate educational demand I have encountered in my career, ignoring as it does individual identity and individual difference.

I espouse a reciprocal relationship between theory on the one hand and teaching practice on the other. Practice informs theory and theory informs practice in a circular, continuing set of relationships. I have never seen much value in talking to teachers only about ideas that confirm their present practice. I have never believed in offering teachers watered-down versions of theories, because in my experience teachers like to get their teeth into the writings of those who challenge their expectations. In the final chapter of this book I contrast child development theory used by educators with what challenges developmental psychologists. Educators must support all learners today, next month, and next year and must teach in areas where there is little appropriate theory and data (take, for example, the topic of biliteracy, which is of enormous global significance). Developmental theorists and researchers work at the cutting edge of significant debates, trying to formulate and clarify new constructs that may take us into the future. The professional tasks of educators and researchers are not as closely aligned as many assume.

In conclusion, I have to agree with a succinct summary provided by Katz and Chard in their book *Engaging Children's Minds: The Project Approach* (1989), which fits well with my thinking about children taking different paths to common outcomes. These authors conclude that a homogeneous curriculum leads to heterogeneous outcomes, and if education systems want homogeneous outcomes they will need to provide heterogeneous opportunities to learn.

14 The Challenge of Literacy Improvement

THE CHALLENGE OF LITERACY IMPROVEMENT is fine-tuning programs that are already satisfactory to get better results. To ensure that by the age of nine no children will have fallen dangerously behind their peers in literacy development, special attention must be paid to the preschool years, the preparatory class at school entry, the first two years of literacy instruction, and early interventions that provide catch-up experiences. From the ages of eight to eleven, some children do not become able to read and write more difficult texts, not only because of different levels of competence but also because of unevenness and weaknesses in some aspects of their literacy processing. Differentiated instruction could help to develop different strengths on different kinds of literacy tasks. When you are doing a job like literacy teaching well, it is hard to think about doing it even better.

You have invited someone to speak to you who has invested most of the end of her working years to bringing together those things that all sensible people know should be kept separate: things like

practice and theory;
research and instruction;
quantitative and qualitative research;
developmental psychologists and educators;

This was an oral address.

classroom education and special education;
writing and reading;
low achievers and average learning rates;
economic poverty and success with literacy.

It becomes more and more difficult to bring such concepts together as people research their separateness. Polarities run for cover into their respective enclaves when challenged. If you try to bring them together in some middle position the attack or counterarguments will come from both sides, and I can vouch for that. I like to be able to reconceptualize the polarities and complete the circles of interactive effects.

One example of this struggle is found in the Reading Recovery (RR) program, for we take in children who are outliers in literacy achievement and end up with them functioning well in ordinary classrooms. (Not every child achieves this.) That makes a lot of people suspicious or incredulous because it defies their experience and expectations. It means that we start in one field of theory and research, like special education, and end up in another relating to ordinary classroom functioning. So we must satisfy critics from both sides. By all the theories I learned about in my training, and taught to others for two-thirds of my career, RR should not work. So even I have found what we have been able to do incredible, suspicious, and hard to accept. But a developmental psychologist (which is my basic discipline and my main teaching subject) focuses on change, so my own doubts became subsumed under the weight of empirical evidence of change, and what we now can see happening to real children in ordinary schools.

As a developmental psychologist working in the area of normal and atypical child development, I have been interested in the diverse needs of learners. As a trained teacher with classroom experience, I have latterly given much of my attention to change over time in school learning, from the high flyers through to those children with the most severe problems, especially in the early years of school. For more than thirty years my job involved training educational psychologists to work to change the learning context for unusual learners in the education system. That is a snapshot view of a many-faceted career.

Awareness of Literacy Before School

Child health programs, preschool experiences that are enriching, and families that support their members well contribute to school success, together with some more obviously direct preparations for going to school. The topic of literacy before school brings to mind baby book packages, reading to children, taking an interest in early writing, family literacy programs, library loans to families, all kinds of read-alouds, and giveaway book schemes, all of which serve to increase children's awareness of literacy in their environment.

Most societies allow parents to bring children through the years before school in any way that suits their lifestyle, given a few legal barriers. Three researchers

(Weinberger, Hannon, and Nutbrown 1990) developed a project on ways of working with parents to promote early literacy development. (I introduced their use of a jigsaw earlier, in Chapter 10.) To encourage parents to notice their own child's awareness of environmental print they gave the parents a graphic of an assembled jigsaw, sometimes empty, and sometimes labeled with different aspects of literacy awareness. Parents shaded in those pieces that described things they had noticed their child doing, or they recorded how their children had demonstrated interest. The jigsaw is a great prompt for parent or preschool teacher observation.

It is easy to write at length about the need for preschool richness in

oral language (any language)
nursery rhyme experience
being read to
exploring with a pencil
interactions with adults
knowledge of the world.

It is also easy to detect a chasm between the aims of preschools and schools. An early childhood position might be

Let them play and explore and enjoy their early childhood.

A school's position might be

Prepare children for literacy learning.

We need a bridge over these troubled waters—troubled waters found across the world—between preschool and school literacy. Part of this problem is being addressed by authors who stress cultural diversity and how important this factor is in learning (Tharp and Gallimore 1988; Delpit 1986; Luke and Freebody 1997). Preschool environments should provide opportunities for literacy events to occur, and adults should interact with literacy awareness shown by the child. In both preschool and school every adult should be alert to any response that a learner is making to literate things, to grab the moment and go with the interest, in some way interact with it, lead it on a little, and then let it go (see Chapter 4).

If preschools do not try to provide opportunities they will see little literacy awareness, and if they deliberately ignore it they provide children with models of people who ignore literate activities.

A Preparatory Year

Different countries have different names for the point at which children enter school—kindergarten in the United States, prep or preparatory year in Australia, reception year or class in the United Kingdom. All provide a transition time from preschool to real school, and "a get ready for school" place. It is an institutional recognition of the fact that children are different one from another. There are two versions of this "get ready for school" goal:

1. Some want the children to be reading and writing during this transition.
2. Others want children only to get ready for reading and writing.

This is a real difference in expectation, producing differences in achievements in different countries. Getting ready in this transitional year involves focusing on aspects of the written code, like letters, sounds, and words. It involves teaching children their letters, or having them listen to stories or complete readiness workbooks. *In some countries there is no real expectation that they will read and write.*

Some time (decades) ago, using a sample of 100 children that was representative of all socioeconomic groups in Auckland, New Zealand, I conducted a study of how children changed from their fifth birthday to their sixth birthday. I recorded and coded my observations weekly in the five schools I was studying, schools in which children were expected to read and write. Children in New Zealand enter school on their fifth birthday and are soon invited to write down a message, "a sentence" as one incredulous mother said to me. But they get all the help they need to do this in an activity shared by the teacher and the children are expected to take part in whatever way they can, if only to insert a fullstop. They then "read" their message back. This happens every day. Soon they are expecting to write and to read. The children assume they can do it (see Chapter 1).

Not to expect children to read and write is quite acceptable, but it is important to recognize that different countries have different expectations of their five-year-olds. Children begin to learn literacy at whatever age societies decree they should, at four, five, six, or seven. The only limitation is that once you have selected a school entry age you have to be able to work out what to expect children to learn and how to deliver appropriate literacy instruction.

If the choice is to *prepare* children for school, this preparation should be extraordinarily rich in all aspects of the emergent literacy jigsaw, with special attention paid to oral language enrichment. It should not be restricted to letter learning, or to listening to stories, or to experimenting with writing. During that rich preparation literacy events should happen often, and teachers should try to interact with every instance of literacy awareness and should try to understand the child's current view. Compared with preschool events, the teachers' interactions in this transition time should last longer and challenge the children more.

I personally prefer to expect that children will actually read and write in their preparatory year; I refer to this as "allowing them to conduct the orchestra." Either approach to school preparation seems to work. However, I think we should understand that there are two different approaches.

Where Are Children After Three to Four Years at School?

Being a developmental psychologist, I think we need to have a concept of our destination. So let me jump ahead and provide one description of satisfactory progress after three to four years at school. I would like to see

language strengths

- a child eager to talk, and read, and write

prior experience with different types of texts

- with processes tuned to continuous texts, like strategies for writing texts and strategies for reading both fiction and nonfiction

a measure of independence

- shown by self-monitoring, self-correction, and self-extending strategies in reading and writing

reading vocabulary

- an extensive knowledge of words accessed quickly, and ways of getting to new words in reading from known words or parts of words

writing vocabulary

- an extensive knowledge of spelling accessed quickly, and ways of getting to new words in writing from reading or hearing parts of words

reciprocity in language activities

- a reading process that extends both writing and reading
- a writing process that extends both reading and writing

biliteracy when appropriate

- with equivalent processes in each language

Just as almost every child constructs an oral language learning system by five years of age so almost every child, if allowed to move at different rates along different paths, can construct a literacy learning system in three to four years at school. The learner not only has item banks of knowledge needed to read more difficult texts but also has constructed the power source that will drive subsequent learning, what I would call a "self-extending system." The reading and writing processes that children have constructed are so sophisticated that they allow children subsequently to learn more about reading by reading and writing, and more about writing by writing and reading. In my theory of what happens (literacy processing theory), these are two powerful self-extending systems, and oral language is another powerful self-extending system.

The First Year of Classroom Instruction

Every society has a formal start to literacy learning, a universal form of social engineering. Experience tells us to be optimistic because 80 percent of children become constructive learners whatever teaching we adopt. The conversations, communications, and teaching that occur in classrooms, which are only a fractional part of a learner's life experiences, contain three components:

Teacher and curriculum	interacting with	the constructive learner
(1)	(2)	(3)

Whatever theory, method, or program of literacy learning suits your fancy can be explained by variations of those components. Most succeed because the learner works on making it come together, whatever resources the educators provide.

Limits to effective outcomes are set when education ignores individuals or, more accurately, ignores the diversity among individuals. The immense diversity in what children have learned before they enter school, after five years of differential socialization, means that students come unequally prepared to take advantage of schools and their practices. The implication of our new awareness of social and cultural issues is that we must acknowledge that prior experiences have been different from one child to another. The opportunity to learn is determined by the cultural contexts in which they spent those first five years.

Most teachers look for indicators of this unequal preparation and make assumptions about what to expect of different children. They then offer learning opportunities that follow from their assumptions. As Garth Boomer, an important literacy educator in Australia, wrote in a paper entitled "Organizing the Nation for Literacy" (1988):

> Some children come to school with schooling in their blood. Others come with wilder strains that fit them if not for rejection, at least for alternative forms of taming.

He recommended that, given the diversity in children's prior learning, teachers should attend first to themselves, to ensure that they are:

- equally hospitable to all,
- equally demanding of all,
- and *un*equally attentive to those who are passive in response to the strangeness of the new environment.

I would add that teachers must also

- lift the number of make-up opportunities
- offer more challenge
- give more thought in planning
- do what works for the learners
- give learners more time
- give learners more individual attention
- and allow more time for individual talk.

These things will help open literacy doors to literacy.

Schools must provide bridges for children to cross into the school situation, *allowing children to bring what they already know how to do to bear on the classroom tasks.* The challenge for the school is to realize the learning potential that exists in every child. Only with effort can teachers understand how, and with whom, the preschooler's prior learning has been operating in the first five years of life. (Boomer colorfully described this as the generating plant constructed so far, referring to the source of power for future learning.)

Teachers have to deal with all kinds of unequal preparation in the same year in which they introduce children to literacy learning, and the implications of their decisions will reverberate throughout the next several years of school. New doors open for many children, but doors also begin to close for others. How do we ensure the kind of equity that delivers to each child useful activities designed for his or her current needs in today's lesson?

The new entrant to school is where he or she is and can be nowhere else. The program must go to where the child is and take him or her to somewhere else. That is where education begins. You have to be concerned about children's transition into literacy, and current practices are not good enough. Such concerns can focus on four things:

teacher expectations,
lack of make-up opportunities,
the timing of opportunities, and
chances missed at first must come around a second time.

Most teachers see little need to change practices that they think have worked in the past. But what if these practices are based on expectations that are no longer acceptable? And what if there is a demand for improved outcomes from existing good programs?

Accommodating Diversity: Positioning the Learner for Success

Every program will have its lowest achievers; the description is a relative one and not a statement of level of performance. No combination of program, teaching, and children can be perfect. Every delivery system is flawed. We will always have low achievers even in high-performing schools. There is not, and never will be, a prescriptive program that will make all children readers and writers. Individual diversity will always prevent this outcome. Even if the program were able to be near perfect, child absences, teacher promotions, and too many snow or storm days would reduce its ultimate effectiveness. We need great classroom programs, but they will never serve the range of individual diversity among learners. There is good reason to plan for safety nets and make-up opportunities.

When a new program, curriculum, or syllabus is selected teachers should sit down together and work out the consequences of the choice made. Consider these questions: What are the program's emphases? Which groups of children could be disadvantaged by the selected program? As every program has its risk areas, how will you make up for the risk areas in the program you have selected? You can minimize the risks for your low achievers by arranging to give them more attention and keeping careful records of progress or watching whether important expected changes occur. By doing this you may, for example, be able to prevent slow word-by-word reading becoming a habit, or writing becoming forgotten while the child works on improving reading.

When children walk through the school door they will have a range of competence from very high to very low. How will you ensure that every child has a chance to use what he or she knows in learning something new? How will you cope with individual differences at the time they begin? Even when the system has optimum teaching from well-trained teachers, some children will still begin to pull away from others, learning at different rates, widening the range of performance. How will you cope with the increasing differences that even good teachers will produce?

Asking colleagues to challenge each other in school team discussions is appropriate to uncover when our teaching practice is closing doors on literacy progress for some children. Team decisions can call up the strengths of individual members and catch the errors of excess, stemming from personal enthusiasms.

What do we usually do in schools? To cater to individual differences we move certain students into slow-learner groups, a practice that Boomer described as potential breeding grounds of inequity and low self-esteem, slotting children into categories and leading us to reduce our teaching efforts. These practices are highly suspect when it becomes clear that certain groups, such as the poor, or those whose first language is not English, or particular ethnic groups make up the bulk of these alternative courses. Boomer was highly critical of this. He wrote,

> In the harshest light, these practices of catering for difference are seen to be, in effect, the agents of indifference, unwitting and unexamined in most instances.
>
> The concept of ability . . . underpins much unexamined . . . practice. The able tend to be those who have got "it," whatever "it" is, in their genes. The less able are those who have got less of "it." The able are expected to do well and do. The less able are expected to do less well and they live up to [those] expectations. This kind of analysis lets teachers, schools and systems nicely off the hook. It reinforces the view that children come to school with inherently different abilities. It is the school's job to help each child to make the most of her or his talents. The analysis draws attention to the child's capacities and deficiencies *and takes the spotlight away from the school's charter to educate each child and to guarantee certain standards of achievement for all.*
>
> . . . And so we begin to grade children like potatoes according to a notion of ability. Kookaburras and koalas, such friendly symbols of separation, are in fact often sinister harbingers of an educational apartheid which will eventually be terminal for some . . . By means of my loaded metaphors, I am [illustrating my conviction] that the notion of natural ability often leads to negative consequences both in terms of equity and excellence in Australian schools . . . [Students] should not be denigrated. *They are to be valued equally but unequally challenged.*

I encourage you to think about the implications from Boomer's quotes:

> Programs should be equally demanding of all, and all learners are to be valued equally but unequally or differentially challenged.
>
> The less-prepared groups need as much challenge, more thought, more time, more attention, and twice as many learning opportunities as the well prepared. What they do *not* need is to be set aside from literacy activity for another year.

Every child who enters school can learn things about literacy, but we must reach into that child's existing ways of learning to discover at what level his or her literacy awareness can be tapped. There is a comfortable match here with my earlier comments on how to build a bridge between literacy awareness in preschool and school.

Quantities of Make-Up Opportunities

Different learning opportunities may have created big gaps between what children are capable of doing and what they are actually able to do. Individual differences on entry to school reflect how children have been treated by the world and what they have selected to attend to. *A need for make-up opportunities for those who have missed out because they gave their attention to other things is an obligation for an education system operating on principles of social justice.* For these children, the first year of school must be rich in the opportunities to learn what other preschoolers have already learned.

This does not mean they should be pressured to catch up; it means giving them twice as much time on tasks as the well prepared need:

- more listening to and acting out of stories,
- doubling up of writing explorations,
- hearing and singing rhymes and songs more often than their fortunate classmates who have been there and done that,
- and massive opportunities to talk with a supportive, attentive, tutoring adult.

Such make-up experiences do not come from being left alone, left waiting for maturation or readiness to appear. It requires an increase in time, attention, and quality learning interactions. Classrooms or schools that do not organize to provide these extras are closing doors on children who begin with low achievement profiles.

We are unnecessarily locked into a slow-learner concept derived from saying "this pupil is not ready for our school," backed by concepts like intelligence, maturation, readiness, and "cognitive unfolding." These are no longer sufficient as explanations of differences in what school beginners have learned; opportunities to learn have been very important. And providing more preschool education does not let schools off the hook. If much of what children can and cannot do on entry to school is a product of learning in the cultural contexts of their homes, then make-up opportunities should begin immediately, *and progress can and must be more rapid than it would have been at a younger age.* The learners are ready, but the school is not ready to demand learning from them and to deliver the opportunities they need.

Recognizing children's diversities we have generously offered them more time, another year before we expect much of them. Can we do anything else? This is not about changing abilities; it is about providing opportunities that were not there, were not available to learn from, or opportunities that were there but from which the learner turned away. The teacher's challenge is to find out which demands are appropriate for a particular child and create opportunities for each child to reveal this. If the needs uncovered are those of a younger child, so be it; the teacher is challenged to provide opportunities in double quantity, and to expect fast learning to occur! *It is not a double dose of classroom expectations that is needed, but a double dose of preschool expectations merging into classroom expectations as the learner responds to the initial approach at his or her own level.*

There is a challenge for teachers in going to where the slowest children are and teaching those children the earliest steps towards literacy learning. Waiting is not good enough. Doing more of what you already do is not enough. Find out where the children are, and go back to that point and teach. I think teachers already do this in beginning writing, but they need to replicate that kind of teaching in oral language and in reading.

The First Two Years of School

A broad and rich literacy curriculum for children in the first years of school that will open doors to literacy will include

make-up opportunities
being read to
a talk environment
rhymes, jingles, poems, and songs
writing one's own messages
all four language activities—speaking, listening, reading, and writing
interactions with adults
quantities of easy reading
opportunity to revisit the familiar often
more make-up-opportunities
a teacher who knows where I am

The doors begin to close on high literacy achievement with the following practices:

- prescriptive curricula, practices, or assessment
- separation of reading and writing
- time away from continuous texts and authentic tasks
- failure to note new learning needs
- failure to teach children how to go further alone
- overcommitment to a concept of ability
- failure to see inequalities of opportunity accumulating in classrooms

and most important of all

- the learner's not being allowed to conduct the orchestra—not being allowed to put it all together for himself or herself.

The difference between the two major approaches to early schooling is that one approach allows the children to "conduct the orchestra" and the other does not.

Talking Is a Neglected Area

What could be more demanding than learning to talk? Yet that is developmentally appropriate before a child comes to school. Learning to talk is harder than learning to read or write, and it is achieved earlier! Think for a moment of "talking," described by Ruth Berman and D. I. Slobin (1994) as "the complex of linguistic, cognitive, and communicative abilities that underlie the human ability to capture and convey events in words" (p. ix). How could we let the exciting era of research and writing on language acquisition that lasted for three decades, through the 1980s, slip into oblivion?

Teachers teach through talk in order to get children to read and write. Children enter school with differences in oral language experiences, and they need rich oral language experiences so that they can better understand the teacher's talk. They need activities that call upon them to produce oral language in order to extend their control, and not just in the service of reading and writing. Oral language must be extended at a fast pace; otherwise children's entry competence may limit what they are able to make of all the subsequent opportunities provided by the education system. For want of a boost to oral language development a child could be lost to education.

Books on language acquisition must always be of interest for the early-grades teacher who asks, "How should I talk with these children to enrich their language?" We rarely see teachers planning language activities for the sake of extending oral language itself. Vivian Paley's book *Wally's Stories* (1981) provides a fantastic account of a classroom in Chicago where talking is given high value. We need to try to do what Paley did! The rank children hold in relation to their peers in oral language levels on entry to school is likely to be their ranking at eight years, unless the teacher does things to make such a prediction false. They can also be locked into a low ranking in literacy achievement if teachers assume that will happen. Teachers can make something different happen for many of those children.

Look for Indicators of Success After the First Year

Teachers need about two years to produce signs of independent reading and writing with most children, longer for some and shorter for the fast learners who take to schooling like ducks to water. In normal circumstances some children will fall behind. *The challenge to teachers is to design experiences for these children so that the gap does not widen.*

Returning again to Boomer's critical paper, I quote:

> The strongest equity measures we can take are those that hold all students engaged in mainstream curriculum which keeps their educational and life options open . . . [This requires] a national strategy for literacy which would

> secure the foundations of literacy by the early primary years . . . [and] ensure that all or nearly all children by, say, age 8 are still in the game, i.e., can read and write to a satisfactory base level . . . this relies on teachers having a belief in the educability of all children . . . It relies on tenacity and persistence to ensure that no one falls dangerously behind.

Today an international spotlight has been turned on literacy learning in the early primary school years. Some calls have been made to see that every child is able to read and write by about the age of nine. This idea is ill conceived and poorly explained, and it exerts pressure without a plan for how it could be achieved. Past experience would tell us that human variation cannot be reduced to a common outcome. It is foolish to make idealistic claims without confronting the obstacles in the way. It brings to our attention, however, the widespread acknowledgment that there is a very important acquisition stage in literacy development lasting three or four years, and a crucial set of learning that underpins all educational progress. We are again being challenged to improve the quality of our instruction and to try to make all children successful in acquiring a literacy processing system in the early years of school.

Good schools provide a rich range of promising possibilities to suit different individuals, and we do not have to decide which banner to get behind. We have to carry *all* the banners and flourish the right one at the right moment to meet a particular child's needs, so no one falls dangerously behind. This is *not* wishy-washy eclecticism. It is a way to superb teaching differentiated for children who have different learning needs. *The tough part is knowing when to do what, with whom—and having the flexibility in your classroom organization to do it!* Having a repertoire of teaching options that collapse the dichotomies and watching the progress of individual children mean that teachers can teach groups during the literacy acquisition phase bearing in mind the diversity of individuals.

Early Intervention

What I am describing is clearly not the collective vision of teachers. One year into school and all around the world teachers and principals argue with Reading Recovery professionals to keep children out of an early intervention program. They do not want children to be given this kind of help at this time. Mainly they want them "left alone" for another year! I need to explore this briefly. Certain children only have to walk in the school door and teachers' expectations drop. The first thing for teachers to do is to examine their own range of assumptions, their expectations, their beliefs about who succeeds and who does not.

You can see the doors to effective literacy learning beginning to close during that first year of school. That is why early intervention programs are suggested—in an attempt to stop doors from closing before it is too late. Or, more accurately, as insurance against those doors closing.

There are three main options for low achievers at the end of the first year. One option is not to intervene at all, for a variety of reasons, but mostly out of kindness, as we like to be optimistic that these children "will come out right." Another option is to provide supplementary help as they drag their way up the grades behind the other children, gaining some learning in remedial education but never quite getting there. A third option is to eliminate the problem at this level, or reduce it to minimum size. To achieve this, low achievers must move out of the intervention into the "average" band. If we can dramatically reduce the number of learners who have extreme difficulty with literacy learning, and the cost of these learners to educational systems, we can minimize the "Matthew effect," which asserts that the good always get better while the low achievers fall further and further behind (Stanovich 1986). Reading Recovery is best described as an insurance policy taken out by a school against the risk of having children with literacy learning difficulties in the middle and upper primary classes. How much insurance is to be taken is up to the school.

In a 1997 International Reading Association poll published in *Reading Today,* all twelve experts interviewed nominated early intervention as an important topic in literacy education today! One dictionary of literacy defines an intervention program as a substitute program, often mounted with government funding, for poor children. That is an extraordinarily narrow view. Interventions usually try to remove some adverse effects in peoples' lives, and early interventions aim to undercut or reduce any adverse effects. They try to *prevent* something from happening.

Theoretically, we can have three kinds of prevention of literacy difficulties. These categories were first applied in the 1960s to mental health work by an American psychiatrist, Gerard Caplan, but they are widely used by other professions.

- *Primary prevention* involves children in a broad and healthy set of experiences between birth and entering school, making them well prepared for problem-solving their way into new learning at school.
- *Secondary prevention* involves early detection of low achievement and providing extra support to keep problems from arising.
- *Tertiary prevention* happens after problems have become established, and entails compensating for those problems.

Most early literacy intervention programs are secondary prevention offered to children after they have had a chance to succeed in ordinary classroom programs. As a supplementary extra by the end of the first year, intensified help in literacy learning can be given to those at the lower end of that widening gap, the ones for whom the good class teaching I have been talking about has not been enough. This is not a judgment of the failure of children or the poor quality of the teaching; rather, it simply recognizes that teachers are doing a better job with some children than with others. Even the best teaching can be a mismatch with the needs of certain individuals. We now have the evidence, from thousands of Reading Recovery children, that if we change the delivery of literacy education for them they can learn and function at average levels. A classroom teacher, given a relatively cheap supplementary apprentice-type training, becomes a more powerful interacting adult when trained to work one on one with the individual strengths of a particular child. The reasons children make a slow start are varied, including the following:

The students may be learning a new culture in the regular classroom.
They may be learning a new language in the regular classroom.
They may have the language development of a younger child.
They may be from different sociocultural backgrounds.
They may have missed or avoided certain learning opportunities.
They may have special learning needs.

Give Extra Attention

Assuming superb teaching for everyone, think of the early years of education as a marathon in which an unequal starting bunch spreads further and further apart the more they run. Can anything be done for the slow movers?

Is the aim to improve their performance scores?

Do we want to give them competencies that they do not yet have?

Do we want to prevent failure in future schooling?

What kind of a safety net can we provide for low achievers? Solutions used in the past have been the following:

- Give them an extra teacher.
- Give them an uncertified assistant who costs less.
- Give them extra time and more repetitions.
- Send them to "special appraisal," get them labeled and into special education, where they will no longer bring down classroom statistics but will join the increasing number of children diagnosed as "learning disabled."

These "educational solutions" leave the lowest in the lowest positions relative to their classmates. Correlations of early progress with later progress are high. I was shocked in my first research to find that a child's rank in relation to his or her peers at the end of the first year of literacy learning was a good predictor of where that child would be subsequently in school in ratings of literacy achievements. We now know we can upset those correlations if we change our delivery system. How might this be done? When first encountering this problem, my thinking proceeded as follows.

First, we need a description of what it is that high-progress children learn to do in the first year of school. This does not mean what the curriculum and teachers expect them to learn. It is another kind of description: from the point of view of development and learning, how do they change over time? How do we get them to control directional behavior, to bring print and language and meaning together, to reach out successfully to read a harder, unpreviewed text? I developed such a description from a yearlong study during which I recorded everything that children said and did as they read and wrote for me every week. The description was cast in terms of the psychology of children's learning, not in terms of the program they were learning from.

Second, we simply have to teach low-progress children to do the things high-progress children do.

Third, they will have to learn fast because while they try to catch up their classmates will be forging ahead. So slow children will have to learn at an accelerated rate.

Fourth, when they catch up they will have to be able to retain their gains and not slip back.

To break the cycle we need to take the lowest achievers, give them short-term help, and ensure both accelerated learning and sustained learning when they are returned to the average band in the classroom. A high proportion of the lowest achievers in first grade should be back in the average band before the end of the first two years of school, competent in both reading and writing.

We would have to begin before the gap to be bridged is too great, and as soon as a reliable choice of candidates can be made, so as not to take in children who do not need the help and not to omit children who do. New Zealand expects children to learn to read and write between their fifth and sixth birthdays, so selecting children at their sixth birthday is a suitable practice. On the evidence we have I think we are making the fewest errors. Reducing errors in selection makes sure that those who need it most get it.

We would need excellent teachers who have been trained well. Teaching and progressions must be detailed and explicit, while at the same time the curriculum must be capable of varying from child to child.

Finally, in my own attempt at solving the problem, in order to get accelerated progress so that children might catch up with average classmates, we did three other things:

1. We designed the program for *daily lessons.* In the development years fewer than daily lessons had not produced satisfactory results.
2. We designed the program to *begin with what children already knew* and to follow the child's own route to the required outcome. This contradicts all classroom teaching, and all group teaching, and is only possible in one-to-one teaching.
3. We designed the program to bring each child as rapidly as possible *to a level in the class where the class teacher's efforts could lift the child further* and judged this to be the "average" rank. These children would be the classroom teacher's responsibility after that.

These decisions worked, and the system intervention, delivered after one year of instruction, is called Reading Recovery. The combined data bases on Reading Recovery include half a million children in three countries already, a fair-sized sample, but still a drop in the proverbial bucket. Not all of the interventions were expected to be successful; relatively small numbers of children needed longer-term help, but this was predicted at the beginning of the study.

In the Reading Recovery program, there is a standard skeleton for the lesson, but the teacher designs each child's lessons and series of lessons to work with what that child already knows, is learning, and needs to be challenged by. The lessons are not sequenced or prescriptive. Teachers are trained on how to construct a series of lessons for a particular child with the aim of getting that child to make the necessary changes to do what good readers do. There is enough flexibility in the program to allow it to

- adapt to individual differences,
- return a child to any classroom program,
- adjust teaching to the different needs of ESL children and other special cases.

Can low-achieving children really accelerate? In Reading Recovery, several drastic alterations in standard classroom learning conditions are made:

- The child has daily lessons.
- The lessons are individually designed.
- They are individually delivered.
- All unnecessary teaching is eliminated. Teachers are told not to teach what the child already knows.
- The child's strengths, and new ones that emerge, guide the instruction.
- The new is embedded in the context of what the child can do.
- Teachers are instructed not to do for the child anything he or she can be encouraged to do independently.
- Increasing knowledge in all knowledge sources is fostered.
- The child is helped to link and compare what he or she knows, and to search for, detect, and correct errors.

The best path of progress will differ from child to child. Weak areas are strengthened in the context of strengthening all other areas in an interactive network of processes. The interrelating of all aspects of literacy acts is as important as the knowledge learned.

Reading Recovery is a workable and appropriate example of what appears to be needed, it comes with sound staff training, and it is designed to minimize problems for schools. Cross-national evidence shows that in a Reading Recovery program children learn and teachers teach effectively. In addition, Reading Recovery is workable in different educational settings with different populations of children.

Who Needs Long-Term Help?

If early intervation is implemented effectively, who needs long-term help? Think of a circular room with many doors opening into it. Children enter the room through any one of these doors and then learn to climb one of the various staircases to higher levels. Many keys unlock the doors, and different staircases all get you to the top. For most children having difficulty, Reading Recovery is like a master key and a safe staircase that takes them from any classroom program and returns them to competence in that program.

A few cannot climb any staircase for more than a few steps. It is possible that another teacher might have been more effective with these children. It is possible that life circumstances did not bring the child and the program together in the right way. It is possible that a particular child has problems that his or her well-trained teacher does not have the skills to work with. And it is also possible that, with more time, many of these children could learn to read and write, but there has to be a cap, or ceiling, on time spent at this level of intervention to keep it cost effective. We must distinguish between short-term and long-term candidates for extra help. On the basis of experience and several research reports, the time children spend in the program has been set at twenty weeks.

The particular matrix of psychological characteristics of a particular child may not be sufficiently served by the tasks used in Reading Recovery; in this case a specialist's report and an even more idiosyncratic program is needed. In an effective, established program, this should not occur in more than 1 to 2 percent of the age cohort. So, having reduced our literacy laggards to 1 or 2 percent, we can then provide that small number with longer-term help. The messages run like this: To preparatory and classroom teachers, keep as many children as you can away from the need for individual help by quality classroom teaching. To early intervention program specialists, take as many of the slowest learners as you can to relative independence in the classroom program and away from long-term help. To administrators, provide longer-term help for those few children who need it immediately following completion of their supplementary one-on-one tutoring.

Many education systems are attending to reform and improvement of classroom instruction as a means of improving literacy. An early prevention program should be an essential part of any literacy improvement strategy. A prevention program aims to eliminate literacy learning difficulty, though that is not the aim of most early intervention programs. Remedial education will never make over completely a dysfunctional reading or writing process that a child has learned and been using for several years. There is a growing consensus that preventative intervention, designed to prevent problems and establish early independence by age eight or nine, is achievable.

A good review is referred to after the original studies are forgotten; it summarizes the position of the research to date, saving readers from having to return to the original sources. Reviewers therefore have a responsibility to understand and report previous research accurately so as not to bias the subsequent course of research, theory, and practice with their conclusions. Whether we like it or not, Herber (1994) has shown that reviews of research do not usually go back more than twenty years. It is twenty years since Reading Recovery began to be developed and nineteen years since the first Reading Recovery research reports were published. The decade of the 1970s is already outside the reviewer's ken. Perhaps partly for these reasons, incorrect information has, unfortunately, been published in several reviews of Reading Recovery literature (Clay 1997). To take just one example, several reviews echo the claim that Reading Recovery has used only in-program tests and has no standardized test as a beyond-program measure. This particular problem we recognized from the beginning. Training sites have used local standardized instruments. In New Zealand the Burt test from the New Zealand Council for Educational Research has been used; in the United States several tests have been used, the most successful being the Woodcock reading test; and in England the British Intelligence Scale (Reading) is favored, although this test is not available for use by teachers.

There Are Still Neglected Problems

Even if we eliminate the problems of most of the younger children, the educational system is left with two further challenges: how to provide long-term help for groups equivalent to Reading Recovery's referred group, and what to do about older children who have slipped through the net. What can be constructed for effective learning among these older children? I recently reviewed current research and found no promising developments (Clay 1998). Reading Recovery teachers have a well-articulated theory that would allow them to develop literacy skills in many of the children in longer-term programs, and with appropriate expert supervision. But the procedures we use are directed toward developing competent seven-year-old readers.

To make literacy processing theory available to special education teachers we would have to proceed by carefully managed trials in selected sites, and with much caution. There is as much challenge in training, say, a certificated teacher of the deaf in a theory of literacy processing (such as the one Reading Recovery uses) as there is in redeveloping the program in Spanish (for the United States), which we have achieved, or in French or Welsh, both of which are under discussion (in Canada and Wales, respectively).

Let me conclude by attending to the middle years of primary school. Assuming that you already do wonderful things in your schools and classrooms, I have tried to identify some places for improvement at certain points in children's progress through the educational system. To recapitulate the foundational changes that can lead to literacy improvements:

Examine literacy awareness in preschool.
Smooth the transition into school.
Provide preschool-level make-up opportunities when children enter school.
Provide a broad range of literacy learning activities.
Open literacy doors and do not allow expectancies to close them.
Provide early intervention to full implementation at school.
Refer children as appropriate for long-term supplementary help.
Go for children's attaining a measure of literacy independence by eight years of age.
And bring 98 percent of that age cohort to literacy independence by the age of nine or ten.

NEEDED: A THEORY OF CHANGE BETWEEN EIGHT AND ELEVEN YEARS

We need more research to clarify how the reading process of successful readers changes between eight and eleven years. Teachers do not have an account of how the processing changes, and they need such an account if they are to help those who are not extending their literacy systems in effective ways. We have islands of knowledge, but we do not have a clear view of the reading process and its changes once the learner becomes a silent reader. We have insight into some factors, thanks to the genre theorists, who taught us about the different challenges of different texts and have moved us forward in this area. They have expanded our understanding of some important challenges to readers and writers that are highly relevant for this age group.

To the question "What do I have to do as a teacher to assist children to continue to read harder and harder materials *while continuing to build and strengthen their literacy systems?*" I know of no published answer. For example, the much-publicized area of phonological knowledge changes over time as good readers get better and better at reading more and more difficult texts loaded with multisyllabic words. We need to know more about these changes, and about word knowledge, and about grammar's contribution, and about processing multiple meanings for the same word, and sorting out ambiguous meanings in texts.

When we get a good description of how successful eight-year-old reading becomes successful eleven-year-old reading, we will have to work out the instructional strategies that will bring about those changes in classrooms; only then will we come within reach of being more effective with below-average readers. Practicing teachers cannot solve this problem on their own by observing surface behaviors; they need the help of theorists and researchers who model or hypothesize what the changes in the processing system look like. However, studying change over time is fraught with difficulties, as I well know, and researchers are unlikely to give us the theory we need in the short term. The biggest hurdle is the fact that at this level literacy processing is silent, rapid, and seemingly automatic. It is hard to observe and analyze.

COMPREHENSION ISSUES

Consider also issues around the theme of comprehension in reading. If your students are having problems with comprehending what they read, there are many things to think about. Comprehending is not just a literacy task (as we may have mistakenly led teachers to think it was). It is what a child is doing when holding a conversation with someone, listening to someone reading aloud, or reading on his or her own, at any time or place. It is not an aspect of thinking that emerges only after children have done the reading or passed through the first two years of school. All educators need to hold as their top priority the expectation that learners will understand what they are reading. The reading process the child builds should involve comprehension, for if we train the child to read without involving these powerful thinking strategies from the beginning, it will be more difficult for some of them to think about content later. *Middle and high school teachers need to support schools in putting thinking at the center of the early years of literacy instruction.* Comprehension lies in what learners say, what is read to them, and what they read and write; learners should know that all literacy acts involve comprehension.

A SECOND SAFETY NET

Schools should take stock of learners' progress in literacy learning for a second time (assuming that there is a check after the first year at school) around ten or eleven years of age. This is a good time to identify learners who clearly have lows in some aspect of their reading or writing activities, and to help by giving them intensive make-up programs. This time, instruction could be in small groups rather than one on one. The problems tackled would be different for different pupils, focusing on, say,

strengthening comprehension,
building interest in reading and/or writing and/or spelling,
approaching texts of various kinds with flexible strategies,
switching genres with ease,
building vocabulary,
increasing awareness of devices used in written language.

An intensive booster program as part of the English curriculum, delivered to small groups who have somewhat homogeneous reading needs for three months, or even for the entire school year for some learners who show two or three crucial problems, could strengthen all subsequent achievements, and maximize the learner's opportunities in high school. Ten- or eleven-year-olds are usually ready to take stock of their literacy skills in both reading and writing, and can be made aware of many of the things that are helpful for them to know and do.

Different achievements in literacy performance occur *not only because of lower levels of general competence but also because of unevenness and weaknesses in some components of literacy processes.* My interest in eight- to eleven-year-olds and a second catch-up effort with special attempts to group children for instruction according to particular needs assumes that tackling more and more difficult texts requires a literacy processing system that continues to change. We need to hypothesize, research, and articulate those changes. We have been given some leads by international studies that are now testing fiction, exposition, and documents as different indicators of literacy progress (Elley 1992).

ENGLISH FOR SPEAKERS OF OTHER LANGUAGES

We should look closely at what we are doing to develop the reading and writing competence of eight- to twelve-year-olds, with a lot of questioning, discussing, and sharing of activities and know-how. In particular, what is being done to ensure that ESL children are expanding their English vocabulary and handling the multiple meanings of words that lie at the heart of understanding? (Native English speakers pick these up in their ordinary life activities.) Early schooling can teach these children a reading process and many how to's, but there is also a language to be learned and expanded if they are to comprehend what they read. And how much attention do we give to checking whether their reading touches them enough to spur them on in a difficult task? I suspect that new energy is needed here.

And Finally, Consider This

When I think about "improved instruction" and trace it through my developmental theories of diversity and individual differences I arrive at a conclusion that you may not want to consider. My guess is that *if we increase literacy achievement with a good preschool, preparatory, and Grade 1 program we will produce a greater need for an early intervention program for the lowest achievers; and we will have created a bigger gap to bridge.* The matter of accommodating diversity and individual differences in learning paths is complex. We must keep our criteria relative and give assistance to the lowest achievers in any program. It is time for us to institutionalize early preventative intervention accessible to all children who need it, as part of the overall system of delivering education, and as the first step in a process of improvement of literacy learning at all levels of schooling.

References

Berman, R. A., and D. I. Slobin. 1994. *Relating Events in Narrative: A Cross-Linguistic Developmental Study.* Hillsdale, NJ: Lawrence Erlbaum.

Boomer, G. 1988. Organizing the Nation for Literacy. In *Working Papers on Public Education,* Vol. 1. Victoria, Australia: State Board of Education.

Caplan, G. 1964. *Principles of Preventive Psychiatry.* London: Tavistock Publications.

Clay, M. M. 1997. Letter to the Editors. *Reading Research Quarterly* 32, 1: 114.

———. 1998. The Development of Literacy Difficulties. In D. Corson et al., eds., *Encyclopedia of Language and Education,* Vol. 2, *Literacy.* Dordrecht, Netherlands: Kluwer Academic.

Delpit, L. D. 1986. Skills and Other Dilemmas of a Progressive Black Educator. *Harvard Educational Review* 56, 4: 379–385.

Elley, W. B. 1992. *How in the World Do Students Read?: The I.E.A. Study of Reading Literacy.* Hamburg: The International Association for the Evaluation of Educational Achievement.

Herber, H. L. 1994. Professional Connections: Pioneers and Contemporaries in Reading. In R. B. Ruddell, M. R. Ruddell, and H. Singer, eds., *Theoretical Models and Processes of Reading.* 3rd ed. Newark, DE: International Reading Association.

Luke, A., and P. Freebody. 1997. Shaping the Social Practices of Reading. In *Literacy: Meeting the Challenge Conference Papers.* New South Wales: Department of School Education.

Paley, V. G. 1981. *Wally's Stories.* Cambridge, MA: Harvard University Press.

Phillips, G., and P. Smith. 1997. *A Third Chance to Learn: The Development and Evaluation of Specialized Interventions for Young Children Experiencing the Greatest Difficulty in Learning to Read.* Wellington: New Zealand Council for Educational Research.

Stanovich, K. E. 1986. Matthew Effects in Reading: Some Consequences of Individual Differences in the Acquisition of Literacy. *Reading Research Quarterly* 2, 4: 360–407.

Tharp, R. G., and R. Gallimore. 1988. *Rousing Minds to Life: Teaching Learning and Schooling in Social Context.* Cambridge, UK: Cambridge University Press.

Weinberger, J., P. Hannon, and C. Nutbrown. 1990. *Ways of Working with Parents to Promote Early Literacy Development.* Sheffield, UK: University of Sheffield Education Research Unit.

15 Ashok's Story from India

I WANT TO SHARE WITH you a vignette, written by a professor of education from India (Kumar 1986) and translated for me by a postgraduate student at the Center for the Study of Reading at the University of Illinois in 1991.

Ashok wanted to be educated. Nobody had gone to school from his family. His father was a farmer with a very small piece of land, and was illiterate. Ashok persuaded his mother and eventually his father, who agreed to send him to a primary school in a nearby village.

In first grade the teacher taught him the alphabet. For weeks she made the students learn the sound of each letter, and she also made them learn to write each letter. She helped children who had difficulty in forming letters by writing with them, holding their hands. In school there was a small, overused blackboard. It was covered so badly with chalk powder that it hurt the eyes to read what was written on it. From August to September this blackboard was covered with letters of the alphabet. Children copied each letter from it several times. Finally in this manner Ashok learned all the Hindi letters.

Then the teacher started paying attention to the textbook. In that textbook there was a letter on each page with a word and a picture. For example, next to *b*, *bird* was written. Ashok knew right from the beginning that *b* meant *bird*. Therefore, he was very happy when the teacher started to teach him words by adding letters. But he didn't know that for the teacher, *b-i-r-d* combined to be *bird*. From his point of view *b* itself was *bird*. The teacher did not have time to understand his point of view. I cannot say if she even knew that Ashok had a point of view. Anyway, she thought that Ashok was saying the word written next to the letter, so she assumed that he was beginning to learn how to read.

Ashok learned the words accompanying each letter. He had already learned how to make letters. He was very happy with his progress at the end of first grade. When he went to second grade and was asked to read a book, he read like this: *b* of *bird, a* of *apple, t* of *table.*

The teacher got annoyed with him when she saw him read like this all the time. After Ashok's every attempt to read she would say to him, "Listen carefully to the other children read and read like they do." Ashok listened very carefully to the other children read, but he could not understand where he was making a mistake. He felt that the others read exactly like him. Why was the teacher so upset with him? Fortunately, the teacher got mad at some other children too, so he did not feel totally isolated. Somehow, he got through second grade too. He gave up his habit of saying *b* of *bird.* Now he read by combining letters and vowel sounds. (*Translation of the article was difficult at this point. Ashok was reading by breaking up the sounds and had no fluency.*)

The teacher rarely asked Ashok to read. Generally, the children sitting near him on the mat read the whole chapter, but Ashok did not feel sad about it. He had memorized one whole poem. When Ashok's turn came to read this poem, while lessons were being revised during the final weeks of second grade, he read it without opening his book to the right page. The teacher became angry with him because he had not looked at the right page. But Ashok was happy that he could read without even looking at the book. The differences between his and his teacher's point of view were becoming sharper.

Third grade started. Many children from Ashok's village had stopped going to school. There was pressure on him, too, to quit, but he remained firm about going to school. He wanted to finish school soon and start making money. The teacher had told the class several times that the kids who would continue progressing in school would become important people later on and would earn a lot of money.

But his problems started right from the beginning of this grade. A new subject called "geography" was introduced in this grade. Ashok could not understand anything that was written in his geography textbook. On the first page of this book it said, "Our district is uneven and rocky . . . It is situated a little above the tropic of Cancer . . . Its construction is like that of a plateau." Many children in the class had learned to read fluently. They stood up and read, and then copied it in their notebooks. When Ashok tried to read slowly, the teacher would become impatient. The same situation existed during science lessons. In a month the teacher got so fed up with Ashok that she stopped saying anything to him. Her anger and impatience, which had tied Ashok to her until this point, changed into indifference. Ashok felt that the teacher did not care about him any more. After Diwali vacation (a festival celebrated in October or November) he did not go back to school.

A few years later there was a survey held in that district. Two representatives from the State Educational Research Board came with several lengthy forms. The purpose of the survey was to find out the reason for the high drop-out rate in primary education. The people conducting the survey selected several villages and went and interviewed the parents. In this manner they collected information about several hundred children who had dropped of school.

I knew that there was an educational survey going on. When I found out the purpose of this survey I decided to give up my laziness and go to the surveyors with my questions. They had finished their work and were in a hurry to leave. I asked them to show me Ashok's data sheet. I wanted to know how Ashok's case would be represented in national statistics. The surveyors were reluctant to pull out one particular data sheet from the hundreds they had. But I mentioned my position and my degree while talking to them and eventually they agreed to find Ashok's data sheet. When I read that sheet it became clear that Ashok had dropped out of school to help his father, because of the family's economic situation. He was counted in the category of children who dropped out because of the "family economic situation." Ashok was declared a child laborer.

Seeing tears form in my eyes, the surveyor became alarmed. He asked, "Is this child related to you?" I said, "No, but I know him very well. I feel that you did not understand his case very well." The surveyor said, "Well, how can one possibly understand every individual case?" Then he changed the topic and asked me, "You live in Delhi. Tell me, when will the New Educational Policy be implemented?"

Reference

Kumar, K. 1986. "Ashok's Story." Department of Education, Delhi University. Unpublished private communication and translation.

16 Accommodating Diversity in Early Literacy Learning

"THE SMALL CHILD GOES INTO school and finds that the school did not have him in mind," wrote Henry Levin (1990), designer of the Stanford Program for Accelerated Schools. The mismatch between what schools require and the individual diversity of learners has been accepted as inevitable and institutionalized in school systems. The delivery system for education is group or whole-class instruction because societies believe they cannot afford to instruct individuals, so classes are instructed. But classes do not learn. Only individuals learn. To adjust for any mismatches, special programs, special education, counseling, psychological services, home schooling, and innumerable special policies for the extremes of diversity are provided. Recent developments in cognitive psychology describing how individuals learn make it imperative that we reconsider how teaching might accommodate diversity among learners. The use of the term *diversity* here refers to any and all the variants of individual difference and is not limited to cultural, ethnic, or linguistic diversity.

Societies and educators agree on certain paths that all children are supposed to traverse—the scheme, the curriculum, the method, the textbook series, the laws and principles of psychology, the educational or developmental sequences described by research. These define average performance for age or time at school, and assessment standards mark the average levels to be attained. Diversity of any kind does not fit well within such expectations. Can educational practice escape from these expectations of average for age, and linked assumptions that children must take common paths to common outcomes? Modern societies may find it essential to address the learning of individuals in order to raise skill levels in a whole population. Modern societies claiming to value diversity, and wishing to mainstream learners who were previously kept apart, need ways of escaping from the tyranny of the average.

One program, called Reading Recovery, has made such an escape. It brings diverse individuals by different routes to full participation in the mainstream of their classroom activities and has been used successfully in the education systems of five countries. This intervention seeks to eliminate literacy learning difficulties in hard-to-teach children and to reduce literacy problems in schools during a "window of opportunity" in children's second year in school. It selects children who are hard to teach for many different reasons and accommodates diversity through one-on-one lessons lasting thirty minutes a day. Teaching interactions specifically tailored to each child's strengths follow an idiosyncratic path such that what is done in Reading Recovery cannot be mimicked or translated into classroom practice. The assumption that "what works well for the hardest-to-teach children would be the best adaptation for most learners" is an example of how we fail to accommodate diversity. In this chapter I analyze Reading Recovery in the context of current debates about cognition and learning because the results of Reading Recovery negate commonsense predictions about "slow learners."

From recent publications we have a better understanding of how learners construct their cognitive processes (although only some of that construction is self-conscious, deliberate, and reflective). Cognition is now understood to be constructed in particular activities, rather than powered by some reservoir of general ability. This notion has generated interest in how learners contribute to their own learning. In a classroom, each learner enters into new learning with different prior experience, and effective teaching may need to be "differentiated teaching" (Hansen and Robenhagen 1993), which takes into account that learners bring different preparation to new tasks. I have argued that when societies begin to teach literacy in schools most children rather quickly construct an "inner control" over a wide range of reading and writing processes by means of which all later literacy learning is learned (Clay 1991). At beginning ages, which range from five to seven years, 80 to 90 percent of children in industrialized countries construct this control quite easily in programs generated by quite different theories and delivered in different languages. Country by country, children become literate by traveling different paths to a common outcome.

Reading Recovery research from English-speaking countries provides evidence that most lowest-achieving children can become readers and writers if the conditions of learning are changed (Clay 1993). Accounts describe how, as if in slow motion with exaggerated moves, such children shift from being passive novices to active processors of information, and apparently from acting on the information in print to being aware of what they need to do. Some begin to talk about their processes, although the program does not require them to do this.

By Different Routes to Common Outcomes

Reading Recovery teachers claim to design individual lessons for each child. Is that possible? Yes, if one assumes that literacy learning is complex and that complexity, like a drive to a large city, might begin at any one of several different starting points and be approached in any one of several different ways. Studies of what preschool children know about literacy show that they are attending to different aspects of literacy and enter kindergarten or school with islands of knowledge that are highly specific with surprisingly little overlap from child to child. This is a little like children learning the rules of their community language from different spoken samples heard in very different homes.

Such idiosyncrasy is not well served by two pervasive expectations in education: either we expect people to make some kind of average response or action like those we encounter most of the time (assumption 1) or we group people according to stereotypes that apply to some subgroup (assumption 2). Children entering school are measured with the yardstick of the "average five- or six-year-old" (assumption 1) or categorized by socioeconomic, ethnic, cultural, linguistic, or maturity stereotypes (assumption 2). Societies and educational systems provide special education for some subgroups. Learners who make very different responses for any number of reasons do not fit the average or stereotypic descriptions. In my role as clinical child psychologist I have had to find special help for such children. Reading Recovery evolved out of my concern to maximize educational outcomes for children who fell outside the "normal" range in any of a myriad of ways.

Reading Recovery provides supplementary assistance for the lowest achievers in literacy learning after the first year at school, not excluding any child in an ordinary classroom for any reason, as soon as it can be reliably determined that what the school provides is resulting in the learner's falling further and further behind his or her age peers. It is assumed that children will need supplementary help for different reasons and that prior learning and other contributing causes will differ from child to child. Rejecting the search for a single important cause or chain of causes for reading and writing difficulties, Reading Recovery recognizes two types of multiple causation: within the group any conceivable cause or causal chain may occur, and a particular learner may have difficulty for several different reasons. Low achievement may arise from lack of learning opportunities, or because the child chose to attend to other things, or because a child has the fine motor skill and language level of a much younger child. Life events and crises in the preschool or early school years may also contribute to low achievement. If children are to learn to read and write, every attempt must be made to help them attend to and learn basic literacy responses. Working with individual strengths may make this possible, although it requires more and different teaching interactions.

Multiple causation makes it highly unlikely that a prescribed sequence of instruction would suit all children with low literacy achievement. Yet historically, literacy difficulties have been addressed by prescriptive programs, with irrational decisions such as a predetermined sequence of instruction for brain-damaged children, no matter where the site or extent of damage, or a severely reductionist attention to letter-sound relationships, no matter how limited the child's language or knowledge of the world. Gittleman (1985) concluded that we have little evidence that such programs work. Most learners in literacy remediation programs make meager gains while continuing to fall further and further behind their classmates.

Children with extremely low achievement in literacy bring to their first Reading Recovery lessons profiles of competencies that differ in level and in pattern. Extreme limitations in prior knowledge or response repertoires make it imperative that the teacher tap every available response among the children's competencies. To create a trajectory of progress in slow learners one must begin with what each child can already do and work with that to bring each learner by different routes to the common outcome of effective performance as quickly as possible. First lessons in Reading Recovery include only what a child already knows (which is limited but different for each child) and call upon learners to move with flexibility around their own current competencies, while challenging them to meet what they know in new juxtapositions.

The end of supplementary help in Reading Recovery comes as soon as learners are judged to be ready to make continuing progress at average levels in their own classes without this support. Learners need to work among their peers, relatively independent and indistinguishable from them. Becoming a competent silent reader by mid-elementary school gives children the resources they need to cope with other school subjects, so the goal of independent survival with a self-extending literacy system becomes both realistic and necessary. Reading Recovery teachers are forced to work with individual differences because they accept a theory of complex learning, two sources of multiple causation, different starting points for every child, different paths to common outcomes, and the common goal of the survival of every child back in the classroom. Levels of success with the hardest-to-teach children are high, although they vary across countries, education systems, populations of children, social class divisions, curricula, dialects, languages, and teachers, and cost-effective results only come with quality implementation of Reading Recovery at the level of the education system. Yet the day-to-day teacher-child interactions are a critical part of such success.

The Tyranny of the Average and Other Mind-Traps

Research studies hide the complexity of child learning by reporting group averages, but a pooled average may not describe any individual. (I have read that no individual Miss World has had a bust measurement that coincided with the average taken from winners' measurements over several years!) Case studies and in-depth ethnographies, in contrast, may describe superbly what exists in a few individual cases and yet this knowledge may not help us in our attempt to accommodate to diversity.

As a consequence of thinking about teaching a class we reason as if it were the class that learns; but only individuals learn. The tyranny of common concepts discussed in this section—the average learner, the curriculum, the stages of development, the sequences of learning, and the poor or slow learner—these are teaching concepts that get in the way of individuals having appropriate opportunities for learning.

Classroom teachers have a sense of high, average, and low progress over time, and can recall exceptional routes taken by a few individual students. From New Zealand research I can draw two illustrations. In 1978 children close to entering high school completed a national survey about the daily news. When children were asked to write down the meanings of some cryptic newspaper-type headlines it was not surprising that items like WORKERS OUT—FACTORY BLACK or DOLLAR DROPS AGAIN were only partially understood by some children. Low-, middle-, and high-level responses and exceptional statements were reported. For DOLLAR DROPS AGAIN an illustrative low-level response was "A man keeps losing his money," a middle-range response was "It's not worth having a dollar any more because it's not worth anything," and a high-level response was "The American dollar has dropped 2.7 percent against the Swiss franc today." Some responses could not be fitted into preselected categories because they were so divergent. To say that such diversity stems from differences in general intellectual ability is not informative; the teacher's challenge is not to predict performance from an IQ score but to move each child along from where he or she is today. The teacher needs to know what strengths this learner can bring to working on this kind of problem.

Similarly, in a study of high school students' confusion about meanings in school texts (Nicholson 1984) I was struck by the lack of opportunities students had to negotiate the various meanings they assigned to those texts. Knowing what thirteen-year-olds could "read" on the average would be no help in addressing the understanding and misunderstanding of these students.

Another disjunction between theory and practice results from collapsing data across age groups and historical time. All children change rapidly, but on somewhat different time scales in different learning domains. Given such diversity, does it help a teacher's responses to a learner to know that all five- to seven-year-olds are at a particular "stage of development"? A stage may sketch a general educational landscape, but it does not help teachers move diverse learners into new territory. When the findings of psychology are used to predict individual change or generate teaching interactions with an individual learner they are always at risk of being inappropriate.

I have found administrators and teachers emphatic about the factors that will prejudice or facilitate a child's progress, taking their predictions from groups and some intuitive averaging of their personal experience, and not acknowledging that such claims are *very often wrong* for individuals. Commonly their own school's delivery system has contributed to the effects they are observing.

Psychology's search for general laws that apply to behavior of human beings of all ages has been as problematic as the tyranny of the average when applied to education. Psychologists have tried to uncover laws to account for sequences of change in children's behavior; societies create sequences of expectancies and learning opportunities for children; and educators like to have variability squeezed into a standard sequence because this makes it easier to think about curricula, outcome standards, and what we will teach today. I have been unable to find a fixed sequence in the development of young children's writing and believe that children enter that complex activity from many different starting points. Some researchers, such as Gentry (1978), have reported sequenced stages for learning writing and spelling, and some curricula, such as the IBM "Writing to Read" program, have been built from such descriptions. Yet recent experiments with young children in Israel (Levin and Tolchinsky Landsmann 1989; Levin and Korat 1993) report lack of sequence. Some basic understandings may in fact be learned sequentially, but in any complex learning it is often impossible to specify a fixed sequence of acquisition.

Shepard (1991) questions the search for developmental sequences in school learning, and educators should consider them, like averages, subgroup stereotypes, and psychological laws, as potential mind-traps. A teacher considering a particular child needs to know that descriptions of average/typical/normal achievement or sequences for learning are always surrounded by error, generate their own exceptions, and do not necessarily constrain what can be true of individuals.

Along with a commitment to normal distributions of competencies is an assumption that toward the "low" end of the normal curve we encounter simple limitations. In fact, to the contrary, as we move from average to low achievers we encounter individuals who know less and less that can be related to the learning task and show several weak spots in their functioning, all of which make teaching them more complicated. It is not a matter of surmounting a particular hurdle of language, cognition, perception, motor skill, or phonemic awareness; it is a matter of multiple weaknesses in the learner creating greater complexity of inappropriate responding, thereby producing less predictability for the teacher about how to proceed.

The clinical child psychologist who works with individual development knows that what is good practice in interacting with most children is often wrong for a particular child. I tried to face each child as a new challenge and never to assume that normal performance, or categories of special problems, or my previous experience with other children would tell me anything about *this child.* I would say to myself, "This child may look like another you have seen but forget that; try to approach this child as a unique person." I brought that view to my longitudinal research of literacy development and into the development of Reading Recovery.

Today we are better than we used to be at accepting cultural difference, language difference, and gender difference, but because we frequently do not acknowledge diversity in ways of learning we have been open to blunders in this area. The average/typical/normal distribution/performance standard/curriculum sequence/developmental sequence may give teachers a sense of the direction in which learners need to move, but when sequence and prescription emerge from scientific studies of groups, all kinds of mismatches can happen between the prescription and the most effective route for particular individuals. We cannot teach well from descriptions of what occurs on the average: it may be a place to start our thinking, but it has little scope for fine-tuning. It is not enough to reveal the learner's knowledge as scores on assignments or tests, for we need to understand in some specific way how he or she negotiates and constructs new meanings in particular contexts.

Fortunately for schools and for society, most individuals become constructive learners who can, on their own, get to successful performance despite the fact that there is noise, error, or mismatch between the prescriptive curriculum and their prior learning. It is in the diverse group of *low achievers* that we find children for whom the prescription was so far from what they needed that they could not engage with the learning process in the classroom. There is some evidence that, supported by responsive and reflective teaching interactions, even these children can do surprising things. With good teaching interactions learners can be helped to construct their cognitions and get good outcomes where poor predictions would have typically been made. If that occurs on a large enough scale, teachers can spoil the correlations on which much educational practice is predicated.

The Negative Critique of Policies for Dealing with Diversity

Many of the arguments in this section (and some of the wording) come from Lori Shepard's (1991) excellent critique of policies for dealing with diversity. She reviewed educational practices in the United States, such as making special placements for the mentally retarded, diagnosing children as learning disabled, holding them back to repeat a grade, and having special kindergarten placements for "unready children." Urging the rejection of such practices, she wrote:

> These placement policies can be seen as part of a recurring pattern in the U.S. educational system to deal with children who have trouble learning by assigning them to a special place where, despite good intentions, they receive systematically poor instruction that lessens their chances for important learning gains. (p. 279)

Against the background of an increasing concern for children of ethnic and linguistic minorities in the United States, she reported that "children from non-mainstream cultural and linguistic backgrounds are disproportionately the victims of these ineffective instructional practices." The intention of the practices was to accommodate diversity by providing instructional help targeted to the needs of individuals, but in retrospect we see that these practices still target groups and not individuals. Negative side effects accrue *as soon as* students are assigned a special place to receive help. Assessment and diagnosis become ways of sorting diverse children into categories and segregating them in special placements. Those labeled as slow learners are given "dumbed-down instruction."

Most of Shepard's criticisms were avoided in the design of the Reading Recovery intervention in 1977, as if I had first listened to the critique before developing Reading Recovery. This is explained by the fact that my work as a trainer of educational psychologists kept me close to the frailties of special education. So Reading Recovery does not prescribe special placement but provides for supplementary teaching for children who remain in, and are brought to full participation in, the activities of their classrooms. "Lowest-achiever status" relative to peers of the same age group is established through observation tasks (with the qualities of tests) that expose the literacy response repertoire of the learner to the prospective teacher. The same systematic observations are used by an independent evaluator to decide when the supplementary program should be withdrawn. Children spend a minimum of time in Reading Recovery, thirty minutes per day for a limited time, varying according to need, from twelve to twenty weeks. This need to lift the child's level of performance to that of most of his or her classmates in the shortest possible time is incompatible with a simplified, sequenced, or massively analytic curriculum. The cessation of help is determined by a procedure that predicts reliably that a child will be able to perform in his or her classroom with a particular teacher and her curriculum. Progress in the next few months is monitored, and competent classroom performance is sustained by high percentages of the children who have participated in the Reading Recovery program.

Children from non-majority cultural and linguistic backgrounds are selected into Reading Recovery only when they fall into the lowest-achiever category. Once in the program, their cultural and linguistic diversity can be accommodated because the planning and delivery of instruction are on an individual basis. Shepard's comments on particular practices sharpens the account of Reading Recovery.

TRACKING

Grouping by intellectual ability developed early this century as schools moved from educating a homogeneous, elite group to deal with an intake of children with more heterogeneous learning levels. It was expected that their achievement would improve when teaching could be tailored to what students were capable of learning. Research evidence shows that such expectations were seldom met; children in the middle and slow groups generally lost academically, their self-concepts were negatively affected, and teachers delivered a simplified curriculum to low-ability classes. These are the consequences of labeling. Other studies show that teachers prefer to teach high-ability students: they hold higher expectations of such students, they expect more homework from them, and they ask these students more challenging questions.

Reading Recovery *works in opposition to tracking:* it seeks to move diverse children from extremely low achievements at entry to full participation in an unstreamed classroom.

SPECIAL EDUCATION PLACEMENT

Originally designed to serve the deaf, blind, and mentally retarded, special education provided instruction that acknowledged and accommodated a child's disability, but later was expanded to serve larger populations with *milder problems* that are *more vaguely defined.* Research shows that students in special education programs receive a watered-down curriculum and therefore lose ground academically compared with control children in ordinary classrooms. The negative effects are greatest for the less severely handicapped students. Minority students are disproportionately represented in special education programs. In addition, the number of children identified as needing special education grew markedly from 1975 to 1990, especially in the learning disabilities (LD) category. Recent criticisms, supported by research studies, are that tests are technically inadequate, that diagnostic signs that occur among successful learners are interpreted as signs of disorder, and that the costs of assessment and staffing leading to LD placement involve an average of six different professionals, with little attempt to reconcile the findings of these professionals in the design of a program to be delivered to the child (Torgeson 1975; Coles 1978; Ysseldyke, Algozzine, and Epps 1983; Aman and Singh 1983; Carrier 1984; Clay 1987; Lyons 1997). Categorizing or labeling a child changes the nature of the classroom teacher's responsibility for that child's learning.

More than half the children labeled LD in schools do not match clinical definitions and are more accurately described as slow learners, children from non-English backgrounds, children from highly mobile families, children with frequent absences, naughty boys, and average achievers in high-achieving districts. It is as if the clinicians have abandoned a scientific definition of LD and ask instead, "Does this child need special help? If so, he [or she] must be LD" (Shepard 1991; see also Clay 1987).

There are no categories of children in Reading Recovery. Individual histories and characteristics are not ignored, but the only selection criteria are low-achievement indicators that suggest the need for supplementary help. There is minimal dependence on testing, and test results are double-checked with observations of complex processing on authentic tasks and with performance in classrooms. Costs of selection are low because the Reading Recovery *teachers* survey the child's competencies with observation tasks (which operate like standardized measures) and use what they find out on these authentic tasks in planning the child's first lessons. As the child's curriculum expands and task difficulty increases, new competencies become available; *the positive effects are most rapid for the least handicapped, but the greatest distance is covered by the most handicapped.*

A well-run program could lead to fewer students being classified for special education provisions outside mainstream education. The school's Reading Recovery team tunes the program to serve that school's own population *because the school accepts responsibility for its own diverse children.* The children selected for supplementary help remain in their classes and move gradually to average performance in a short period of time. If a child remains in the program for about twenty weeks and has not reached average performance, the child's progress is reviewed by the school's Reading Recovery team, and a decision may be taken to refer the child for an individual appraisal from a specialist, who would probably recommend that the education system provide assistance of a somewhat different kind for a longer period. Most but not every child can succeed in this program; in New Zealand 1 percent or less of the age cohort are referred to other forms of assistance.

GRADE RETENTION

Nonpromotion was the nineteenth century's answer to diversity, so the practice is older than tracking and special education. Grade retention is the intervention of choice in the United States for children who lack prerequisite skills for the next grade but whose problems are not serious enough to trigger special education placement. Beliefs about the efficacy of retention are strong, even though research shows that repeating a grade does not improve achievement, that retained students have lower achievement than control students who went directly on to the next grade, and that retainees are 20 to 30 percent more likely to leave school without graduating than similar students who had never been retained. There is a negative effect on personal adjustment in the majority of studies.

A special form of retention occurs at the kindergarten level. Solutions designed to ensure more success and less stress among first-grade children stem from Gesell's theories (Gesell and Ilg 1946) and similar developments in the 1980s in the United States. They take a variety of forms, have different philosophies, and differ in the type of children defined as "at risk." They include simple retention (repeating kindergarten), two-year programs such as developmental kindergarten before kindergarten, and transition rooms before first grade (also called junior-first, prefirst, and readiness rooms).

Children are given the gift of another year before first grade, which is used in one of three ways. It provides wait time until readiness occurs; or it provides remediation following a curriculum that closely resembles the tasks of readiness tests; or it merely provides a second run through the same kindergarten program. Children may be selected because of *immaturity* or *academic deficiencies;* boys are frequently targeted. The results are not positive. As Shepard (1991) states:

> A review of 16 controlled studies now available shows typically no difference academically between unready children who spend an extra year before first grade and at-risk controls who went directly on to the first grade. (p. 287)

There is also a tendency to group "unready children" together in kindergartens, so all children who need the resource are placed in one classroom, with a curriculum dominated by drill on isolated readiness skills.

Reading Recovery cannot work alongside such early retention practices. If children were retained in kindergarten and given a Reading Recovery program there would be no activities in the kindergarten to support what they were learning in their Reading Recovery lessons, and when these lessons were discontinued there would be no suitable classroom program to extend and support children's continued learning. Children need a Grade 1 classroom to support their Grade 1 competencies. It would waste resources to hold children in kindergarten and put them through Reading Recovery. The contract must be to promote (rather than to retain) children and to place them in Reading Recovery. (Indeed, one should ask why the kindergarten program is creating a call for retention.)

Shepard concluded that millions of public school children in many countries are failing because of, not in spite of, the concerted effort vested in special programs. Sorted and labeled by fallible tests and teacher judgments, children are assigned to treatments that are intended to provide better instruction for homogeneous groups and at the same time match instruction to student ability. Analysis of these policies shows that children segregated under such arrangements with special curricula are likely to receive poorer instruction delivered at a slow pace, with an overemphasis on certain elements and a neglect of complexity, and that children from linguistically and culturally different backgrounds are more likely to be selected for these programs.

Older Psychological Theories

Shepard also described how older psychological theories about human ability and learning support these unsatisfactory special education practices. Two types of old theories, which were used to sort children into categories, led to the practices described above.

Psychology began as a study of individual differences, with particular emphasis on differences in human intellectual capacity. (Tracking, described above, is predicated on sorting children by measured potential, such as intelligence.) The theory of intelligence as inherited, which did not allow for much influence of past learning on current status, has been discredited by the criticisms of IQ tests, by the evidence of the influence of environment on observed capacities, and by demonstrations that children can be taught to think intelligently. Scientists have steadily revised their estimates of the relative influence of heredity downward; but, according to Shepard, teachers and the public "have not kept pace with the research insights from cognitive psychology, sociology, or cultural anthropology." The simple public view is that heredity plus environment "or the sum of these two contributions sets fairly firm limits on how much children can learn" (p. 290).

A newer, environmental theory has taken the place of the theory of heredity in the minds of many teachers. While most of them would find it socially and politically unacceptable today to talk about a child's limited genetic endowment for school learning, they often substitute an environmental explanation for school failure that denigrates the child's home experiences, an explanation that has come to be known as the deficit model. They talk about this environmentally determined inability as though it were permanent and unalterable, yet they rarely respond to missed opportunities to learn with make-up opportunities. To be specific, a child who enjoys regular bedtime stories acquires book knowledge that is helpful in learning to read; a child who has no such experience needs a rich and accelerative set of encounters to make up for missed experience. Similarly, a child who has never noticed people writing, or explored with a pencil or "danced with a pen" (Learning Media 1992), needs make-up opportunities to watch writers writing and to try out this activity. This is not an indictment of the child's home, but of the schools that do not provide the make-up opportunities.

Reading Recovery does not use measured intelligence for selection of children because (1) too many errors arise in such measurements to allow it to predict individual success with learning literacy, (2) we cannot predict the interaction of environment with heredity even when we can locate a problem in the genes, and (3) a systemwide early intervention program must depend on selection by teachers rather than by psychologists. So, whatever the hereditary, physical, or cultural limitations of the child, the Reading Recovery teacher provides the low achiever with a second chance to learn. By working with the learning opportunities of the present, by assuming that responses that are the consequence of environmental learning are alterable, effective literacy learning responses can be drawn out of idiosyncratic response repertoires irrespective of attributed cause. With supplementary instruction the teacher tries to bring the learner to independent problem-solving in under twenty weeks; for a very small percentage of children such intensive efforts do not produce the desired outcome and longer-term help is sought. The challenge of accommodating diversity is met by temporary and time-limited teaching that is idiosyncratically responsive to the learner.

Shepard identified the dominant theory of learning in the United States since the 1950s as being responsible for poor results in special education. Educators assumed that complex learning could be broken down into constituent skills and taught to students in fragments in a prescribed sequence, from the simplest to the more complex (Resnick and Resnick 1990; Stallman and Pearson 1990). Once learned, these separate elements were supposed to transform themselves into complex competency; little attention was given to how the parts were to be integrated to achieve conceptual understanding. This reductionist model led to particularly poor results for learners who could not spontaneously (that is, without instruction) combine the separate elements. The teaching of constituent skills usually took place out of the contexts to which they were to be applied (for example, the long-standing and common practice of occupying children with workbook exercises rather than having them use literacy for specific, real-world tasks, like making a record of what was seen on a class walk).

Problematic in these practices was the common assumption that the development of "high-order" skills like thinking and comprehension could be postponed until after students had mastered the elements of learning. Despite overwhelming evidence from cognitive psychology that complex learning involves thinking, including how a three-year-old negotiates the meaning of a simple story, instruction predicated on the old model resulted in some programs that denied students the opportunity to think until they had mastered prerequisites. Successful students made this practice appear to work because they created their own opportunities for complex learning.

Such interpretations of learning theory had numbing effects on the quality of instruction delivered to low-achieving students and became translated into the expectations held by their teachers. McGill-Franzen and Allington (1990) found that good readers were expected to be self-directed, and their assignments implied that the purpose of reading was the comprehension of meaning. Poor readers, however, were taught in a markedly different way; for them, externally controlled fluent decoding was emphasized. Teachers interrupted poor readers more often, asked poor readers fewer comprehension questions, and assigned more skill-in-isolation work (p. 149). Because Reading Recovery is based on my thesis that teachers need many different ways of interacting with diversity to meet the needs of low-achieving students, this prescriptive and sequential bit-by-bit learning model is inappropriate for children engaged in Reading Recovery.

New Theories, New Practices, and General Principles

New theories have emerged in cognitive psychology, in constructivist developmental psychology, and in the broader framework of sociocultural theory for understanding learning. All stress that learning, social or academic, is an active, constructive process, but the multiple meanings of *constructivism* make it hard to define. To illustrate how these newer theories relate to Reading Recovery I will discuss two of the constructivist principles reported by Shepard.

INTELLIGENCE AND REASONING ARE DEVELOPED

First, *intelligence and reasoning are developed abilities.* According to Shepard's account humans learn how to think based on the models of thinking they have the opportunity to try out. Metacognitive processes are constructed by the learner. Planning and evaluating during problem-solving, self-checking for comprehension during reading, developing a mental representation of a problem, drawing analogies to previously learned concepts *are all learned,* some "naturally," some in interaction with a more expert person, and some in more formal tutoring situations. Some learning-to-learn strategies can be quite content specific. Cognitive researchers are concerned primarily with the construction of meaning that goes on inside an individual's head (for example, the building of knowledge structures, the linking of related information, and the strategic learning of how to work with content-specific solutions). Most acknowledge that such learning is socially constructed (Bruner 1990). Anthropologists, sociologists, and developmental psychologists (Valsiner 1987; McNaughton 1995) are interested in the co-construction and negotiation of meaning among individuals in a culture.

Teachers can teach with constructiveness in mind if they create more effective teaching interactions, and the new theory of cognitive development should direct attention to how teachers can critique their teaching interactions with students on their own and with colleagues. Here are some suggestions for change.

Observe Individual Learners Closely. What the learner contributes to the teaching-learning interaction in signaling the construction of understanding is likely to be different, child for child. Change will begin at different starting points for different learners; it will proceed in different ways and at different rates. Teachers must come to understand that each learner is taking new learning aboard by the very processes that make him or her different! In fact, if a teacher can ever find a homogeneous group, good teaching should rapidly make the participants heterogeneous.

Tune in to Individual Differences. For decades teachers have thought about the physical, age, and personality differences between learners, and have adjusted in small part to the huge implications of each one's having a different sociocultural upbringing. The improvement of teaching interactions requires something additional: it requires the teacher to tune in to the way the learner takes in new information, the individual nature of the process of learning. The teacher should consider questions like: How does this child work in the literacy domain? communicate with the teacher? get a sense of mastery and assurance? In what contexts does the learner work well? Of immediate importance, what is this learner attending to within the complexity of the current task? Does the learner catch miscues and mismatches? Does he or she initiate problem-solving? What specifically makes this task so difficult for the learner to understand? What would make a difference to how this learner works at this activity? In sum, the expert teacher acknowledges differences that recur in teaching interactions and uses them constructively.

Converse with Individual Learners. While managing all of the above, teachers must create opportunities for individuals to negotiate what they do not understand with someone who does. The one-room schoolhouse, so successful in teaching individuals, provided just this opportunity for learners to talk about their work with the teacher. Today's theories on how learners construct their understanding call for talking through, playing back, and rounding out understanding in conversation.

Systematically managed individualization in many content areas, which came to schools with specially developed materials and technology in the form of programmed learning, and then computer learning rarely provides for the negotiation of understanding with the teacher or instructor. Today the term *individualization* is ill defined and glibly used, and does not refer to teaching individuals. As Scriven (1975) wrote, "I see it swinging especially between the exaggeration of its value in order to keep up with each new fashion and the inevitable disheartening recognition that the promised marvels have not been flawlessly achieved in classrooms."

The Teacher Must Interact with "the Constructive Child." What is a constructive child? Two decades of research on language acquisition left us with excellent descriptions of how a child learns to speak and with the conviction that the young child works out what he or she needs to learn in order to be understood without direct teaching but through negotiations of meaning that take place in conversations. The miracle of language acquisition occurs as parents and siblings who know the individual well *talk with the individual child.* Nothing like the "group delivery" of the classroom occurs. From those interactions *children take what they want,* constructing their own cognitive competence.

Conversations that negotiate meaning provide a starting point for thinking about how to improve teaching interactions in classrooms, displacing much current and unsatisfactory teacher talk (Cazden 1988). We must learn how to enlist the child's constructiveness in the interests of his or her own progress, and having done this we need to know how to pass the initiative to the child so he or she can "go it alone" much of the time and do without us as teachers. We do not have to solve the problems of teaching with diversity entirely on our own: we have the constructive learner as our strongest ally.

Cazden (1992) highlights the need not only to talk with the child but to personalize the conversation or assignment; she illustrates this concept with an example of a Samoan boy in a social studies lesson, who was asked to compare his life with that of a Neanderthal man. He asked the teacher, "Which of my three lives should I compare?" and enumerated his island life in Samoa, his city life in Auckland, and his church life. Giving learners opportunities to reveal their range of experience will allow their personal construction of meaning to enter into the teaching interaction. This point is stressed in Shepard's article.

STUDENTS SHOULD USE WHAT THEY KNOW

A second principle is that *instruction should allow students to use what they already know to arrive at new understandings.* If learning is to be a constructive process, learners should engage in tasks that have meaning for them (that is, the tasks should be situated in comprehensible contexts) and that allow what they already know to enter into new learning. Prior knowledge is not just prior prescribed school learning; it includes all the images, language patterns, social relations, and personal experiences that a student relies on to make sense of something new.

Tasks with Scope. Change will need to occur in the policies of administrators, in research department evaluations, in curriculum design, and in teacher expectations, but I want to emphasize that a theory of the constructive learner demands an essential change in lesson delivery. We have to escape from notions of stepwise progressions of the child's learning new concepts in set sequences. Any prescribed sequence of instruction leaves some children behind early in the sequence without providing any means for catching up. In one sense Reading Recovery provides an opportunity to return again.

A valuable and different approach that should be part of a teacher's repertoire is the use of what I call "tasks with scope." These allow children to enter a classroom task with whatever they bring to it, using the task as a vehicle for learning to problem-solve and construct new knowledge. If the teacher designs the task so that any child can enter at his or her own level (as in "Write a story about what we did" or "Reread the text to discover something you did not notice the first time"), there is scope for each learner to move from where he or she is to somewhere else as a result of the encounter. This occurs routinely in conversation. In contrast, tasks directed to the learning of items of knowledge, skills, or concepts in a prescribed order do not allow for different starting points, and the sequence of the curriculum does not allow for different routes to different outcomes. On rare occasions prescribed learning may be necessary, but whereas formal sequencing has become the predominant mode of delivering education, prime emphasis needs to be placed on constructive learning in early education. "Tasks with scope" also provide the opportunity for serendipitous learning when active learners learn much more than the teacher had expected.

Reading Recovery has a framework for lessons, which some critics have mistaken for prescriptive teaching. Each required segment of the lesson is a "task with scope" within which teachers create learning opportunities for individuals who are coming to complex learning from different directions. In every lesson a child (1) reads familiar books, (2) rereads yesterday's book, (3) does a few minutes of work with letters singly or in making and breaking up words, (4) composes and writes a story, (5) reassembles that story as a puzzle from its parts, (6) is introduced to a new reading book, and (7) reads that book for the first time. What occurs in each part of the lesson increases in difficulty on an individual schedule until the activities are as advanced as those completed by most children in the learner's classroom. The tasks remain whole because the teacher shares any part of the task needed to support the learner's participation, occasionally completing some part of the task. It would be possible for teachers to use this framework prescriptively, but training helps the teacher to provide scope for the constructive child.

Change the Delivery Variables. Appropriate instruction for diverse pupils in Reading Recovery requires a different delivery system from the traditional classroom arrangement and a change in the design of the learning opportunities. The lessons are individually designed by teachers who have additional training over and above their classroom expertise and who can use a wide range of alternatives for working with the limited response repertoires of the children. This results in stduents learning at a faster rate than their classmates, producing the necessary accelerated progress needed to catch up. The teacher's daily records of child responses demonstrate the idiosyncratic paths to success, can be used by a school's Reading Recovery team to ensure that the program is effective, and are available for research analysis.

When classroom teachers try to teach all children as individuals they cannot find enough time for such individual teaching. Consequently sessions become too widely spaced. New biases develop. The teacher can hear several good readers read in the time it takes to hear one who is struggling, so distortions of attention develop. Individual teaching is not a preferred way to teach in classrooms, but individual interactions with and between learners throughout the school day *in conversations that construct knowledge* are essential if we are to accommodate individual differences.

Henry Levin in his Accelerated Schools program is working to change whole schools, Stan Pogrow (1990a, 1990b) with the HOTS (Higher Order Thinking Skills) program delivers supplementary help to upper elementary students in math and science, and Reading Recovery targets individual children at a critical time in literacy learning, when there is "a window of opportunity." All three programs aspire to change and improve schooling; all three share a belief in the learning abilities of all children, in building on strengths, and in the empowerment of both teacher and learner, by giving them decision-making roles and the responsibility for results. The whole school should be involved in supporting such change, and the purpose of intervention is always to serve the local education system and the individual learner.

A drastic change in the education delivery system is *the hardest part* of the change process, but the importance of organizational and delivery factors in teaching-learning changes should not be underestimated.

Tolerate Different Routes to Desired Learning Outcomes. Given a diverse group of students with multiple weak spots in some complex area of cognitive activity, how can teachers bring them to some satisfactory level of functioning? Because they ignore how much learners bring to their tasks, fixed sequences of instruction create impediments in many areas of education, especially for immigrants and adults.

Reading Recovery selects children who are noticeably and consistently at extremely low levels of performance for their age group. They form a diverse group who must learn faster than their classmates if they are to move out of Reading Recovery, but they travel by different routes and need different learning conditions in order to achieve the school's common outcome for the age group.

Constructing Cognitions About Complex Tasks

Once literacy competencies are constructed, reading becomes an easy task and allows the learner's attention to focus on meaning. Writing continues to offer challenges. Both reading and writing require that a complex set of competencies be put in place in the first two to three years of literacy instruction.

ATTEMPTING A COMPLEX TASK

Learning a language is complex, yet young children successfully learn to talk (Lindfors 1987). Individual "tuition" takes place in conversations without formal instruction. Different homes use language differently; vocabulary, structures, dialects, content, interaction style, exposure to different genres, and opportunities to talk differ from child to child. Children themselves differ in the use they make of available opportunities. Yet from this diversity children learn the forms of English, the rules for constructing utterances, and ways of extending their language competence out of the control they have already. They come by different routes to two general outcomes: understanding how their language works, and knowing how to extend their own control over it.

In Reading Recovery literacy learning occurs in a somewhat analogous way. Teachers assume that literacy learning is complex learning, and they help each child to attend to those aspects of the task that challenge him or her. They arrange complex tasks in a tentative gradient of difficulty assuming that what the child is able to do at any one time is an organized totality (Ferreiro 1993). Initial, primitive responses are used to construct more complex responses (Lewin 1954). Learners are given authentic tasks, like reading stories and writing messages, that are sufficiently meaningful and allow the learners to recognize whether the ways in which they are working are successful or not.

Close observation of children as they read stories and write messages in the daily lessons of Reading Recovery reveal to the teacher the points at which a particular child struggles. So the teacher puzzles this out. What, within the complexity of the activity, is making *this* task difficult for *this* child? The teacher knows the child's performance repertoire (recorded in the detailed daily records) and his or her performance history (over the short-term supplementary program), and these provide a sound basis for thinking through where and how to help the child move forward. This analysis of the complexity of the task and what might be needed is carried out during every interaction. The teacher may devise a trial task or two to test his or her assumptions. The learner takes a big step forward adding some items of new knowledge by learning how to select from multiple sources of information (world knowledge, cognition, perception, language, and movement) to arrive at one decision.

Reading Recovery teachers work from a common model of children's decision-making about continuous texts derived from research on children learning to read and write successfully (Clay 1991). This model assumes that children need to attend to (and work with) a network of information in written texts in order to make choices among possible responses. Through experiences with texts, meanings, words, letters, and sounds learners build reservoirs of item knowledge, but these will not, of themselves, enable readers to understand what they read. In addition to the general perceptual, cognitive, and linguistic strategies they use in all conscious activity, literacy learners must develop strategic behaviors for working with language presented visually in printed continuous texts. Developing phonemic awareness and phonological links to visual texts are known to be special challenges. Young learners in classrooms build these strategic behaviors out of the experiences they gain in reading texts and writing texts, and the processing systems they construct change to cope with new occurrences.

Classroom teachers operating from a constructivist theory support the completion of whole tasks in which the children handle some of the complexity and the teachers in various ways share the tasks and introduce challenges for the learners. But Reading Recovery teachers have a theory of progress in complex learning that is more specific and detailed than classroom teachers need. It is a dynamic theory open to change as new information becomes available, and it is used as a tool until better tools become available. If new ideas can establish their credibility (1) in practice, (2) under research conditions, and (3) among the professional networks, they may be accepted alternative routes for Reading Recovery teaching.

CAN WE ASK LEARNERS HOW THEY THINK?

If every teacher needs to know where individual learners are and how they are thinking, can we just ask them? No, not in Reading Recovery, for if learners can engage in that kind of dialogue they are ready to leave the program. This claim warrants further analysis.

Neo-Piagetians saw the requirement that children verbalize the logic of their thinking as one of the limitations of Piaget's work: he asked children to explain how they were thinking, and not all learners can do that. Older children are better than younger children at telling us what they are thinking, and those who are so articulate are no longer novices to turning an introspective eye on their own products and processes. Most teachers recognize that there are individual differences in how easily young children can give a metacognitive commentary on their thinking, learning, remembering, forgetting, and understanding. Sometimes theorists attribute "thinking about learning" to what is merely the ability to talk one's way through a lesson using the same words as their teacher. Reading Recovery children can learn to mimic the teacher's talk, but as to metacognitive processing, first they have to learn some ways of working effectively with print, and then they have to move from effective acts in reading and writing tasks to awareness of how they are working on text in both activities. We know when they are becoming aware of how they are responding because we can watch them problem-solving "the hard bits" in the texts, and this has its own way of making learners aware. If we listen to a child's verbalizing about what he or she is doing, it is not easy to determine whether the learner is merely mimicking the teacher's talk or really reflecting and responding productively. Some children reveal their thinking to the teacher; others learn well but find reflection difficult. Hard-to-teach children often begin as passive learners, but as independence in problem-solving increases they begin to talk about what they are doing and reveal to the teacher the generative links between their experience and their literacy work. Once children begin to comment on what they are doing and why, using some of the language of the lesson, dialogue between teacher and learner about how the tasks can be carried out is improved. But with novice learners who have little successful experience in related domains, a direct call to articulate how they think and learn is very likely to result in refusals to initiate responses or in attempts to oblige the teacher. The early shifts in young children are from acts to awareness, as productive responding increases to strategic use of what is learned; in some children this leads to metacognitive reflection. Perhaps this is another example of a language-specific aspect of cognitive functioning.

It is particularly inappropriate to ask learners what they are thinking about when what has to be learned involves fast perceptual decision-making with minimum attention, or smooth and fast execution of skilled actions such as the visual-motor learning of directional behavior and the visual perception of letters, letter clusters, and words. While I accept the Brunerian notion that the processes involved in perceptual and cognitive domains are similar (Bruner 1957), young readers and writers must choose within a second which of the perceptual cues to use; there is no time for a slow cognitive internal debate. What the teacher hears is a comment that is an *outcome* of the child's thinking, not the process itself. Examples abound, such as the boy who asked the teacher about a test booklet with changed-around letter and word order, saying, "Did you buy this book at a regular bookshop?" and the boy who found the word *and* in *landed* as well as in *sandwiches* and said in surprise, "Wow! there it is again, just like in the other book!" as if he were just discovering how to work with letter clusters. Perceptual-motor aspects of literacy acquisition are impeded by an overdose of cognitive attention prompted by unnecessary teacher talk about "remembering" and "thinking," which can distract the human processor from the real purpose of the reading (Johnston 1985). The successful learner with fast perceptual responding is free to give attention to the messages. We might ask learners who are *diverse and competent* what they think they are doing or trying to do, but to ask hesitant, nonachieving children to be metacognitive about their processes is unproductive. Reading Recovery teachers infer how children are working on print from recorded observations of behavior, and they must be tentative and wary of mistakes in their inferences. What children say and how they understand or misunderstand the teacher provides him or her with interesting information, as do their commentaries on the stories they are reading and writing. Teachers may even arrange situations that reveal to them the ways in which the learners are thinking (Cazden 1992).

Features Specific to Reading Recovery

What is necessary for Reading Recovery in addition to a theory of constructiveness? Beginning the program close to the onset of confusion, and limiting the time allowed for the program (twelve to twenty weeks) are specific to literacy learning. There is a growing sense among experienced trainers of Reading Recovery teachers that "a lesson every day" is essential if both teacher and learner are going to be able to tap yesterday's learning trace and consolidate it. But teachers also strive for generative outcomes: they want the child to learn how to work with certain features of print and require that once a "how to" is established the learner, working independently but not without nudging, will apply it to new encounters with print. Breaking the complex task into parts and teaching them separately would prevent the opportunity for children to attempt complex decision-making and orchestrate complex skilled actions. Teachers cannot proceed through a set sequence of learning if they are to allow diverse learners to leap forward, up the gradient of difficulty, as soon as their processing strategies permit this (of course, this should be allowed to happen in good classroom teaching also).

Reading Recovery teachers work collaboratively with learners who are reading and creating printed texts; they explore the stories, prompt the children to problem-solve the detail and recall known responses, support learners in meeting new challenges, foster independent attempts, accept approximations as moves towards new achievements, acknowledge shifts towards correct responding, applaud "mastery" because it frees learners to attend to problem-solving at the boundaries of knowledge, and raise task difficulty gradually. Throughout the program the teacher knows that for ultimate success even the learner's weak areas of functioning must also contribute to performance. Teachers must ward off students' dependency and release that student as an independent thinker and learner.

Teaching Individuals with Diversity in Mind

We are reminded of human variability when our own personal characteristics or those of our loved ones do not fit described stereotypes or sequences. It is then that we say, aha, yes, individuals vary. We think daily about divergence from normality when it comes to superiority: sporting prowess, high intelligence, giftedness in art, music, and figure-skating. We accept differences in personal attributes like looks, physique, reaction time, need for sleep, visual perception, auditory perception, sight, hearing, muscle power, singing ability, and we do this so readily that we find identical twins strange and even disturbing. We grossly underrate how different each child's history of learning opportunities has been, how much families differ, and how we have each been closed out from certain experiences in life. For these reasons literacy instruction must be culturally responsive.

Education has responded to diverse learners by slowing down the pace of learning and simplifying the content, but we have also invented ways to teach complex things to diverse learners. In literacy learning learners should be helped to perform complex activities, moving up a steep gradient of difficulty while maintaining success. In addition to a constructivist view of cognition we need a theory of literacy learning as a complex task directed to messages in continuous texts. In particular, knowing what successful learners learn to do as they move up a gradient of difficulty in texts would allow teachers to help different students make the same kinds of shifts, although not necessarily through similar lessons.

If hard-to-teach children are to become literate we also need theories about (1) the psychological competencies that make up the substructure of effective performance (including language learning and perceptual learning), (2) the influence of social contexts on learning and on teaching interactions, (3) how to train teachers to use large teaching repertoires from which they select for diverse learners, and (4) how to implement effective programs in education systems. Delivery of an effective early intervention program like Reading Recovery draws upon large bodies of such theory.

Reading Recovery teachers accept all children as potential learners and find each learner's starting point. They observe how children work on easy tasks when everything goes well; they spend extended time responding to children's initiatives and interacting with their thoughtfulness; they observe learners closely as they work on novel things and are always prepared to be surprised by talent they had not predicted. This personalized analysis includes identifying strengths that will provide the "firm ground" on which to build while tentatively challenging learners in weak areas. The activities, the books, the progressions made by the children have to be allowed to vary with the idiosyncratic progress of a particular child, and the lesson framework was designed to allow for this. Emphases in tomorrow's lesson will arise out of today's observations but will be used in the context of the child's engagement with tomorrow's authentic tasks of reading and writing stories. Teaching interactions change from one child to another so that all these activities would be realized differently with each of the four to six pupils taught daily.

Reading Recovery teachers need a vast repertoire of alternative teaching moves to bring diverse children to classroom competence and further independent literacy learning. That calls for training over and above what is required for quality classroom teaching. The principles of constructivism and an enhanced repertoire of teaching alternatives are new to most Reading Recovery teachers when they begin training: they need to become interactive experts who support children as they construct a literacy system. These teachers' yearlong in-service course runs in parallel with their first year of working with hard-to-teach children. It takes a year of practice and discussion for their teaching to become responsive to diversity in their pupils. Faced with a puzzling pupil they brainstorm possible ways to work with that child.

How can such teachers be kept at a peak level of tentativeness and flexibility in designing their lessons for diverse individuals? The "average" expectations and subgroup stereotypes that creep back into the thinking of Reading Recovery teachers have to be challenged to prevent them from doing what they do so well, which is to search for common characteristics and disregard the uncommon. It is imperative that these teachers remain responsive to the individual variability of children and that they teach in response to this variability. Their decisions need to be tentative ones that they can readily change in response to interactions with learners. Tentativeness and flexibility are bywords of the program. This is why Reading Recovery encourages communication networks between teachers, schools, tutors, trainers, and countries—professionals who support each other in ongoing processes of problem-solving.

Classroom teachers are probably correct in arguing that the demands and ambiguities of classroom instruction cannot be informed by what goes on in such special-delivery conditions. Fortunately classroom teachers have many constructive learners among their students who work with, rather than against, the teacher to negotiate understanding. If the newer theories of cognitive development lead to more focus on the quality of teacher-child exchanges in classrooms and on individual differences, the experience of Reading Recovery may be more generally applicable. For example, the experience of Reading Recovery might inform a shift towards more personalized teaching interactions in the classrooms of the future and encourage a closer monitoring of learners when they begin to work on new subjects, such as foreign languages, particular sciences, and branches of mathematics. But the Reading Recovery model of accommodating diversity has the most to offer in fields of special education, where inclusion or mainstreaming policies operate for the hard-of-hearing, for those labeled "dyslexic," and for mildly subnormal learners.

References

Allington, R. 1984. Content Coverage and Contextual Reading in Reading Groups. *Journal of Reading Behavior* 16: 85–95.

Aman, M. G., and Singh. 1983. Specific Reading Disorders: Concepts of Etiology Reconsidered. In K. D. Gadow and I. Bailer, eds., *Advances in Learning and Behavioral Disabilities,* Vol. 3, pp. 1–47. Greenwich, CT: JAI Press.

Bruner, J. S. 1957. On Perceptual Readiness. *Psychological Review* 64: 123–152.

———. 1990. *Acts of Meaning.* Cambridge, MA: Harvard University Press.

Carrier, J. G. 1984. Comparative Special Education: Ideology, Differentiation, and Allocation in England and the United States. In L. Barton and S. Tomlinson, eds., *Special Education and Social Interest,* pp. 35–64. Beckenham: Croom Helm.

Cazden, C. B. 1988. *Classroom Discourse: The Language of Teaching and Learning.* Portsmouth, NH: Heinemann.

———. 1992. *Whole Language Plus: Essays on Literacy in the United States and New Zealand.* New York: Teachers College Press.

Clay, M. M. 1982. *Observing Young Readers: Selected Papers.* Portsmouth, NH: Heinemann.

———. 1985. Reading Recovery: Systemic Adaptation to an Educational Innovation. *New Zealand Journal of Educational Studies* 22, 1: 35–58.

———. 1987. Learning to Be Learning Disabled. *New Zealand Journal of Educational Studies* 22: 155–173.

———. 1991. *Becoming Literate: The Construction of Inner Control.* Auckland, NZ: Heinemann.

———. 1993. *Reading Recovery: A Guidebook for Teachers in Training.* Auckland, NZ: Heinemann.

Clay, M. M., and C. B. Cazden. 1990. A Vygotskyan Interpretation of Reading Recovery. In L. B. Moll, ed., *Vygotsky and Education: Instructional Implications and Applications of Sociohistorical Psychology,* pp. 206–222. Cambridge, UK: Cambridge University Press. Reprinted in Cazden.

Coles, G. S. 1978. The Learning-Disabilities Test Battery: Empirical and Social Issues. *Harvard Educational Review* 48: 313–339.

Ferreiro, E. 1993. Some Remarks About the Acquisition of Written Language as a Conceptual Object. European Science Foundation, Second Workshop on Written Language and Literacy, Wassenaar, the Netherlands. October.

Ferreiro, E., and A. Teberosky. 1982. *Literacy Before Schooling.* Portsmouth, NH: Heinemann.

Gaffney, J., and R. Anderson. 1991. Two-Tiered Scaffolding: Congruent Processes of Teaching and Learning. Technical Report No. 523, Center for the Study of Reading, University of Illinois at Urbana-Champaign.

Gentry, J. R. 1978. Early Spelling Strategies. *Elementary School Journal* 79: 88–92.

Gesell, A., and F. L. Ilg. 1946. *The Child from Five to Ten.* New York: Harper.

Gittleman, R. 1985. Controlled Trials of Remedial Approaches to Reading Disability. *Journal of Child Psychology and Psychiatry* 26: 843–846.

Hansen, V. R., and O. Robenhagan. 1993. *Abdullah's Genuine Indonesian Curry Powder.* Copenhagen: The Danish National Institute for Educational Research.

Johnston, P. H. 1985. Understanding Reading Disability: A Case Study Approach. *Harvard Educational Review* 55: 153–177.

Learning Media. 1992. *Dancing with a Pen.* Wellington, NZ: Ministry of Education.

Levin, H. 1990. *Building School Capacity for Effective Teacher Empowerment: Applications to Elementary Schools with At-Risk Students.* Stanford, CA: Stanford University School of Education.

Levin, I., and O. Korat. 1993. Sensitivity to Phonological, Morphological, and Semantic Cues in Early Reading and Writing in Hebrew. *Merril-Palmer Quarterly* 39, 2: 213.

Levin, I., and L. Tolchinsky Landsmann. 1989. Becoming Literate: Referential and Phonetic Strategies in Early Reading and Writing. *International Journal of Behavioral Development* 12, 3: 369–384.

Lewin, K. 1954. Behavior and Development as a Function of the Total Situation. In L. Carmichael, ed., *Manual of Child Psychology.* New York: Wiley.

Lindfors, J. W. 1987. *Children's Language and Learning.* 2nd ed. Englewood Cliffs, NJ: Prentice-Hall.

Lyons, C. A. 1997. Reading Recovery and Learning Disability: Issues, Challenges, and Implications. In S. L. Swartz and A. F. Klein, eds., *Research in Reading Recovery.* Portsmouth, NH: Heinemann.

McGill-Franzen, A., and R. L. Allington. 1990. Comprehension and Coherence: Neglected Elements of Literacy Instruction in Remedial and Resource Room Services. *Journal of Reading, Writing, and Learning Disabilities* 6: 149–180.

McNaughton, S. 1995. *Patterns of Emergent Literacy: Development and Transition.* Auckland, NZ: Oxford University Press.

Nicholson, T. 1984. Experts and Novices: A Study of Reading in the High School Classroom. *Reading Research Quarterly* 19, 4: 436–451.

Pogrow, S. 1990a. Challenging At-Risk Students: Findings from the HOTS Program. *Phi Delta Kappan* (January): 389–397.

———. 1990b. A Socratic Approach to Using Computers with At-Risk Students. *Educational Leadership* (February): 61–66.

Resnick, L. B., and D. P. Resnick. 1990. *Tests as Standards of Achievement in Schools.* Proceedings of the ETS Invitational Conference on the Uses of Standardized Tests in American Education. Princeton: Educational Testing Service.

Scriven, M. 1975. Problems and Prospects for Individualization. In H. Talmage, ed., *Systems of Individualized Instruction.* Chicago: National Society for the Study of Education Yearbook.

Shepard, L. 1991. Negative Policies for Dealing with Diversity: When Does Assessment and

Diagnosis Turn into Sorting and Segregation? In E. Hiebert, ed., *Literacy for a Diverse Society: Perspectives, Practices and Policies,* pp. 279–298. New York: Teachers College Press.

Stallman, A., and D. Pearson. 1990. Formal Measures of Early Literacy. In L. M. Morrow and J. K. Smith, eds., *Assessment for Instruction in Early Literacy.* Englewood Cliffs, NJ: Prentice-Hall.

Stanovich, K. E. 1986. Matthew Effects in Reading: Some Consequences of Individual Differences in the Acquisition of Literacy. *Reading Research Quarterly* 21, 4: 360–407.

Torgeson, J. 1975. Problems and Prospects in the Study of Learning Disabilities. In E. M. Hetherington, ed., *Review of Child Development Research* 5: 385–440.

Valsiner, J. 1987. *Culture and the Development of Children's Action.* Chichester, UK: Wilkey.

Ysseldyke, J. E., B. Algozzine, and S. Epps. 1983. A Logical and Empirical Analysis of Current Practice in Classifying Students as Handicapped. *Exceptional Children* 50: 160–166.

17 Child Development and Literacy Learning

IN 1991 THE INTERNATIONAL READING Association and the National Council of Teachers of English produced a volume entitled *Handbook of Research on Teaching the English Language Arts.* It is a comprehensive guide to what we know about literacy teachers, the processes involved in learning to read and write, and language arts instruction. The articles in this collection explore most aspects of language arts, from the history of the profession to ethnographic research, child development, and learning, to teacher preparation and evaluation, and classroom environments. The first part of the book covers theoretical bases for English language arts teaching in related disciplines, like linguistics, psychology, anthropology, literary theory, and child development, and the last named was the chapter that I was asked to write. I was pleased to do this because developmental psychology is my academic discipline, and my commitment is first and foremost to the child as learner.

Perhaps a brief introduction will help readers understand why some of the legitimate activities of researchers do not necessarily lead to changes in the classroom activities of teachers. In essence, theorists and researchers must push the boundaries of understanding how children change and why they succeed; teachers must teach tomorrow, and the next day, and the next day.

Though academic developmental psychology and child development for educators share common interests in oral language, writing, and reading, their aims are different. Developmental psychologists, on the one hand, seek explanations, explore competing alternatives, and describe change over time in literacy behaviors.

Teachers and educators, on the other hand, try to use the ideas of informed experts to optimize opportunities for children's enhanced development in effective programs. Developmental psychologists need questions that will lead to a breakthrough in understanding; teachers need answers that can be built into practice.

In addition, theories of developmental psychology are constructed from research findings, which are strongly influenced by the research designs that are required to separate out this from that. Many times the researcher's questions are not asked with teaching in mind; they are asked to clarify complex and challenging issues.

Teachers are concerned with moving children of very different competencies as far as possible over a change process lasting usually a school year; developmental psychologists often explore overarching explanations that cover much longer periods of time, and try to explain what causes developmental change.

Finally, teaching involves the interactions of child with task, of teacher with child, and of child with child, and requires that interactions be different with different children. However, interactions are hard to study and have been largely avoided by researchers, who find it more informative to measure outcomes.

Thus, there are good reasons why these two disciplines, despite their mutual interest in children and their learning, should be so different in their activities. But if the two sets of activities do not in the end present the same picture—that is, agree with each other—then either or both of their formulations are wrong or misleading. The two lenses must present the same view.

Theories in developmental psychology and theories about teaching the English language arts are furthest apart when developmental psychology has nothing to say about teaching, when it focuses on the evidence that individual children construct their own knowledge, and when it fails to address the roles assigned to teachers by society. Conversely, when teaching is seen as the delivery into children of content and skill by didactic instruction, or the use of teacher-proof curricula that calls for no developmental wisdom, or nothing more than publishers' programs, it ignores the highly relevant insights about children's learning that are provided by developmental psychology. The work of both disciplines is closely allied when researchers document in precise ways the effects on children of real-world interactions and when they search for theoretical explanations of how and why children's responses change over time. The two disciplines have shared interests in recent studies of parent-child interaction, tutoring by novice tutors, and adults talking with children, especially in schools (Cazden 1988), all of which show how the learner gradually assumes a self-monitored role.

The child study movement of the early 1900s emerged from the innovation and international interchange of the 1930s as developmental psychology (Senn 1975). Like its parent discipline of psychology, developmental psychology placed high value on empirical evidence gained under controlled conditions and theories grounded in such data. The methodological and theoretical uniqueness and challenge of a developmental orientation (Baltes 1983) are reflected in its goals, namely

1. to describe change over time in behaviors, abilities, and processes,
2. to explain what occurs, and
3. to optimize opportunities for enhanced development.

The last goal may call for interventions that establish external or internal resources to allow for optimal development or programs that modify problematic behavior. A diversity of philosophical, theoretical, and methodological orientations are always found at the cutting edge of current debates in developmental psychology (Lerner 1983), but there is a major focus today on internal, cognitive, strategic, and affective variables as prior and causative. Learning contexts influence behaviors and cognitive processes in important ways, and the problem of how to study the process of learning during interactions is a challenge to researchers.

Interpreted broadly, formal education fits comfortably into this goal of optimization: its central enterprise can be seen as a myriad of interventions in children's lives during formative years of change. Educational researchers also record cumulative change over time as children learn, with empirical evidence ranging from that gained under controlled conditions (evaluation or assessment) to telling accounts in individual biographies. In such descriptive research, learning is conceptualized broadly as something that occurs in or out of school, with or without instruction. Such research recognizes that some changes in children occur under the control of historical and societal factors, some are determined by the child's selection of what to attend to, more are brought about in interaction with significant others, and some result from what is delivered more formally, in classroom programs.

There is no clear distinction between the two disciplines when educational researchers pursue questions to the level of explanatory theory tested against competing alternatives, or when developmental psychologists test theories in interventions in the real world of schools. More commonly, developmental psychologists focus more on research designs and questions that will yield explanations, and educational researchers aim for effective optimization. Taken together, the two search for both a better explanation and a more effective program.

Since 1970, the need of societies to solve social problems by changing the next generation of schoolchildren produced different research pressures in psychology and education, which complicated the transfer of information between them. Education received calls for accountability and for higher standards on the one hand and for a narrowing of its focus on the other, its critics seemingly blind to what was known about child development, while the scope of developmental psychology was broadened from a concentration on highly controlled experimental studies to a consideration of the ecologies within which children learned (Bronfenbrenner 1979). This led to a more culturally aware and activist stance, with developmental psychologists becoming involved in interventions with underprivileged children, among others (Weikart et al. 1971).

In this chapter, brief comments on research interests shared by the two disciplines in oral language, writing, and reading are followed by a more general analysis of congruence and communicative distance between them.

The Acquisition of Language

ORAL LANGUAGE

Language acquisition has been richly challenging to educators. It is, clearly, cumulative, its foundation is laid before entry to school, and most of it is completed in interaction with significant others but without direct instruction (Lindfors 1987). Preschoolers store information from their experiences and acquire processes for accessing that information. They derive order and structure for language from massively different and diverse samples, they test and refine their values for production, and all the while are barely conscious of any of these processes. The learning is often initiated by the child, although adults and older children may pace the learning and provide appropriate information that the child is able to use. *Learning does not proceed by accurate performance with the use of correct grammar.* How could children construct self-monitoring and self-correction processes if they never made an imperfect response? By being partially correct, the child progresses to more control over complexity in the use of language. Accuracy is the outcome, not the process, of learning.

In the 1960s, as psychologists came to terms with linguists' conceptual approaches to syntax, attention to detailed protocols of individual progress placed the spotlight on the importance of interrelationships between parts of the utterance and the organization of language on several levels. When linguists began to explore the links between structure and meaning, developmental psychologists found themselves in familiar territory with knowledge about cognition and how we understand language. As interest turned to the pragmatics of language use, it was easy for educators to recognize the influence of familiar contextual variables—settings, home influences, cultural factors, discourse factors, dialect differences. By 1975, oral language was seen in rich perspective, as having important implications for teaching, for the valuing of cultures, and for bilingual education. Since then, the interactions of language, culture, and education have received attention as ethnomethodological approaches have been tested and refined (Heath 1983), cultural factors explored (Au and Kawakami 1984), and classroom discourse analyzed (Cazden 1988).

Perhaps because children seem to have well-formed response systems for comprehending and producing language prior to entering school, the continuing development of oral language during schooling is not often seen by teachers to be important. In fact individual differences in oral language achievement vary greatly. While teachers see oral language as central to writing and reading acquisition, they often do not recognize the need to foster its further development. Multicultural or bilingual challenges in most English-speaking countries have led to a new awareness of oral language issues, which may direct more attention to the ways in which the language of the child at home undergoes further development during schooling.

WRITING

By 1978, three slim volumes detailed observations of young children writing (Clay 1975; Graves 1978; Read 1975). Graves placed prime emphasis on the observation of the writing processes used by children who were encouraged to be writers. Read discovered children who analyzed the sounds they could hear in their own pronunciation of sentences and invented a writing system for themselves. I collected weekly writing samples from an age cohort of children in five schools throughout their first year of school. The study of how children learn to write, which had been constrained by beliefs about motor incoordination, a striving for correctness, a need to learn reading before writing, and a notion of getting images of spellings into the brain, began to expand with new vigor. Attention focused on

how to look at children's writing,
how to look for processes of change, and
how to evaluate change.

Writing acquisition, it turned out, had surprising similarities to oral language. Children made responses that were systematic rather than random, and they occurred across children, even across countries and languages (Ferreiro and Teberosky 1982; Goodman 1990), as if children were operating on rules they had discovered for themselves. It was hard to shift children from what they appeared to believe toward new understanding and this pointed to some cognitive involvement. Questions were needed to elicit the rules or assumptions that children were using. Researchers could almost see cognitive processes in operation as they recorded children in classrooms composing messages and monitoring their oral production against their written composition at sound, sound cluster, word, or phrase level within the text as a whole, using recursive strategies of reviewing and revising (Graves 1983; King and Rentel 1979).

READING

By analogy, reading acquisition might also have been viewed constructively—that is, as something that the child put together, except that reading instruction has a long history of polarized theoretical positions. In lay minds, there are two superficial descriptions of beginning reading instruction, one at the letter level (phonics) and one at the word level (sight vocabulary). A wealth of writing on communication, information, and linguistic theory (Miller 1951) showed how language transmits information on several levels. Research directed the attention of teachers to variables that found no place in the stripped-down versions of decoding and sight vocabulary theories—research on children's syntactic errors in reading, the role of context and meaning, the links within stretches of texts called cohesive variables (Chapman 1983), and memory experiments that showed how children related prior experience to new text. These research results were consistent with textual approaches to reading and writing.

Strategic reading is seen by many educators as something that older readers learn: rereading to comprehend (Gamer, Wagoner, and Smith 1983), skimming ahead for organizational structure, using context to process unfamiliar words (Potter 1982), summarizing text to ensure understanding and remembering (Palincsar and Brown 1984), and monitoring comprehension (Wagoner 1983). That earlier forms of each of these strategies occur in the young reader (Baker 1984; Clay 1979), if instruction allows for it, is inconsistent with the advocacy of "decoding first and comprehension later." Unlike oral language and writing research, there have been few continuous longitudinal studies of reading processes in formation (Tierney 1991), with a result that young speakers and writers are seen as building their own competencies and young readers receive them from their teachers and/or texts. The weight of research on early reading is on how cognition and teaching interact at the level of phonological awareness, to the neglect of other levels of language knowledge that might be powering the progress. Recent attention to the interactions of reading with writing may take us out of this strange situation (Langer 1986).

The Contribution of Developmental Theory

In the first half of this century psychoanalytic theory, with its focus on the study of the individual child, provided a strong developmental emphasis for the education of young children in British education, from the time of Susan Isaacs (1935) to the Plowden Report (1967). In the United States, the strong influence of psychology on education was from associationist or behavioral theories, which could be applied to children being instructed in groups; at that time developmental psychology studied children before they went to school and in their out-of-school lives. In contrast to Britain and the United States, the Soviet Union's developmental psychology was directed, even in the 1930s, to pedagogical issues (although it only reached Western countries in translation in the 1960s); work from that period is central to research on children's learning today (Vygotsky 1962; Wertsch 1985).

For fifty years Piaget's theory of cognitive development has evolved and expanded, providing a theory that might be called an "inclusive model" of learning (Cairns and Valsiner 1984). According to this theory, children not only carry out cognitive operations, but also use processing strategies, code their experiences, and compile records of their experiences, which they store as memory schemas. Piaget's description of assimilatory and accommodation processes presents teachers with the option of going with the child or against the child in one-to-one teaching, but provides only very general guidance for the design of day-to-day cumulative instruction of groups for children in classrooms (Goodman 1990). Critical evaluation of the contribution of Piagetian theory to teaching has led to the concept of the competent preschooler (Donaldson 1979) and to theories that challenge the role of conflict in cognitive change (Bryant 1982, 1984).

Current analysis of Vygotsky's theory focuses not on his theory of inner speech, only partially on his social theory, but mostly on his concept of the zone of proximal development. His challenge to current teaching practice is that he sanctions shared activity between tutors and learners so that the learners can complete more difficult tasks with help that they would not complete on their own. Learners are supported in the beginning but gradually take over the entire task. The help of the expert becomes unnecessary as learners become able to assume control. Education does not have to be an activity on which the child must always work solo on new material. While these ideas can be easily fitted to concepts of teaching, they do not reflect the depth of Vygotsky's theory, which claims that shared and supported activity allows the child to construct some inner generating system. That allows the child to initiate and manage learning of this kind independently on future occasions.

Many abilities are now regarded in developmental psychology as "alterable variables" and potential targets for education. Researchers study the procedures children use to get to solutions, like cognitive strategies and self-monitoring (Flavell 1982), and provide explanations of how speech and texts are understood, arguing that "scripts" have causal effects on achievement (Schank and Abelson 1977). Even intelligence is seen as a matter of dynamic processes, rather than fixed static states (Sternberg 1984; Pintrich et al. 1986).

How do developmental theories influence teachers' assumptions about children? The explanations provided, particularly in language and cognitive areas, have given teachers a vocabulary and knowledge structures that allow them to think beyond what children do to what may be occurring in their heads. It is the purpose of scientific study to go beyond the details of individual difference and the surface features of what is observed to less obvious phenomena and more general statements of relationships. Education needs to know *why* developmental psychology works in the ways it does.

The need to test particular developmental theories on certain age groups has led to an uneven spread of information, with most attention going to the preschool years (ages four to six), followed by the early elementary years (ages six to nine) and the intermediate years (ages nine to twelve) (McCandless and Geis 1975), with adolescence poorly researched. Recent research on infants and toddlers has overcome an earlier neglect, and life-span developmental psychology is theoretically strong but empirically young. Such research coverage serves early childhood education well, but not schooling in later years.

Theories of child development influence teachers' assumptions about why children behave the way they do, rather than their decisions about how and what to teach. There are particular risks when the theories applied belong to another age, or arose from a different knowledge base. For example, Wertsch (1985) had to use Soviet authorities who wrote long after Vygotsky's death to explicate Vygotsky's work; Gesell's (Gesell and Ilg 1946) attempt to characterize the mismatch between some children's learning needs and instruction demands is used today to exclude children from instruction and so from opportunities to learn. Bloom's (1971) theory of how the scores of average achievers can be lifted two standard deviations by teaching in certain ways was applied as a concept of mastery learning that amounted to pouring content into empty vessels more demandingly.

The Contribution of Methodology

Critical for more effective interchange between developmental psychology and education is a need to appreciate the logical linkages between theoretical issues, research designs, statistical analyses, and interpretations (Baltes, Reese, and Nesselroade 1977; Bryant and Bradley 1985; Pintrich et al. 1986). Theory testing and experimental controls in psychology are necessary to answer some kinds of questions for which observational and participant-observation methodologies are not feasible; the approaches address important, but different, questions.

Experimental or longitudinal studies that compare age groups with widely spaced observations can only produce descriptions of change in children consistent with discrete stages. Gradual change in process or knowledge, which is more like what teachers see in classrooms, is more likely to emerge from intensive longitudinal studies of change over short intervals.

When developmental psychology pays close attention to what happens in the course of children's development, with manipulative and precise measurement of change in children's responses, it provides good models for education, and for teachers to monitor whether desired outcomes are occurring. Ideas of where, when, and how to begin teaching, of the changes that may be expected over time, of the track that most children take, of the variability to be expected, and of different developmental paths to the same outcomes could emerge from developmental research so designed.

Piaget's clinical method, used to study children's cognitions in depth, had an important impact on the acceptability of talking to children about their understanding (Ferreiro and Teberosky 1982; Karmiloff-Smith 1979). Roger Brown (1973) and his eminent students began a search for descriptions of language acquisition with in-depth data from the language of three children. This approach required researchers to carefully record daily change, arrange small-scale manipulations, and analyze particular features, trying to model the inner structure of language competence to account for the outer behaviors. Studies in the Soviet Union of sensory features used a similar kind of detailed observation, in an effort to perceive what was behind the behavior change.

Longitudinal research is highly relevant to the understanding of change over time needed in education; it is essential for the study of prediction, for understanding the origins of individual differences, and for the evaluation of outcomes of educational programs (Sontag 1971). It is a method too rarely used, and is almost never applied to a total cohort of children across the whole normal curve, varying in age as they do in real classrooms and under the normal school conditions within which children are taught. Yet descriptive data of learning processes in classrooms are very useful in education (Nicholson 1984). If teachers became researchers of change over time in the day-to-day, small-scale sense (Pinnell and Matlin 1989), assessment and evaluation of children's progress could be enriched.

Detailed description of changes in successful learners may well provide teachers with appropriate guides for what poor learners need to be taught in what education regards as "basic" subjects (Clay 1985).

Different Priorities

While there are many points of congruence between the two disciplines, there are many reasons for communicative distance to arise between research on teaching the English language arts and research in developmental psychology. A recognition of some of these reasons may improve the potential for dialogue between them.

QUESTIONS AND ANSWERS

While developmental psychology must take time to pose its questions and test its explanations systematically in a scientific way, education must act on today's best available knowledge for current programs and tomorrow's plan for changes. Teachers need answers to build into their practice: psychologists want questions that will lead to breakthroughs in understanding. Researchers in both disciplines solve problems in similar areas but with different goals. What counts as relevant is different for each group, and this is liable to lead one group to ignore the findings of the other.

SELECTING THE SUBJECTS

Teachers must deal with all children; they present the kind of diversity that developmental psychology seeks to control in its research designs. Teachers face the average (the majority), the extreme (the minority), and particular individuals with learning challenges all at the same time. Developmental psychologists, however, in order to obtain a clear test of a hypothesis, select appropriate samples of children. The findings may be clear, but they usually apply only to some of the children in a mixed classroom; only extremely rarely will they apply to all. This can lead educators to become impatient with psychological research and unwilling to consider its findings.

THE WHOLE LEARNER VERSUS PARTICULAR PROCESSES

The teacher's job is to work with all aspects of the child's functioning as applied to a single task. Teachers know that the individual child interacts in some holistic way with the specific task at a particular time. Developmental psychologists try to keep in mind the whole organism, directing research to the links between perception and reading, cognition and language, culture and learning, classroom discourse and child learning, and contexts and outcomes. However, it is the nature of developmental psychology to search for explanations in specialized areas, to tease out the specific, eschew the complex, explicate processes, avoid global theory, and oppose unwarranted generalization; it thus tends to exclude holistic theories.

Common Research Problems

ACHIEVEMENT OUTCOMES DO NOT DEFINE CURRICULA INPUTS

Research findings of what children typically do at selected ages describe in stepwise form sequences of achievements, which are the outcomes of learning. Those error-free end results, which are the outcome of many false starts, half-correct processes, and much self-correction en route to a recognizable product or achievement, have sometimes been built into curricula by educators in their perfected form. The appropriate research questions relate to how this now-perfect performance was acquired, and records of the changes that took place en route to perfect performance will provide a better guide for the curricula of learning than study of the perfect outcomes of instruction.

Education is not about putting in the outcomes; it is about knowing what inputs, in what contexts, give rise to the desired outcomes. In current debates about phonological segmentation in reading, metacognitive awareness in oral language, or the importance of correctness in writing, the distinction is not made between where you begin and how you get to where you end up but is merely between inputs that give rise to outcomes.

For example, if learners construct knowledge from learning interactions, then finding that competent readers score well on tests of phonological awareness does not imply that one should teach phonics, but rather that one should study change over time in younger children and document the sequences of interactions by which they reach that final state of competence. Perhaps, as in language acquisition, many different kinds of input contribute to the ability to read. The fact that most children learn to read in very different instructional programs suggests that this may be the case. Developmental psychology can contribute to our understanding of this process in a slightly different form. It accepts that what changes over time must be observed through studying individuals who change over time. Language acquisition research has illustrated how individuals learn from different language samples on different time scales, taking different paths to the same goal: talking fluently. What these individuals need to learn cannot be interpolated from the average scores of separate samples of three-, four-, five-, six- and seven-year-olds. Designers of educational interventions in the school years commonly try to achieve change in individuals on the basis of evidence derived from cross-sectional norms. Differences between individuals do not describe what is required to achieve change within or by individuals; interventionists in both developmental psychology and education have often failed to recognize this (Montada and Fillip 1976). A normative description of change is a gross approximation and does not provide a satisfactory basis for designing an instructional sequence.

INTERACTIONS ARE HARD TO STUDY

Riegel (1979) was impressed by the dialectical worldview of developmental psychology, and he chided the discipline for describing either the responses of the adult (parent or teacher) or the child during learning interactions and not doing the harder task of studying the interactions themselves. Two design and analysis problems that make such study difficult are that interactions occur in sequences, and that any one response affects the subsequent responses of either or both parties. (That is, of course, one description of instruction.) Research designs in behavioral psychology, language acquisition, classroom discourse, and ethnomethodology, as well as the work of Bruner (Bruner and Sherwood 1976; Bruner and Garton 1978), could be the source of innovative approaches for interaction study. Sensitive observation of children can shift easily to the observation of interactions, and a guide to the observation of interactions (Bakeman and Gottman 1986) would be helpful.

Some Final Thoughts

A BEGINNING HAS BEEN MADE

Vygotsky's theories (1962; Wertsch 1985) of the support system provided by others for learners at the growing edge of their competence (Bruner 1986) almost confirm recent developments (Au and Kawakami 1984; Clay 1985; Palincsar and Brown 1984). Adults have been shown to work in this way tutoring preschool children (Wood, Bruner, and Ross 1976). "Teachers scaffold budding reading skills through prompts and examples and then foster individual control of reading by gradually removing social supports" (Pintrich et al. 1986). There is more than a scaffold involved, however, because learning in the language and cognitive areas leaves children not only with the ability to produce desired performance but with the inner structures and functions capable of generating that performance (Karmiloff-Smith 1986).

UPDATING THE KNOWLEDGE BASE

A somewhat disturbing claim in recent years has been that we can predict very little about the way an individual will change from infancy to adulthood (Lipsitt

1982), or about the way selected behaviors are achieved from one historical era to another (Baltes, Reese, and Nesselroade 1977; Elder 1974; Lerner 1983). Group predictions often do not hold up for individuals, and they do not hold up even for groups if the social contexts in which we learn are undergoing change. Still, these claims are disturbing, because education operates on assumptions about children's accumulating expertise and continually changing in expected directions during childhood (Kagan 1983), and both the degree and the direction of the expected change are derived from the average majority. That such claims are made implies that knowledge about children gained from research should be checked at quite short intervals, since today's research populations may be responding differently from the original research populations. Replication studies should be funded, as neither developmental psychologists nor educators would want outdated information to limit the learning opportunities of today's children.

References

Au, K., and A. Kawakami. 1984. Vygotskian Perspectives on Discussion Processes in Small Group Reading Lessons. In P. Peterson, L. Wilkinson, and M. Hallinan, eds., *The Social Context of Instruction: Group Organization and Group Processes.* New York: Academic Press.

Bakeman, R., and J. M. Gottman. 1986. *Observing Interaction: An Introduction to Sequential Analysis.* Cambridge: Cambridge University Press.

Baker, L. 1984. Children's Effective Use of Multiple Standards for Evaluating Their Comprehension. *Journal of Educational Psychology* 76: 588–597.

Baltes, P. B. 1983. Lifespan Developmental Psychology: Observations on History and Theory Revisited. In R. M. Lerner, ed., *Developmental Psychology: Historical and Philosophical Perspectives,* pp. 79–111. Hillsdale, NJ: Lawrence Erlbaum.

Baltes, P. B., H. W. Reese, and J. R. Nesselroade. 1977. *Lifespan Developmental Psychology: Introduction to Research Methods.* Monterey, CA: Brooks/Cole.

Bloom, B. 1971. Mastery Learning. In J. H. Block, ed., *Mastery Learning: Theory and Practice.* New York: Holt, Rinehart & Winston.

Bronfenbrenner, U. 1979. *The Ecology of Human Development.* Cambridge, MA: Harvard University Press.

Brown, A. L., and A. S. Palincsar. 1982. Inducing Strategic Learning from Text by Means of Informed Self-Control Training. In S. J. Samuels, ed., *Issues in Reading Diagnosis (Special Issue), Topics in Learning and Learning Disabilities* 2: 1–17.

Brown, R. 1973. *A First Language: The Early Stages.* Great Britain: Allen & Unwin.

Bruner, J. S. 1986. *Actual Minds: Possible Worlds.* Cambridge, MA: Harvard University Press.

Bruner, J. S., and A. Garton, eds. 1978. *Human Growth and Development.* Oxford: Clarendon Press.

Bruner, J. S., and V. Sherwood. 1976. Early Rule Structure: The Case of Peek-a-Boo. In R. Harré, ed., *Life Sentences: Aspects of the Social Role of Language.* New York: Wiley.

Bryant, P. E. 1982. The Role of Conflict and Agreement Between Intellectual Strategies in Children's Ideas About Measurement. *British Journal of Psychology* 73: 243–252.

———. 1984. Piaget, Teachers, and Psychologists. *Oxford Review of Education* 10, 3: 251–259.

Bryant, P. E., and L. Bradley. 1985. *Children's Reading Problems.* Oxford: Blackwell.

Cairns, R. B., and J. Valsiner. 1984. Child Psychology. In M. R. Rozenweig and L. W. Porter, eds., *Annual Review of Psychology* 35: 553–578.

Cazden, C. B. 1988. *Classroom Discourse: The Language of Teaching and Learning.* Portsmouth, NH: Heinemann.

Chapman, L. J. 1983. *Reading Development and Cohesion.* London: Heinemann.

Clay, M. M. 1975. *What Did I Write?* Auckland, NZ: Heinemann.

———. 1979. *Reading: The Patterning of Complex Behavior.* Auckland, NZ: Heinemann.

———. 1985. *The Early Detection of Reading Difficulties.* Auckland, NZ: Heinemann.

Donaldson, M. 1979. *Children's Minds.* New York: Norton.

Elder, G. H. 1974. *Children of the Great Depression.* Chicago: University of Chicago Press.

Ferreiro, E., and A. Teberosky. 1982. *Literacy Before Schooling.* Portsmouth, NH: Heinemann.

Flavell, J. J. 1982. On Cognitive Development. *Child Development* 53: 1–10.

Gamer, R., S. Wagoner, and T. Smith. 1983. Externalizing Question-Answer Strategies of Good and Poor Comprehenders. *Reading Research Quarterly* 16: 439–447.

Gesell, A., and F. L. Ilg. 1946. *The Child from Five to Ten.* New York: Harper.

Goodman, Y. M. 1990. *Literacy Development: Psychogenesis and Pedagogical Implications.* Newark, DE: International Reading Association.

Graves, D. H. 1978. *Balance the Basics: Let Them Write.* New York: Ford Foundation.

———. 1983. *Writing: Teachers and Children at Work.* Portsmouth, NH: Heinemann.

Heath, S. B. 1983. *Ways with Words.* Cambridge: Cambridge University Press.

Isaacs, S. 1935. *Children We Teach.* London: University of London Press.

Kagan, J. 1983. Developmental Categories and the Premise of Connectivity. In R. M. Lerner, ed., *Developmental Psychology: Historical and Philosophical Perspectives.* Hillsdale, NJ: Lawrence Erlbaum.

Karmiloff-Smith, A. 1979. *A Functional Approach to Child Language.* Cambridge, UK: Cambridge University Press.

———. 1986. From Meta-Processes to Conscious Access: Evidence from Children's Metalinguistic and Repair Data. *Cognition* 23: 95–147.

King, M., and V. Rentel. 1979. Towards a Theory of Early Writing Development. *Research in the Teaching of English* 13, 3: 243–253.

Langer, J. A. 1986. *Children Reading and Writing: Structures and Strategies.* Norwood, NJ: Ablex.

Lerner, R. M., ed. 1983. *Developmental Psychology: Historical and Philosophical Perspectives.* Hillsdale, NJ: Lawrence Erlbaum.

Lindfors, J. W. 1987. *Children's Language and Learning.* 2nd ed. Englewood Cliffs, NJ: Prentice-Hall.

Lipsitt, L. P. 1982. Infancy and Life-Span Development. In T. M. Field, A. Huston, H. C. Quay, L. Troll, and G. E. Finlay, eds., *Review of Human Development.* New York: Wiley.

McCandless, B. R., and M. F. Geis. 1975. Current Trends in Developmental Psychology. In H. W. Reese, ed., *Advances in Child Development and Behavior* 10: 1–8. New York: Academic Press.

Miller, G. A. 1951. *Language and Communication.* New York: McGraw-Hill.

Montada, L., and S. H. Fillip. 1976. Implications of Life-Span Developmental Psychology for Childhood Education. In H. W. Reese, ed., *Advances in Child Development and Behavior* 11: 253–266. New York: Academic Press.

Nicholson, T. 1984. Experts and Novices: A Study of Reading in the High School Classroom. *Reading Research Quarterly* 19, 4: 436–451.

Palincsar, A. S., and A. L. Brown. 1984. Reciprocal Teaching of Comprehension Monitoring Activities. *Cognition and Instruction* 2: 117–175.

Pinnell, G. S., and M. L. Matlin. 1989. *Teachers and Research: Language Learning in the Classroom.* Newark, DE: International Reading Association.

Pintrich, P. R., D. R. Cross, R. B. Kozma, and W. J. McGeachie. 1986. Instructional Psychology. In M. R. Rozenweig and L. W. Porter, eds., *Annual Review of Psychology,* pp. 611–654. Palo Alto, CA: Annual Reviews.

Plowden, B. 1967. *Children and Their Primary Schools.* London: Her Majesty's Stationery Office.

Potter, F. 1982. The Use of Linguistic Context: Do Good and Poor Readers Use Different Strategies? *British Journal of Educational Psychology* 52: 16–23.

Read, C. 1975. *Children's Categorizations of Speech Sounds in English.* Urbana, IL: National Council of Teachers of English.

Riegel, K. F. 1979. *Foundations of Dialectical Psychology: Some Historical and Ethical Considerations.* New York: Academic Press.

Schank, R. C., and R. P. Abelson. 1977. *Scripts, Plans, Goals, and Understanding.* Hillsdale, NJ: Lawrence Erlbaum.

Senn, M. J. E. 1975. Insights on the Child Development Movement in the United States. Monograph. *The Society for Research in Child Development* 40, 3–4: 1–107.

Sontag, L. W. 1971. The History of Longitudinal Research: Implications for the Future. *Child Development* 42: 987–1002.

Sternberg, R. J., ed. 1984. *Mechanisms of Cognitive Development.* New York: W. H. Freeman.

Tierney, R. J. 1991. Studies of Reading and Writing Growth: Longitudinal Research on Literacy Development. In J. Flood, J. M. Jensen, D. Lapp, and J. R. Squire, eds., *Handbook of Research on Teaching the English Language Arts,* pp. 176–194. New York: Macmillan.

Vygotsky, L. S. 1962. *Thought and Language.* Cambridge, MA: MIT Press.

Wagoner, S. 1983. Comprehension Monitoring: What It Is and What We Have to Know About It. *Reading Research Quarterly* 18: 328–346.

Weikart, D. P., L. Rogers, C. Adcock, and D. McClelland. 1971. *The Cognitively-Oriented Curriculum.* Urbana, IL: University of Illinois.

Wertsch, J. V. 1985. *Vygotsky and the Social Formation of Mind.* Cambridge, MA: Harvard University Press.

Wood, D., J. S. Bruner, and G. Ross. 1976. The Role of Tutoring in Problem-Solving. *Journal of Child Psychology and Child Psychiatry* 17: 89–100.

REFERENCES

This list is a compilation of all the sources cited in the text. Citations within chapters are found in the reference section at the end of each chapter.

Adams, M. J. 1990. *Beginning to Read: Thinking and Learning About Print.* Cambridge, MA: MIT Press.

Allington, R. 1984. Content Coverage and Contextual Reading in Reading Groups. *Journal of Reading Behavior* 16: 85–95.

Aman, M. G., and Singh. 1983. Specific Reading Disorders: Concepts of Etiology Reconsidered. In K. D. Gadow and I. Bailer, eds., *Advances in Learning and Behavioral Disabilities,* Vol. 3, pp. 1–47. Greenwich, CT: JAI Press.

Anderson, R. C., and B. B. Armbruster. 1990. *Some Maxims for Learning and Instruction.* Technical Report No. 491. Champaign, IL: Center for the Study of Reading, University of Illinois.

Art in New Zealand Schools. 1978. Wellington, NZ: School Publications Department of Education.

Au, K., and A. Kawakami. 1984. Vygotskian Perspectives on Discussion Processes in Small Group Reading Lessons. In P. Peterson, L. Wilkinson, and M. Hallinan, eds., *The Social Context of Instruction: Group Organization and Group Processes.* New York: Academic Press.

Bakeman, R. and J. M. Gottman. 1986. *Observing Interaction: An Introduction to Sequential Analysis.* Cambridge: Cambridge University Press.

Baker, L. 1984. Children's Effective Use of Multiple Standards for Evaluating Their Comprehension. *Journal of Educational Psychology* 76: 588–597.

———. 1994. Fostering Meta-Cognitive Development. In H. W. Reese, ed., *Advances in Child Development and Behavior,* Vol. 25, pp. 201–239. San Diego: Academic Press.

Baltes, P. B. 1983. Lifespan Developmental Psychology: Observations on History and Theory Revisited. In R. M. Lerner, ed., *Developmental Psychology: Historical and Philosophical Perspectives,* pp. 79–111. Hillsdale, NJ: Lawrence Erlbaum.

Baltes, P. B., H. W. Reese, and J. R. Nesselroade. 1977. *Lifespan Developmental Psychology: Introduction to Research Methods.* Monterey, CA: Brooks/Cole.

Barr, R. 1984. Beginning Reading Instruction: From Debate to Reformation. In P. D. Pearson, R. Barr, M. L. Kamil, and P. Rosenthal, eds., *Handbook of Reading Research,* Vol. 1, pp. 545–581. New York: Longman.

Berman, R. A., and D. I. Slobin. 1994. *Relating Events in Narrative: A Cross-Linguistic Developmental Study.* Hillsdale, NJ: Lawrence Erlbaum.

Biemiller, A. 1970. The Development of the Use of Graphic and Contextual Information as Children Learn to Read. *Reading Research Quarterly* 6: 75–96.

Bissex, G. L. 1980. *Gnys at Wrk: A Child Learns to Write and Read.* Cambridge, MA: Harvard University Press.

Bloom, B. 1971. Mastery Learning. In J. H. Block, ed., *Mastery Learning: Theory and Practice.* New York: Holt, Rinehart & Winston.

Bloom, L., and M. Lahey. 1978. *Language Development and Language Disorders.* New York: Wiley.

Boomer, G. 1988. Organizing the Nation for Literacy. In *Working Papers on Public Education,* Vol. 1. Victoria, Australia: State Board of Education.

Brailsford, A. 1985. Kindergarten Children's Literacy Experiences. Ph.D. diss., University of Alberta.

Brogan, M. 1981. *I'll Tell You About Your Painting.* Auckland, NZ: Play Centre Journal.

Bronfenbrenner, U. 1979. *The Ecology of Human Development.* Cambridge, MA: Harvard University Press.

Brown, A. L. 1980. Metacognitive Development and Reading. In R. J. Spiro, C. Bruce, and W. F. Brewer, eds., *Theoretical Issues in Reading Comprehension,* pp. 453–481. Hillsdale, NJ: Lawrence Erlbaum.

Brown, A. L., and A. S. Palincsar. 1982. Inducing Strategic Learning from Text by Means of Informed Self-Control Training. In S. J. Samuels, ed., *Issues in Reading Diagnosis (Special Issue), Topics in Learning and Learning Disabilities* 2: 1–17.

Brown, A. L., and S. S. Smiley. 1978. The Development of Strategies for Studying Texts. *Child Development* 49: 1076–1088.

Brown, R. 1973. *A First Language: The Early Stages.* Great Britain: Allen & Unwin.

———. 1977. Introduction. In C. E. Snow and C. A. Ferguson, eds., *Talking to Children: Language Input and Acquisition.* New York: Cambridge University Press.

Bruer, J. T. 1994. *Schools for Thought: A Science of Learning in the Classroom.* Cambridge, MA: MIT Press.

Brugelmann, H. J. 1986. Discovering Print: A Process Approach to Initial Reading and Writing in West Germany. *The Reading Teacher* 40, 3: 294–298.

Bruner, J. S. 1957. On Perceptual Readiness. *Psychological Review* 64: 123–152.

———. 1983. *Child's Talk: Learning to Use Language.* London: Norton.
———. 1986. *Actual Minds: Possible Worlds.* Cambridge, MA: Harvard University Press.
———. 1990. *Acts of Meaning.* Cambridge, MA: Harvard University Press.
Bruner, J. S., and A. Garton, eds. 1978. *Human Growth and Development.* Oxford: Clarendon Press.
Bruner, J. S., and H. Haste. 1987. *Making Sense: The Child's Construction of the World.* London: Methuen.
Bruner, J. S., and V. Sherwood. 1976. Early Rule Structure: The Case of Peek-a-Boo. In R. Harré, ed., *Life Sentences: Aspects of the Social Role of Language.* New York: Wiley.
Bryant, P. E. 1982. The Role of Conflict and Agreement Between Intellectual Strategies in Children's Ideas About Measurement. *British Journal of Psychology* 73: 243–252.
———. 1984. Piaget, Teachers, and Psychologists. *Oxford Review of Education* 10, 3: 251–259.
Bryant, P. E., and L. Bradley. 1985. *Children's Reading Problems.* Oxford: Blackwell.
Bussis, A. M., E. A. Chittenden, and M. Amarel. 1976. *Beyond the Surface Curriculum.* Boulder, CO: Westerview Press.
Butler, D. 1980. *Babies Need Books.* London: Bodley Head.
———. 1986. *Five to Eight.* London: Bodley Head.
Butler, D., and M. M. Clay. 1979. *Reading Begins at Home.* Auckland, NZ: Heinemann.
Cairns, R. B., and J. Valsiner. 1984. Child Psychology. In M. R. Rozenweig and L. W. Porter, eds., *Annual Review of Psychology* 35: 553–578.
Campione, J. C. 1987. Metacognitive Components of Instructional Research with Problem Learners. In F. E. Weinert and R. H. Kluwe, eds., *Metacognition, Motivation, and Understanding,* pp. 117–140. Hillsdale, NJ: Lawrence Erbaum.
Caplan, G. 1964. *Principles of Preventive Psychiatry.* London: Tavistock Publications.
Carrier, J. G. 1984. Comparative Special Education: Ideology, Differentiation, and Allocation in England and the United States. In L. Barton and S. Tomlinson, eds., *Special Education and Social Interest,* pp. 35–64. Beckenham: Croom Helm.
Cazden, C. B. 1972. *Child Language and Education.* New York: Holt, Rinehart & Winston.
———. 1974. Play with Language and Meta-Linguistic Awareness: One Dimension of Language Experience. *Organization Mondiale Pour l' Education Prescolaire* 6: 12–24.
———. 1988a. *Classroom Discourse: The Language of Teaching and Learning.* Portsmouth, NH: Heinemann.
———. 1988b. *Interactions Between Maori Children and Pakeha Teachers.* Auckland, NZ: Auckland Reading Association.
———. 1991. Active Learners and Active Teachers. In J. F. Flood, J. Jensen, D. Lapp, and J. R. Squire, eds., *Handbook of Research on Teaching the English Language Arts.* New York: Macmillan.
———. 1992. Revealing and Telling: The Socialization of Attention in Learning to Read and Write. *Educational Psychology* 12, 3–4: 305–313.
———. 1995. Bernstein's Visible and Invisible Pedagogies: Reading Recovery as a Mixed System. Paper presented at AERA, San Francisco.
Cazden, C. B., and H. Mehan. 1989. Principles from Sociology and Anthropology: Context, Code, Classroom, and Culture. In M. C. Reynolds, ed., *Knowledge Base for the Beginning Teacher.* Oxford: Pergamon.
Chall, J. 1967. *Learning to Read: The Great Debate.* New York: McGraw-Hill.

———. 1979. *Stages of Reading Development.* New York: McGraw-Hill.

Chapman, L. J. 1983. *Reading Development and Cohesion.* London: Heinemann.

Chomsky, C. 1969. *The Acquisition of Syntax in Children Five to Ten.* Cambridge, MA: MIT Press.

———. 1975. How Sister Got into the Grog. *Early Years* (November): pp. 36–39.

Church, J. 1966. *Three Babies: Biographies of Cognitive Development.* New York: Random House.

Clark, M. M. 1976. *Young Fluent Readers.* London: Heinemann.

Clay, M. M. 1966. Emergent Reading Behaviour. Ph.D. diss., University of Auckland.

———. 1967. The Reading Behaviour of Five-Year-Old Children: A Research Report. *New Zealand Journal of Educational Studies* 2, 1: 11–31.

———. 1968. A Syntactic Analysis of Reading Errors. *Journal of Verbal Learning and Verbal Behavior* 7: 434–438.

———. 1969. Reading Errors and Self-Correction Behaviour. *British Journals of Educational Psychology* 39: 47–56.

———. 1970. An Increasing Effect of Disorientation on the Discrimination of Print: A Developmental Study. *Journal of Experimental Psychology* 9: 297–306.

———. 1974. Orientation to the Spatial Characteristics of the Open Book. *Visible Language* 8, 3: 275–282.

———. 1975. *What Did I Write?* Auckland, NZ: Heinemann.

———. 1977. *Write Now: Read Later.* Auckland, NZ: Auckland Council of the International Reading Association.

———. 1979. *Reading: The Patterning of Complex Behavior.* Auckland, NZ: Heinemann.

———. 1982. *Observing Young Readers: Selected Papers.* Portsmouth, NH: Heinemann.

———. 1983. Getting a Theory of Writing. In B. M. Kroll and G. Wells, eds., *Explorations in the Development of Writing.* Chichester, UK: Wiley.

———. 1985a. *The Early Detection of Reading Difficulties.* 3rd ed. Auckland, NZ: Heinemann. (Includes test booklets "Sand" and "Stones.")

———. 1985b. Engaging with the School System: A Study of New Entrant Classrooms. *New Zealand Journal of Educational Studies* 20, 1: 20–38.

———. 1985c. Reading Recovery: Systemic Adaptation to an Educational Innovation. *New Zealand Journal of Educational Studies* 22, 1: 35–58.

———. 1987a. Learning to Be Learning Disabled. *New Zealand Journal of Educational Studies* 22: 155–173.

———. 1987b. Sailing On-Course: Language Development. *New Zealand Childcare Quarterly* 7, 3: 21–27.

———. 1987c. *Writing Begins at Home: Preparing Children for Writing Before They Go to School.* Auckland, NZ: Heinemann.

———. 1989. Concepts About Print: In English and Other Languages. *The Reading Teacher* 42, 4: 268–277.

———. 1991. *Becoming Literate: The Construction of Inner Control.* Auckland, NZ: Heinemann.

———. 1993a. *An Observation Survey of Early Literacy Achievement.* Auckland, NZ: Heinemann.

———. 1993b. *Reading Recovery: A Guidebook for Teachers in Training.* Auckland, NZ: Heinemann.
———. 1997a. Letter to the Editors. *Reading Research Quarterly* 32, 1: 114.
———. 1997b. *Using Concepts About Print with School Entrants.* In SET Special, Wellington, NZ: New Zealand Council for Educational Research.
———. 1998. The Development of Literacy Difficulties. In D. Corson et al., eds., *Encyclopedia of Language and Education,* Vol. 2, *Literacy.* Dordrecht, Netherlands: Kluwer Academic.
Clay, M. M., and C. B. Cazden. 1990. A Vygotskyan Interpretation of Reading Recovery. In L. Moll, ed., *Vygotsky and Education: Instructional Implications and Applications of Sociohistorical Psychology,* pp. 206–222. Cambridge, UK: Cambridge University Press.
Clay, M. M., M. Gill, T. Glynn, T. McNaughton, and K. Salmon. 1983. *Record of Oral Language* and *Biks and Gutches.* Auckland, NZ: Heinemann.
Coles, G. S. 1978. The Learning-Disabilities Test Battery: Empirical and Social Issues. *Harvard Educational Review* 48: 313–339.
Dalgren, G., and L. E. Olsson. 1986. The Child's Conception of Reading. Paper presented to the American Education Research Association, San Francisco, CA, April.
Day, H. D., and K. C. Day. 1980. The Reliability and Validity of the Concepts About Print and Record of Oral Language. *Resources in Education,* ED 179–932. Arlington, VA: ERIC Document Reproduction Service.
Day, K. C., H. D. Day, R. Spicola, and M. Griffin. 1981. The Development of Orthographic Linguistic Awareness in Kindergarten Children and the Relationship of This Awareness to Later Reading Achievement. *Reading Psychology* 2, 2: 76–87.
Delpit, L. D. 1986. Skills and Other Dilemmas of a Progressive Black Educator. *Harvard Educational Review* 56, 4: 379–385.
———. 1992. Acquisition of Literate Discourse. *Theory into Practice* 3: 296–302.
Dewey, G. 1970. *English Spelling: Roadblock to Reading.* New York: Teachers College Press, Columbia University.
Diack, H. 1960. *Reading and the Psychology of Perception.* Nottingham, England: Peter Skinner.
Donaldson, M. 1979. *Children's Minds.* New York: Norton.
Downing, J. 1970. Children's Concepts of Language in Learning to Read. *Educational Research* 12: 106–112.
———. 1971–72. Children's Developing Concepts of Spoken and Written Language. *Journal of Reading Behavior* 4, 1: 1–19.
———. 1979. *Reading and Reasoning.* New York: Springer.
Downing, J., and C. K. Leong. 1982. *Psychology of Reading.* New York: Macmillan/Collier.
Duckworth, E. 1979. Either We're Too Early and They Can't Learn It or We're Too Late and They Know It Already: The Dilemma of "Applying Piaget." *Harvard Educational Review* 49, 3: 297–312.
———. 1984. Teaching as Research. *Harvard Educational Review* 56, 4: 273–274.
Dyson, A. H. 1982. The Emergence of Visible Language: Interrelationships Between Drawing and Early Writing. *Visible Language* 6: 360–381.

———. 1983. The Role of Oral Language in Early Writing Processes. *Research in the Teaching of English* 17: 1–30.

———. 1987. Individual Differences in Beginning Composing: An Orchestral Vision of Learning to Compose. *Written Communication* 4: 411–442.

———. 1990. *Weaving Possibilities: Rethinking Metaphors for Early Literacy Development.* Occasional Paper 19. Berkeley: University of California, Center for the Study of Writing.

———. 1994. Viewpoints: The Word and the World Reconceptualizing Written Language Development or Do Rainbows Mean a Lot to Little Girls? In R. B. Ruddell, M. R. Ruddell, and H. Singer, eds., *Theoretical Models and Processes of Reading.* 3rd ed. Newark, DE: International Reading Association.

Ehri, L. C. 1987. Learning to Read and Spell Words. *Journal of Reading Behavior* 19: 5–31.

———. 1991. Development of the Ability to Read Words. In R. Barr, M. L. Kamil, P. Mosenthal, and P. D. Pearson, eds., *Handbook of Reading Research,* Vol. 2, pp. 383–417. White Plains, NY: Longman.

———. 1994. Development of the Ability to Read Words: Update. In R. B. Ruddell, M. R. Ruddell, and H. Singer, eds., *Theoretical Models and Processes of Reading.* 4th ed. Newark, DE: International Reading Association.

Elder, G. H. 1974. *Children of the Great Depression.* Chicago: University of Chicago Press.

Elkonin, D. B. 1971. The Development of Speech. In A. V. Zaporozhets and D. B. Elkonin, eds., *The Psychology of Preschool Children,* pp. 111–185. Cambridge, MA: MIT Press.

———. 1973. Reading in the USSR. In J. Downing, ed., *Comparative Reading,* pp. 551–580. New York: Macmillan.

Elley, W. B. 1992. *How in the World Do Students Read?: The I.E.A. Study of Reading Literacy.* Hamburg: The International Association for the Evaluation of Educational Achievement.

Escamilla, K., A. M. Andrade, A. G. M. Basurto, and O. A. Ruiz. 1994. *Instrumento de Observación de los logros de la lecto-escritura inicial: Spanish Reconstruction of* An Observation Survey: *A Bilingual Text.* Portsmouth, NH: Heinemann.

Ferreiro, E. 1993. Some Remarks About the Acquisition of Written Language as a Conceptual Object. European Science Foundation, Second Workshop on Written Language and Literacy, Wassenaar, the Netherlands. October.

Ferreiro, E., and A. Teberosky. 1982. *Literacy Before Schooling.* Portsmouth, NH: Heinemann.

Flavell, J. J. 1982. On Cognitive Development. *Child Development* 53: 1–10.

Fletcher-Flinn, C., and H. Snelson. 1997. The Relation Between Metalinguistic Ability, Social Metacognition, and Reading: A Developmental Study. *New Zealand Journal of Psychology* 26, 1: 20–28.

Frith, U. 1985. Beneath the Surface of Developmental Dyslexia. In K. E. Patterson, J. C. Marshall, and M. Coltheart, eds., *Surface Dyslexia,* pp. 301–330. London: Erlbaum.

Frith, U., and J. M. Volers. 1980. *Some Perceptual Prerequisites for Reading: The World of Two-Dimensional Space.* Newark, DE: International Reading Association.

Gaffney, J., and R. Anderson. 1991. Two-Tiered Scaffolding: Congruent Processes of Teaching and Learning. Technical Report No. 523, Center for the Study of Reading, University of Illinois at Urbana-Champaign.

Gamer, R., S. Wagoner, and T. Smith. 1983. Externalizing Question-Answer Strategies of Good and Poor Comprehenders. *Reading Research Quarterly* 16: 439–447.

Genishi, C., and A. Dyson. 1984. *Language Assessment in the Early Years.* Norwood, NJ: Ablex Publishing.

Gentry, J. R. 1978. Early Spelling Strategies. *Elementary School Journal* 79: 88–92.

Gesell, A., and F. L. Ilg. 1946. *The Child from Five to Ten.* New York: Harper.

Gibson, E. J. 1965. Learning to Read. *Science* 148: 1066–1072.

———. 1969. *Principles of Perceptual Learning and Development.* New York: Appleton-Century-Crofts.

Gibson, E., and H. Levin. 1975. *The Psychology of Reading.* Cambridge, MA: MIT Press.

Girling-Butcher, W., G. W. Phillips, and M. M. Clay. 1991. Fostering Independent Learning. *The Reading Teacher* 44, 9: 694–697.

Gitomer, D. H., and R. Glaser. 1987. If You Don't Know It Work on It: Knowledge, Self-Regulation and Instruction. In R. E. Snow and M. J. Farr, eds., *Aptitude, Learning, and Instructions: Vol. 3, Conative and Affective Process Analyses,* pp. 301–325. Hillsdale, NJ: Lawrence Erlbaum.

Gittleman, R. 1985. Controlled Trials of Remedial Approaches to Reading Disability. *Journal of Child Psychology and Psychiatry* 26: 843–846.

Goodman, Y. M. 1981. Test Review: Concepts About Print. *The Reading Teacher* 34, 4: 445–448.

———. 1990a. *Literacy Development: Psychogenesis and Pedagogical Implications.* Newark, DE: International Reading Association.

———, ed. 1990b. *How Children Construct Literacy: Piagetian Perspectives.* Newark, DE: International Reading Association.

Goodnow, J. 1977. *Children's Drawing.* Glasgow, Scotland: Fontana.

Gough, P. B. 1972. One Second of Reading. *Visible Language* 6, 4: 291–320. Republished in R. B. Ruddell, M. R. Ruddell, and H. Singer, eds. 1985. *Theoretical Models and Processes of Reading,* 3rd ed., pp. 661–686. Newark, DE: International Reading Association.

Gough, P. B., and M. L. Hillinger. 1988. Learning to Read: An Unnatural Act. *Bulletin of the Orton Society* 30: 179–196.

Grace, P. 1987. *Electric City and Other Stories.* Auckland, NZ: Penguin.

Graves, D. H. 1978. *Balance the Basics: Let Them Write.* New York: Ford Foundation.

———. 1983. *Writing: Teachers and Children at Work.* Portsmouth, NH: Heinemann.

Griffin, M., R. Spicola, A. Banks, and E. Reyes. 1985. *A Comparison of Developmental Patterns in Print Awareness in Indian, Mexican-American, and Black Children, Ages 3 to 7.* Denton, TX: College of Education, Texas Woman's University.

Grossi, E. P. 1990. Applying Psychogenesis Principles to the Literacy Instruction of Lower-Class Children in Brazil. In Y. Goodman, ed., *How Children Construct Literacy: Piagetian Perspectives,* pp 99–114. Newark, DE: International Reading Association.

Haber, R. N. 1978. Visual Perception. *Annual Review of Psychology* 29: 31–59.

Hall, N. 1987. *The Emergence of Literacy.* Portsmouth, NH: Heinemann.

Hanlon, N. 1977. Patterns of Verbal Interaction: The Effect of Situational Influences on the Language of Performance of Eight-Year-Old Children. Ph.D. diss., University of Waikato, Hamilton, New Zealand.

Hansen, V. R., and O. Robenhagan. 1993. *Abdullah's Genuine Indonesian Curry Powder.* Copenhagen: The Danish National Institute for Educational Research.

Harris, T., and R. E. Hodges, eds. 1995. *The Literacy Dictionary: The Vocabulary of Reading and Writing.* Newark, DE: International Reading Association.

Heath, S. B. 1982. What No Bedtime Story Means: Narrative Skills at Home and at School. *Language in Society* 11: 49–76.

———. 1983. *Ways with Words.* Cambridge: Cambridge University Press.

Herber, H. L. 1994. Professional Connections: Pioneers and Contemporaries in Reading. In R. B. Ruddell, M. R. Ruddell, and H. Singer, eds., *Theoretical Models and Processes of Reading.* 3rd ed. Newark, DE: International Reading Association.

Herdan, G. 1956. *Language as Choice and Chance.* Growingen: P. Noordhof.

Hobsbaum, A., S. Peters, and K. Sylva. 1996. Scaffolding in Reading Recovery. *Oxford Review of Education* 22, 1: 17–35.

Holdaway, D. 1979. *The Foundations of Literacy.* Sydney: Ashton Scholastic.

Ilg, F. L., and L. B. Ames. 1950. Developmental Trends in Reading Behavior. *Journal of Genetic Psychology* 76: 291–312.

Isaacs, S. 1935. *Children We Teach.* London: University of London Press.

Iturrondo, A. M. 1985. *Story Reading and the Knowledge of Printed Spanish: Exploring Their Relationship in the Preschool Classroom.* Research Report. Rio Piedras: University of Puerto Rico.

Jamieson, P. 1977. Adult-Child Talk. In G. MacDonald, ed., *Early Childhood Conference Papers.* Massey University, Wellington: New Zealand Council for Educational Research.

Johns, J. L. 1980. First Graders' Concepts About Print. *Reading Research Quarterly* 15, 4: 529–549.

Johnston, P. H. 1985. Understanding Reading Disability: A Case Study Approach. *Harvard Educational Review* 55: 153–177.

Juel, C. 1988. Learning to Read and Write: A Longitudinal Study of 54 Children from First Through Fourth Grades. *Journal of Educational Psychology* 80: 437–447.

———. 1991. Beginning Reading. In R. Barr, M. L. Kamil, P. Mosenthal, and P. D. Pearson, eds., *Handbook of Reading Research,* Vol. 2, pp. 759–788. White Plains, NY: Longman.

Juel, C., and J. A. Leavell. 1988. Retention and Nonretention of At-Risk Readers in First Grade and Their Subsequent Reading Achievement. *Journal of Reading Disabilities* 21: 571–580.

Kagan, J. 1983. Developmental Categories and the Premise of Connectivity. In R. M. Lerner, ed., *Developmental Psychology: Historical and Philosophical Perspectives.* Hillsdale, NJ: Lawrence Erlbaum.

Karmiloff-Smith, A. 1979. *A Functional Approach to Child Language.* Cambridge, UK: Cambridge University Press.

———. 1986. From Meta-Processes to Conscious Access: Evidence from Children's Metalinguistic and Repair Data. *Cognition* 23: 95–147.

———. 1992. *Beyond Modularity: A Developmental Perspective on Cognitive Science.* Cambridge, MA: MIT Press.

Katz, I., and H. Singer. 1982. The Substrata-Factor Theory of Reading: Differential Development of Subsystems Underlying Reading Comprehension in the First Year. In J. A. Niles and L. A. Harris, eds., *New Inquiry in Reading Research and Instruction.* (Thirty-

First Yearbook of the National Reading Conference.) Rochester, NY: National Reading Conference.

———. 1984. The Substrata-Factor Theory of Reading: Subsystem Patterns Underlying Achievement in Beginning Reading. In J. A. Niles, ed., *Thirty-Third Yearbook of the National Reading Conference.* Rochester, NY: National Reading Conference.

Katz, L. G., and S. C. Chard. 1989. *Engaging Children's Minds: The Project Approach.* Norwood, NJ: Ablex.

Kephart, N. C. 1960. *The Slow Learner in the Classroom.* Columbus, OH: Charles E. Merrill.

Kerin, A. 1987. One-to-One Interaction in Junior Classes. Master's thesis, University of Auckland.

King, M. L. 1977. Evaluating Reading. *Theory into Practice* 16, 5: 407–418.

———. 1980. Learning How to Mean in Written Language. *Theory into Practice* 19, 3: 163–169.

King, M. L., and V. Rentel. 1979. Towards a Theory of Early Writing Development. *Research in the Teaching of English* 13, 3: 243–253.

Kolers, P. 1970. Three Stages of Reading. In H. Levin and J. Williams, eds., *Basic Studies on Reading,* pp. 90–118. New York: Basic Books.

Kontos, S., and J. G. Nicholas. 1986. Independent Problem-Solving in the Development of Metacognition. *Journal of Genetic Psychology* 147: 481–495.

Kumar, K. 1986. "Ashok's Story." Department of Education, Delhi University. Unpublished private communication and translation.

Langer, J. A. 1986. *Children Reading and Writing: Structures and Strategies.* Norwood, NJ: Ablex.

Learning Media. 1992. *Dancing with a Pen.* Wellington, NZ: Ministry of Education.

Lerner, R. M., ed. 1983. *Developmental Psychology: Historical and Philosophical Perspectives.* Hillsdale, NJ: Lawrence Erlbaum.

Levin, H. 1990. *Building School Capacity for Effective Teacher Empowerment: Applications to Elementary Schools with At-Risk Students.* Stanford, CA: Stanford University School of Education.

Levin, I., and O. Korat. 1993. Sensitivity to Phonological, Morphological, and Semantic Cues in Early Reading and Writing in Hebrew. *Merril-Palmer Quarterly* 39, 2: 213.

Levin, I., and L. Tolchinsky Landsmann. 1989. Becoming Literate: Referential and Phonetic Strategies in Early Reading and Writing. *International Journal of Behavioral Development* 12, 3: 369–384.

Lewin, K. 1954. Behavior and Development as a Function of the Total Situation. In L. Carmichael, ed., *Manual of Child Psychology.* New York: Wiley.

Lindfors, J. W. 1987. *Children's Language and Learning.* 2nd ed. Englewood Cliffs, NJ: Prentice-Hall.

Lipsitt, L. P. 1982. Infancy and Life-Span Development. In T. M. Field, A. Huston, H. C. Quay, L. Troll, and G. E. Finlay, eds., *Review of Human Development.* New York: Wiley.

Luke, A., and P. Freebody. 1997. Shaping the Social Practices of Reading. In *Literacy: Meeting the Challenge Conference Papers.* New South Wales: Department of School Education.

Lyons, C. A. 1997. Reading Recovery and Learning Disability: Issues, Challenges, and Implications. In S. L. Swartz and A. F. Klein, eds., *Research in Reading Recovery.* Portsmouth, NH: Heinemann.

Mattingly, I. G. 1972. Reading, the Linguistic Process, and Linguistic Awareness. In J. F. Kavanagh and I. G. Mattingly, eds., *Language by Ear and Eye,* pp. 133–147. Cambridge, MA: MIT Press.

———. 1978. The Psycholinguistic Basis of Linguistic Awareness. Paper presented at the annual meeting of the National Reading Conference, St. Petersburg, FL.

———. 1979. Reading, Linguistic Awareness and Language Acquisition. Paper presented at the International Reading Association–University of Victoria International Research Seminar on Linguistic Awareness and Learning to Read, Victoria, BC.

McCandless, B. R., and M. F. Geis. 1975. Current Trends in Developmental Psychology. In H. W. Reese, ed., *Advances in Child Development and Behavior* 10: 1–8. New York: Academic Press.

McGill-Franzen, A., and R. L. Allington. 1990. Comprehension and Coherence: Neglected Elements of Literacy Instruction in Remedial and Resource Room Services. *Journal of Reading, Writing, and Learning Disabilities* 6: 149–180.

McKenzie, M. 1981. *Extending Literacy.* London: Inner London Educational Authority Centre for Primary Education.

———. 1986. *Journeys into Literacy.* Huddersfield, UK: Schofield and Sims.

McLane, J. B., and G. D. McNamee. 1990. *Early Literacy.* Cambridge, MA: Harvard University Press.

McNaughton, S. 1995. *Patterns of Emergent Literacy: Development and Transition.* Auckland, NZ: Oxford University Press.

Meade, A. 1982. Who Talks to William? and Karla, and Susan, and Michael, and . . . ? Adult-Child Interaction, Particularly in Conversation, in Early Childhood Centres. SET No. 1. Wellington: New Zealand Council for Educational Research.

Meek, M. 1982. *Learning to Read.* London: Bodley Head.

———. 1988. *How Texts Teach What Readers Learn.* Stroud, UK: The Thimble Press.

Metge, J., and P. Kinloch. 1978. *Talking Past Each Other: Problems of Cross-cultural Communication.* Wellington, NZ: Victoria University Press.

Miller, G. A. 1951. *Language and Communication.* New York: McGraw Hill.

———. 1981. *Language and Speech.* San Francisco: Freeman.

Ministry of Education, Israel. 1995. *Concepts About Print: A Tool for Assessing the Buds of Knowledge.* Jerusalem: Ministry of Education.

Montada, L., and S. H. Fillip. 1976. Implications of Life-Span Developmental Psychology for Childhood Education. In H. W. Reese, ed., *Advances in Child Development and Behavior* 11: 253–266. New York: Academic Press.

Moore, D. W. 1981. First and Last, One and Two, Letter and Word: Concept Formation in Papua–New Guinean Community Schools. Paper presented to the Fourth National Conference on Mathematics, Lae, Papua–New Guinea.

New Zealand Ministry of Education. 1985. *Reading in the Junior Classes.* Wellington, NZ: Learning Media.

———. 1996. *The Learner as a Reader: Developing Reading Programs.* Wellington, NZ: Learning Media.

Nicholson, T. 1984. Experts and Novices: A Study of Reading in the High School Classroom. *Reading Research Quarterly* 19, 4: 436–451.

Ninio, A., and C. E. Snow. 1988. Language Acquisition Through Language Use: The Functional Sources of Children's Early Utterances. In Y. Levy, I. M. Schlesinger, and M. D. S. Braine, eds., *Categories and Processes in Language Acquisition*, pp. 11–30. Hillsdale, NJ: Lawrence Erlbaum.

O'Leary, S. 1997. *Five Kids: Stories of Children Learning to Read.* Bothell, WA: Wright Group.

Paley, V. G. 1981. *Wally's Stories.* Cambridge, MA: Harvard University Press.

Palincsar, A. S., and A. L. Brown. 1984. Reciprocal Teaching of Comprehension Monitoring Activities. *Cognition and Instruction* 2: 117–175.

———. 1986. Interactive Teaching to Promote Independent Learning from Text. *The Reading Teacher* 39, 8: 771–777.

Paris, S. G., and P. Winograd. 1990. How Metacogntion Can Promote Academic Learning and Instruction. In B. F. Jones and L. Idol, eds., *Dimensions of Thinking and Cognitive Instruction*, pp. 15–51. Hillsdale, NJ: Lawrence Erlbaum.

Perkins, K. C. 1978. *Developmental Observations of Kindergarten Children's Understanding in Regard to Concepts About Print, Language Development, and Reading Behavior.* Denton, TX: College of Education, Texas Woman's University.

Phillips, G. E. 1997. An Analysis of the Co-Construction of Context in Beginning Reading Instruction. Ph.D. diss., University of Auckland.

Phillips, G. E., and P. Smith. 1997. *A Third Chance to Learn: The Development and Evaluation of Specialized Interventions for Young Children Experiencing the Greatest Difficulty in Learning to Read.* Wellington: New Zealand Council for Educational Research.

Pick, H. L. 1992. Eleanor J. Gibson: Learning to Perceive and Perceiving to Learn. *Developmental Psychology* 28, 5: 787–794.

Pickard, P. M. 1975. *The Activity of Children.* London: Longmans Green.

Pinnell, G. S., M. D. Fried, and R. M. Estice. 1990. Reading Recovery: Learning How to Make a Difference. *The Reading Teacher* 43: 282–295.

Pinnell, G. S., and M. L. Matlin. 1989. *Teachers and Research: Language Learning in the Classroom.* Newark, DE: International Reading Association.

Pintrich, P. R., D. R. Cross, R. B. Kozma, and W. J. McGeachie. 1986. Instructional Psychology. In M. R. Rozenweig and L. W. Porter, eds., *Annual Review of Psychology*, pp. 611–654. Palo Alto, CA: Annual Reviews.

Plowden, B. 1967. *Children and Their Primary Schools.* London: Her Majesty's Stationery Office.

Pogrow, S. 1990a. Challenging At-Risk Students: Findings from the HOTS Program. *Phi Delta Kappan* (January): 389–397.

———. 1990b. A Socratic Approach to Using Computers with At-Risk Students. *Educational Leadership* (February): 61–66.

Potter, F. 1982. The Use of Linguistic Context: Do Good and Poor Readers Use Different Strategies? *British Journal of Educational Psychology* 52: 16–23.

Rayner, K., and A. Pollatsek. 1987. Eye Movements in Reading: A Tutorial Review. In M. Coltheart, ed., *Attention and Performance 12: The Psychology of Reading.* Hillsdale, NJ: Lawrence Erlbaum.

Read, C. 1975. *Children's Categorization of Speech Sounds in English.* Urbana, IL: National Council of Teachers of English.

———. 1986. *Children's Creative Spelling.* London: Routledge and Kegan Paul.

Reid, J. 1966. Learning to Think About Reading. *Educational Research* 9, 1: 56–62.

Resnick, L. B., and D. P. Resnick. 1990. *Tests as Standards of Achievement in Schools.* Proceedings of the ETS Invitational Conference on the Uses of Standardized Tests in American Education. Princeton: Educational Testing Service.

Richardson, E. S. 1964. *In the Early World.* Wellington, NZ: New Zealand Council of Educational Research.

Riegel, K. F. 1979. *Foundations of Dialectical Psychology: Some Historical and Ethical Considerations.* New York: Academic Press.

Robinson, H. M. 1967. Insights from Research: Children's Behavior While Reading. In W. D. Page, ed., *Help for the Reading Reacher: New Directions in Research.* National Conference on Research in English.

Robinson, S. E. 1973. Predicting Early Reading Progress. Master's thesis, University of Auckland.

Rodriguez, I. 1983. Administration of the Concepts About Print SAND Test to Kindergarten Children of Limited English Proficiency Utilizing Four Test Conditions. Ph.D. diss., Texas Woman's University, Denton, TX.

Rowe, M. B. 1986. Wait Time: Slowing Down May Be a Way of Speeding Up. *Journal of Teacher Education* 37: 43–50.

Ruddell, R. B., M. R. Ruddell, and H. Singer, eds. 1994. *Theoretical Models and Processes of Reading.* 4th ed. Newark, DE: International Reading Association.

Rumelhart, D. E. 1994. Toward an Interactive Model of Reading. In R. B. Ruddell, M. R. Ruddell, and H. Singer, eds., *Theoretical Models and Processes of Reading,* 4th ed., pp. 864–894. Newark, DE: International Reading Association.

Samuels, S. J. 1994. Toward a Theory of Automatic Information Processing in Reading, Revisited. In R. B. Ruddell, M. R. Ruddell, and H. Singer, eds., *Theoretical Models and Processes of Reading,* 4th ed., pp. 816–837. Newark, DE: International Reading Association.

Schank, R. C., and R. P. Abelson. 1977. *Scripts, Plans, Goals, and Understanding.* Hillsdale, NJ: Lawrence Erlbaum.

Schmidt, E. 1982. A Comparison of United States and Danish Children's Emerging Learnings of Written Language. Reading by All Means: Selected Proceedings, 12th New Zealand Conference of IRA. (Hvad ved skolebegyndere om bøgernes sprog? Serien Laese Rapport, 6. *Laesning.* Copenhagen: Danish Reading Association.)

Scriven, M. 1975. Problems and Prospects for Individualization. In H. Talmage, ed., *Systems of Individualized Instruction.* Chicago: National Society for the Study of Education Yearbook.

Senn, M. J. E. 1975. Insights on the Child Development Movement in the United States. Monograph. *Society of Research and Child Development* 40, 3–4: 1–107.

Seymour, P. H. K. 1986. *Cognitive Analysis of Dyslexia.* London: Routledge and Kegan Paul.

Shanahan, T., ed. 1990. *Reading and Writing Together: New Perspectives for the Classroom.* Norwood, MA: Christopher-Gordon.

Shepard, L. 1991. Negative Policies for Dealing with Diversity: When Does Assessment and

Diagnosis Turn into Sorting and Segregation? In E. Hiebert, ed., *Literacy for a Diverse Society: Perspectives, Practices and Policies,* pp. 279–298. New York: Teachers College Press.

Sinclair, A., R. J. Jarvella, and W. J. M. Levelt, eds. 1978. *The Child's Conception of Language.* New York: Springer.

Singer, H. 1994. The Substrata-Factor Theory of Reading. In R. B. Ruddell, M. R. Ruddell, and H. Singer, eds., *Theoretical Models and Processes of Reading.* 4th ed., pp. 895–925. Newark, DE: International Reading Association.

Smith, F. 1978. *Understanding Reading: A Psycholinguistic Analysis of Reading and Learning to Read.* 2d ed. New York: Holt, Rinehart & Winston.

Sontag, L. W. 1971. The History of Longitudinal Research: Implications for the Future. *Child Development* 42: 987–1002.

Spiro, R. J. 1980. Constructive Processes in Prose Comprehension and Recall. In R. J. Spiro, B. C. Bruce, and W. F. Brewer, eds., *Theoretical Issues in Reading Comprehension,* pp. 453–481. Hillsdale, NJ: Lawrence Erlbaum.

Stallman, A., and D. Pearson. 1990. Formal Measures of Early Literacy. In L. M. Morrow and J. K. Smith, eds., *Assessment for Instruction in Early Literacy.* Englewood Cliffs, NJ: Prentice-Hall.

Stanovich, K. E. 1986. Matthew Effects in Reading: Some Consequences of Individual Differences in the Acquisition of Literacy. *Reading Research Quarterly* 2, 4: 360–407.

Sternberg, R. J., ed. 1984. *Mechanisms of Cognitive Development.* New York: W. H. Freeman.

Stevens, A. L., and D. E. Rumelhart. 1975. Errors in Reading: Analysis Using an Augmented Network Model of Grammar. In D. A. Norman, D. E. Rumelhart, and the NLR research group. *Explorations in Cognition.* San Francisco: Freeman.

Sulzby, E. 1985a. Children's Emergent Reading of Favorite Storybooks: A Developmental Study. *Reading Research Quarterly* 20: 458–481.

———. 1985b. Kindergartners as Writers and Readers. In M. Farr, ed., *Advances in Writing Research,* Vol. 1, *Children's Early Writing Development,* pp. 127–199. Norwood, NJ: Ablex.

Sulzby, E., and W. H. Teale. 1991. Emergent Literacy. In R. Barr, M. L. Kamil, P. Mosenthal, and P. D. Pearson, eds., *Handbook of Reading Research,* Vol. 11, pp. 727–757. White Plains, NY: Longman.

Sutton-Smith, B. 1981. *The Folkstories of Children.* Philadelphia: University of Pennsylvania Press.

Teale, W. H., and E. Sulzby, eds. 1986. *Emergent Literacy: Writing and Reading.* Norwood, NJ: Ablex.

Tharp, R. G., and R. Gallimore. 1988. *Rousing Minds to Life: Teaching Learning and Schooling in Social Context.* Cambridge, UK: Cambridge University Press.

Tierney, R. J. 1991. Studies of Reading and Writing Growth: Longitudinal Research on Literacy Development. In J. Flood, J. M. Jensen, D. Lapp, and J. S. Squire, eds., *Handbook of Research on Teaching the English Language Arts,* pp. 176–194. New York: Macmillan.

Tierney, R. J., J. E. Readence, and E. K. Dishner. 1990. *Reading Strategies and Practices: A Compendium.* 3rd ed. Needham Heights, MA: Allyn & Bacon.

Tizard, B., and M. Hughes. 1984. *Young Children Learning.* London: Fontana.

Tolchinsky Landsmann, L. 1990. Literacy Development and Pedagogical Implications: Evidence from the Hebrew Writing System. In Y. Goodman, ed., *How Children Construct Literacy,* pp. 26–44. Newark, DE: International Reading Association.

Tompkins, G. E., and L. M. McGee. 1986. Visually Impaired and Sighted Children's Emerging Concepts About Written Language. In D. Yaden, ed., *Metalinguistic Awareness: Findings, Problems, and Classroom Applications.* Portsmouth, NH: Heinemann.

Torgeson, J. 1975. Problems and Prospects in the Study of Learning Disabilities. In E. M. Hetherington, ed., *Review of Child Development Research* 5: 385–440.

Tough, J. 1975. *Focus on Meaning: Talking to Some Purpose with Young Children.* London: Unwin Education Books.

———. 1981. *A Place for Talk.* London: Ward Lock Educational.

Treiman, R. 1993. *Beginning to Spell: A Study of First-Grade Children.* New York: Oxford University Press.

Trelease, J. 1982. *The Read-Aloud Handbook.* Harmondsworth, UK: Penguin.

———. 1989. *The New Read-Aloud Handbook.* New York: Penguin.

Valsiner, J. 1987. *Culture and the Development of Children's Action.* Chichester, UK: Wilkey.

Vernon, M. 1960. The Development of Perception in Children. *Educational Research* 3: 2–11.

———. 1971. *Reading and Its Difficulties.* London: Cambridge University Press.

Vygotsky, L. S. 1962. *Thought and Language.* Cambridge, MA: MIT Press.

———. 1978. *Mind in Society.* Cambridge, MA: Harvard University Press.

Wagoner, S. 1983. Comprehension Monitoring: What It Is and What We Have to Know About It. *Reading Research Quarterly* 18: 328–346.

Watson, A. J., R. D. Phillips, and C. Y. Wille. 1995. What Teachers Believe About Teaching Composite Classes. *South Pacific Journal of Teacher Education* 23, 2: 133–164.

Watson, B. 1980. Teaching Beginning Reading: An Observation Study. Master's thesis, University of Auckland.

———. 1994. Facilitating Independent Learning Early in the First Year of School. Ph.D. diss., University of Auckland.

Weaver, P., and F. Shonkoff. 1979. *Research Within Reach: A Research-Guided Response to the Concerns of Reading Educators.* Newark, DE: International Reading Association.

Weber, R. 1968. The Study of Oral Reading Errors: A Survey of the Literature. *Reading Research Quarterly* 4: 96–119.

———. 1970. A Linguistic Analysis of First Grade Reading Errors. *Reading Research Quarterly* 5: 427–451.

Weikart, D. P., L. Rogers, C. Adcock, and D. McClelland. 1971. *The Cognitively-Oriented Curriculum.* Urbana, IL: University of Illinois.

Weinberger, J., P. Hannon, and C. Nutbrown. 1990. *Ways of Working with Parents to Promote Early Literacy Development.* Sheffield, UK: University of Sheffield Education Research Unit.

Wellman, H. M., and J. D. Lempers. 1977. The Naturalistic Communicative Abilities of Two-Year-Olds. *Child Development* 48: 1052–1057.

Wells, G. 1981. *Learning Through Interaction: The Study of Language Interaction.* London: Cambridge University Press.

———. 1986. *The Meaning Makers: Children Learning Language and Using Language to Learn.* Portsmouth, NH: Heinemann.

Wertsch, J. V. 1978. Adult-Child Interaction and the Roots of Metacognition. *Quarterly Newsletter of the Institute of Comparative Human Development* 2: 15–18.

———. 1985. *Vygotsky and the Social Formation of Mind.* Cambridge, MA: Harvard University Press.

White, D. N. 1984. *Books Before Five.* Portsmouth, NH: Heinemann.

Williams, J. 1995. Phonemic Awareness. In T. Harris and R. E. Hodges, eds., *The Literacy Dictionary: The Vocabulary of Reading and Writing,* pp. 185–186. Newark, DE: International Reading Association.

Wood, D., J. S. Bruner, and G. Ross. 1976. The Role of Tutoring in Problem-Solving. *Journal of Child Psychology and Child Psychiatry* 17: 89–100.

Yendovitskaya, T. V., V. P. Zinchenko, and A. G. Ruzskaya. 1971. Development of Sensation and Perception. In A. V. Zaporozhets and D. B. Elkonin, eds., *The Psychology of Preschool Children,* pp. 1–65. Cambridge, MA: MIT Press.

Yopp, H. K. 1995. A Test for Assessing Phonemic Awareness in Young Children. *The Reading Teacher* 49, 1: 20–29.

Yopp, H. K., and H. Singer. 1994. Toward an Interactive Reading Instructional Model: Explanation of Activation of Linguistic Awareness and Meta-Linguistic Ability in Learning to Read. In R. B. Ruddell, M. R. Ruddell, and H. Singer, eds., *Theoretical Models and Processes in Reading,* pp. 381–390. Newark, DE: International Reading Association.

Ysseldyke, J. E., B. Algozzine, and S. Epps. 1983. A Logical and Empirical Analysis of Current Practice in Classifying Students as Handicapped. *Exceptional Children* 50: 160–166.

Zaporozhets, A. V. 1965. The Development of Perception in the Preschool Child. *Monographs of the Society for Research in Child Development* 30, 2: 82–101.

Zaporozhets, A. V., and D. B. Elkonin, eds. 1971. *The Psychology of Preschool Children.* Cambridge, MA: MIT Press.

Zinchencko, V. P., and B. F. Lomov. 1960. The Functions of Hand and Eye Movements in the Process of Perception. *Problems of Psychology* 1 and 2: 102–116.

(continued from page ii)

Chapter 6: "A Fable" by Marie M. Clay. Copyright © 1993. Presidential Column. *Reading Today* (April/May). Reprinted by permission.
Chapter 7: "Looking and Seeing in the Classroom" by Marie M. Clay. Copyright © 1982 by the National Council of Teachers of English. *English Journal* 2: 90–92. Reprinted by permission.
Chapter 8: "Using the Concepts About Print Task with School Entrants" by Marie M. Clay. Copyright © 1997. *set Special: Language and Literacy* 12: 1–4. Reprinted by permission of NZCER.
Chapter 9: "Concepts About Print: In English and Other Languages" by Marie M. Clay. Copyright © 1989. *The Reading Teacher* 42, 4: 268–276. Reprinted by permission.
Chapter 11: "Fostering Independent Learning" by Wendy Girling-Butcher, Gwenneth Phillips, and Marie M. Clay. Copyright © 1991. *The Reading Teacher* 44, 9: 694–697. Reprinted by permission.
Chapter 12: "Introducing a New Storybook to Young Readers" by Marie M. Clay. Copyright © 1991. *The Reading Teacher* 45, 4: 264–273. Reprinted by permission.
Chapter 13: "Constructive Processes: Talking, Reading, Writing, Art, and Craft" by Marie M. Clay. Copyright © 1986. *The Reading Teacher* 39, 4: 764–770. Reprinted by permission.
Chapter 14: Unpublished paper presented to "Literacy: Meeting the Challenge Conference" of the New South Wales Department of School Education, August 1997. Copyright © 1997 Marie M. Clay. Reprinted by permission.
Chapter 15: From "World Literacy: Future Directions and Challenges" by Marie M. Clay. Copyright © 1997. Auckland Council of the New Zealand Reading Association. Reprinted by permission.
Chapter 16: "Accommodating Diversity in Early Literacy Learning" by Marie M. Clay. Copyright © 1996. In D. R. Olson and N. Torrance, eds. *The Handbook of Education and Human Development*, pp. 202–224. Oxford: Blackwell. Reprinted by permission.
Chapter 17: "Child Development" by Marie M. Clay. Copyright © 1991. In Flood, Jensen, Lapp, and Squire, eds. *Handbook of Research on Teaching the English Language Arts*, pp. 40–45. New York: Macmillan; sponsored by the International Reading Association and the National Council of Teachers of English. Reprinted by permission.